PETER PARKER THE SPECTACULAR
SPIDER-MAN

AMAZING
FANTASY

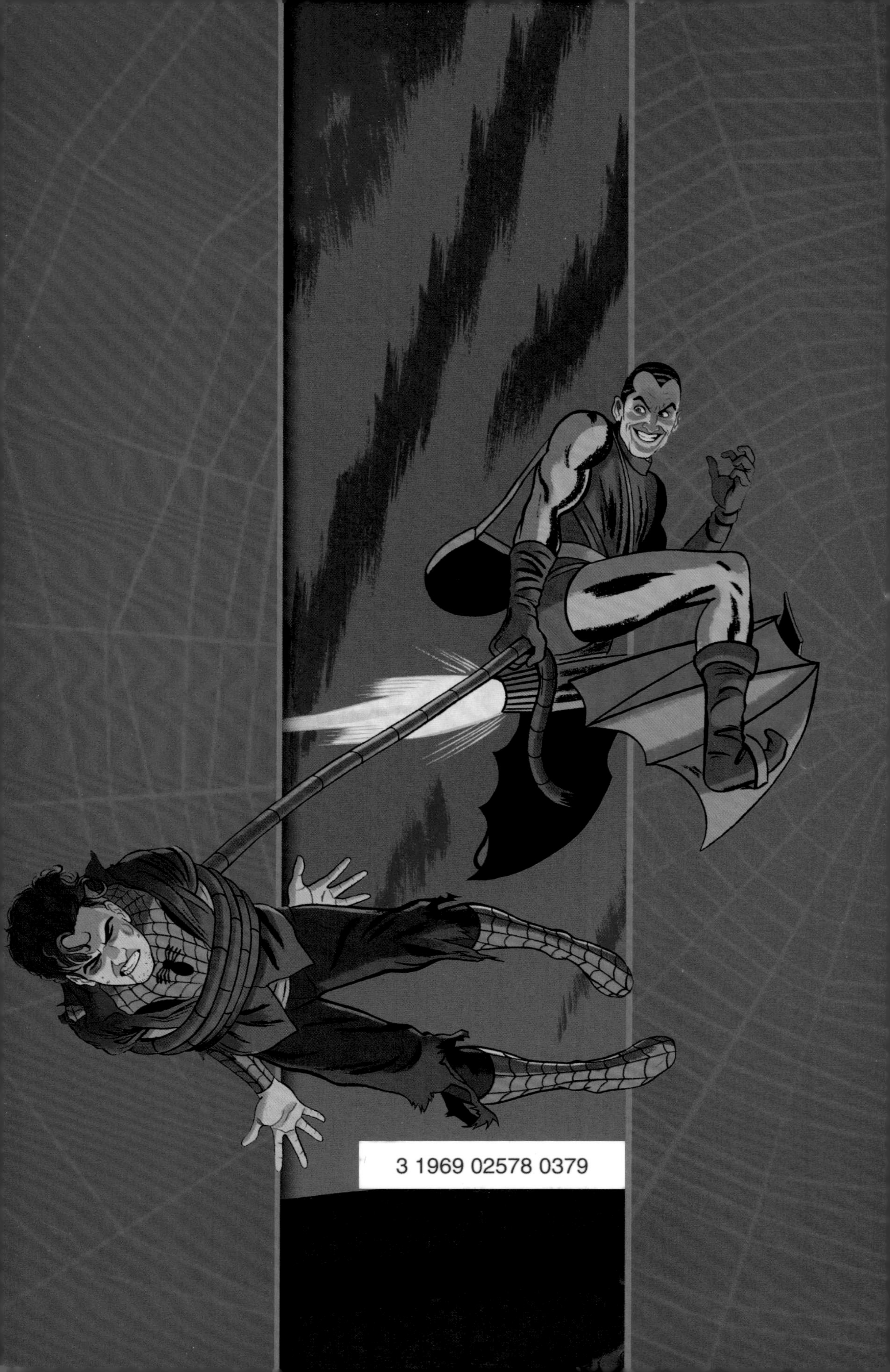

PETER PARKER: THE SPECTACULAR SPIDER-MAN

AMAZING FANTASY

CHIP ZDARSKY
WRITER

JOE QUINONES
PENCILER

JOE RIVERA (#301-303) WITH **JOE QUINONES** & **PAOLO RIVERA** (#303)
INKERS

JORDAN GIBSON (#301-303) WITH **JOE QUINONES** (#303)
COLORISTS

ANNUAL #1

"PAPER TRAIL"

CHIP ZDARSKY
WRITER

MICHAEL ALLRED
ARTIST

LAURA ALLRED
COLOR ARTIST

"WHATEVER HAPPENED TO THE SPIDER-MAN FOR ALL SEASONS"

MIKE DRUCKER
WRITER

CHRIS BACHALO
PENCILER & COLORIST

JAIME MENDOZA, VICTOR OLAZABA, WAYNE FAUCHER, LIVESAY & **TIM TOWNSEND**
INKERS

VC's TRAVIS LANHAM
LETTERER

JOE QUINONES & **MICHAEL** AND **LAURA ALLRED** (ANNUAL #1)
COVER ART

TOM GRONEMAN & **KATHLEEN WISNESKI**
ASSISTANT EDITORS

DEVIN LEWIS
ASSOCIATE EDITOR

NICK LOWE
EDITOR

COLLECTION EDITOR: **MARK D. BEAZLEY**
ASSISTANT EDITOR: **CAITLIN O'CONNELL**
ASSOCIATE MANAGING EDITOR: **KATERI WOODY**
SENIOR EDITOR, SPECIAL PROJECTS: **JENNIFER GRÜNWALD**
VP PRODUCTION & SPECIAL PROJECTS: **JEFF YOUNGQUIST**
SVP PRINT, SALES & MARKETING: **DAVID GABRIEL**
BOOK DESIGNER: **ADAM DEL RE**

EDITOR IN CHIEF: **C.B. CEBULSKI**
CHIEF CREATIVE OFFICER: **JOE QUESADA**
PRESIDENT: **DAN BUCKLEY**
EXECUTIVE PRODUCER: **ALAN FINE**

SPIDER-MAN CREATED BY **STAN LEE** & **STEVE DITKO**

PETER PARKER: THE SPECTACULAR SPIDER-MAN VOL. 3 — AMAZING FANTASY. Contains material originally published in magazine form as PETER PARKER: THE SPECTACULAR SPIDER-MAN #301-303 and ANNUAL #1. First printing 2018. ISBN 978-1-302-91118-8. Published by MARVEL WORLDWIDE, INC., a subsidiary of MARVEL ENTERTAINMENT, LLC. OFFICE OF PUBLICATION: 135 West 50th Street, New York, NY 10020. **Printed in Canada.** DAN BUCKLEY, President, Marvel Entertainment; JOHN NEE, Publisher; JOE QUESADA, Chief Creative Officer; TOM BREVOORT, SVP of Publishing; DAVID BOGART, SVP of Business Affairs & Operations, Publishing & Partnership; DAVID GABRIEL, SVP of Sales & Marketing, Publishing; JEFF YOUNGQUIST, VP of Production & Special Projects; DAN CARR, Executive Director of Publishing Technology; ALEX MORALES, Director of Publishing Operations; DAN EDINGTON, Managing Editor; SUSAN CRESPI, Production Manager; STAN LEE, Chairman Emeritus. For information regarding advertising in Marvel Comics or on Marvel.com, please contact Vit DeBellis, Custom Solutions & Integrated Advertising Manager, at vdebellis@marvel.com. For Marvel subscription inquiries, please call 888-511-5480. **Manufactured between 6/22/2018 and 7/24/2018 by SOLISCO PRINTERS, SCOTT, QC, CANADA.**

10 9 8 7 6 5 4 3 2 1

I LOVE TIME-TRAVEL STORIES!

DO YOU LIKE ALIEN INVASION STORIES, TOO?

HECK YES I DO!!!

GOOD, SINCE THIS IS BOTH! BECAUSE THE ONLY SOLUTION TO STOP AN ATTACK IN
PRESENT-DAY NEW YORK FROM AN ALIEN SPECIES CALLED THE VEDOMI
REQUIRES SPIDER-MAN TO TRAVEL…INTO THE PAST!

THIS IS ALL THE TINKERER'S FAULT. I CAN'T BELIEVE HE SIDED WITH A BUNCH OF ALIEN
A.I.s OVER HUMANITY!

LUCKILY, SPIDEY'S GOT SOME TOP-NOTCH ALLIES OF HIS OWN!
LIKE TERESA DURAND! PETER'S SORT-OF SISTER/FORMER S.H.I.E.L.D. AGENT.

OKAY! TERESA'S GREAT IN A FIGHT. WHO ELSE? THE HUMAN TORCH? BLACK PANTHER?

OH, Y'KNOW…J. JONAH JAMESON…

JAMESON?! THEY BROUGHT HIM BACK IN TIME?!

HEY, J.J.J. CAN BE PRETTY RESOURCEFUL. HE WAS THE MAYOR OF NYC, AFTER ALL.

I HAVE SO MANY BAD FEELINGS ABOUT THIS…
MAYBE SOME HEROES FROM THE PAST WILL HELP SPIDEY OUT, TOO?

MAYBE!!! TURN THE PAGE AND FIND OUT!

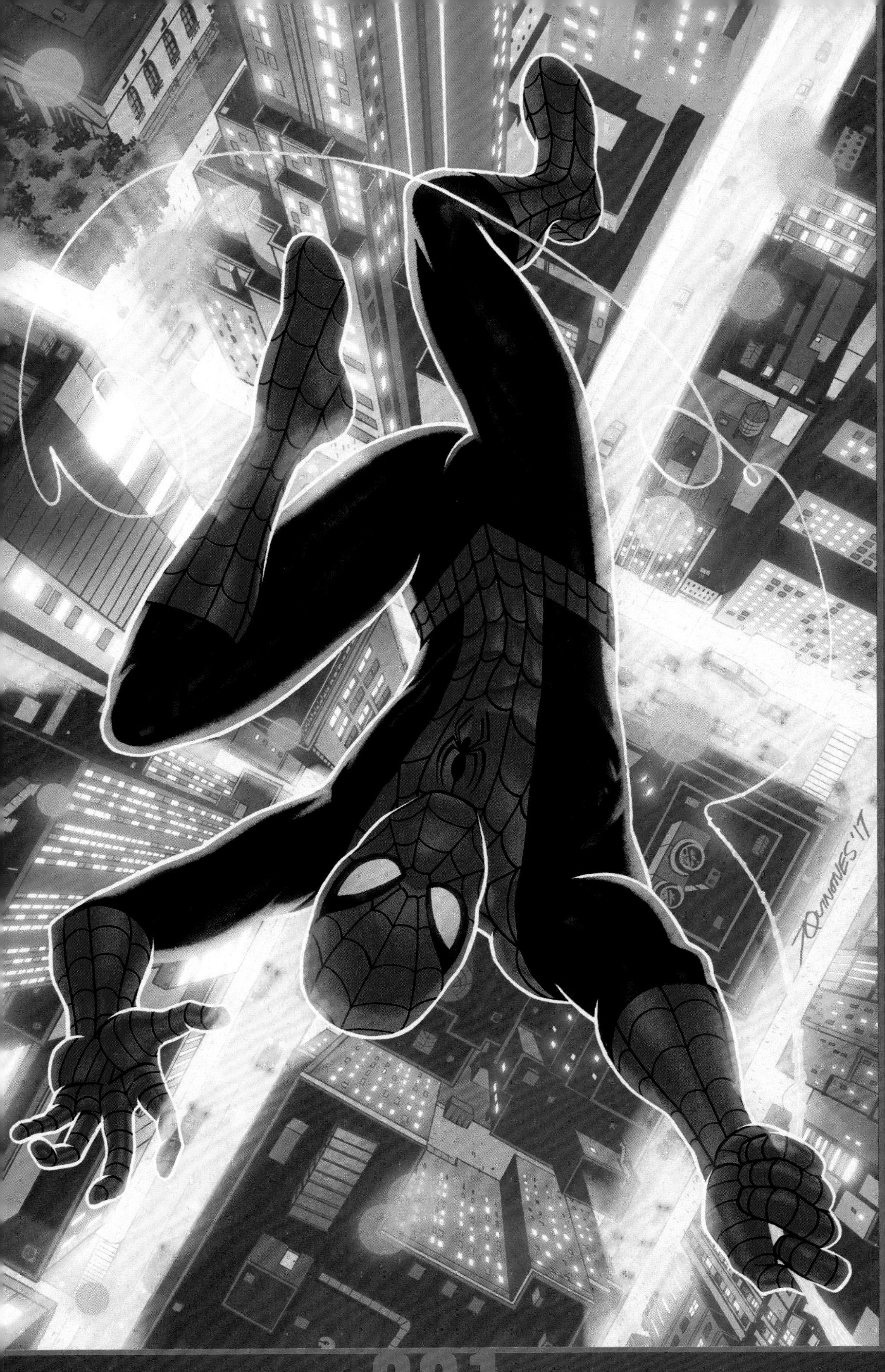

301

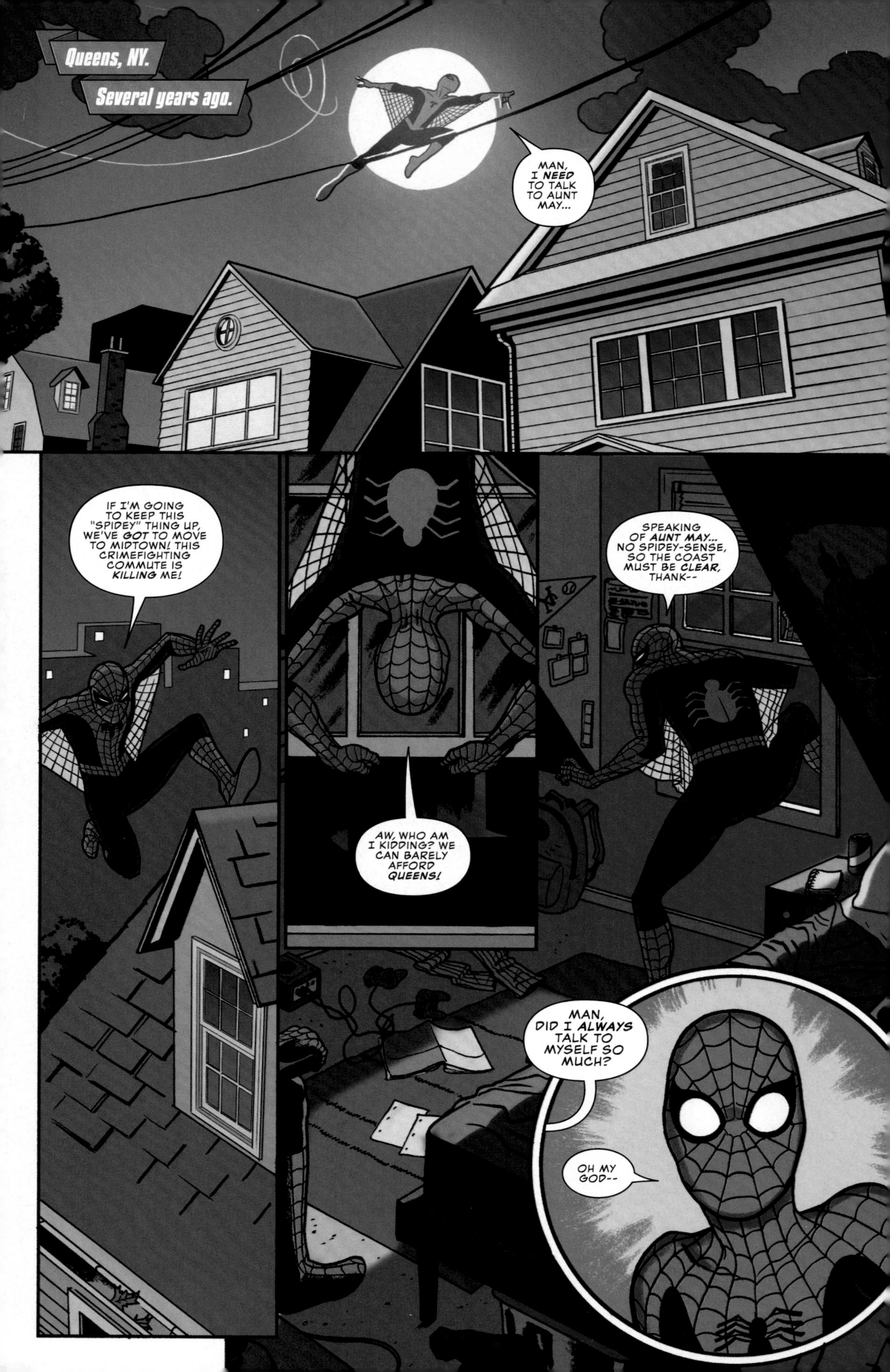

Queens, NY.
Several years ago.
MAN, I NEED TO TALK TO AUNT MAY...
IF I'M GOING TO KEEP THIS "SPIDEY" THING UP, WE'VE GOT TO MOVE TO MIDTOWN! THIS CRIMEFIGHTING COMMUTE IS KILLING ME!
AW, WHO AM I KIDDING? WE CAN BARELY AFFORD QUEENS!
SPEAKING OF AUNT MAY... NO SPIDEY-SENSE, SO THE COAST MUST BE CLEAR, THANK--
MAN, DID I ALWAYS TALK TO MYSELF SO MUCH?
OH MY GOD--

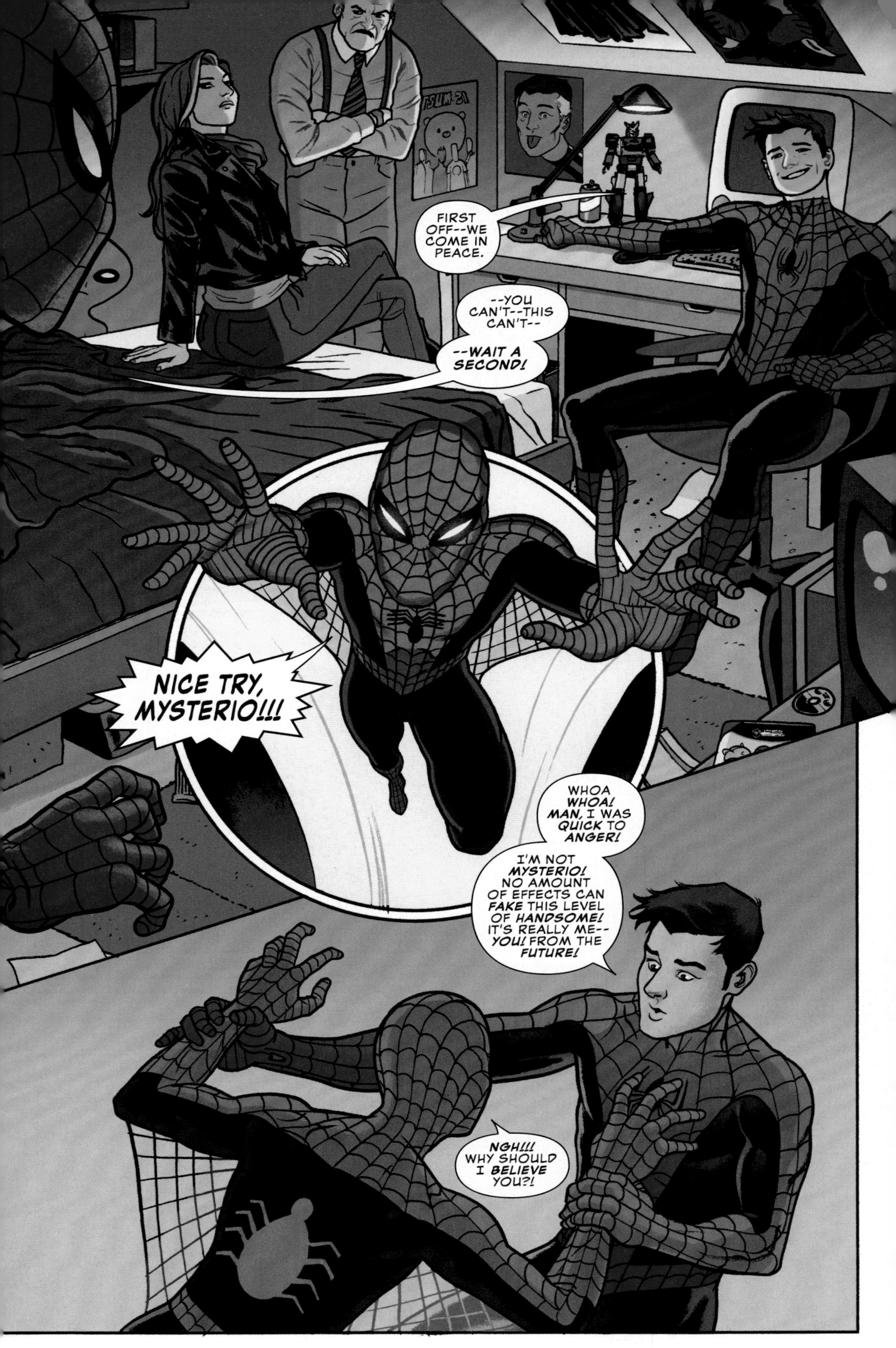
FIRST OFF--WE COME IN PEACE.
--YOU CAN'T--THIS CAN'T--
--WAIT A SECOND!
NICE TRY, MYSTERIO!!!
WHOA WHOA! MAN, I WAS QUICK TO ANGER!
I'M NOT MYSTERIO! NO AMOUNT OF EFFECTS CAN FAKE THIS LEVEL OF HANDSOME! IT'S REALLY ME--YOU! FROM THE FUTURE!
NGH!!! WHY SHOULD I BELIEVE YOU?!

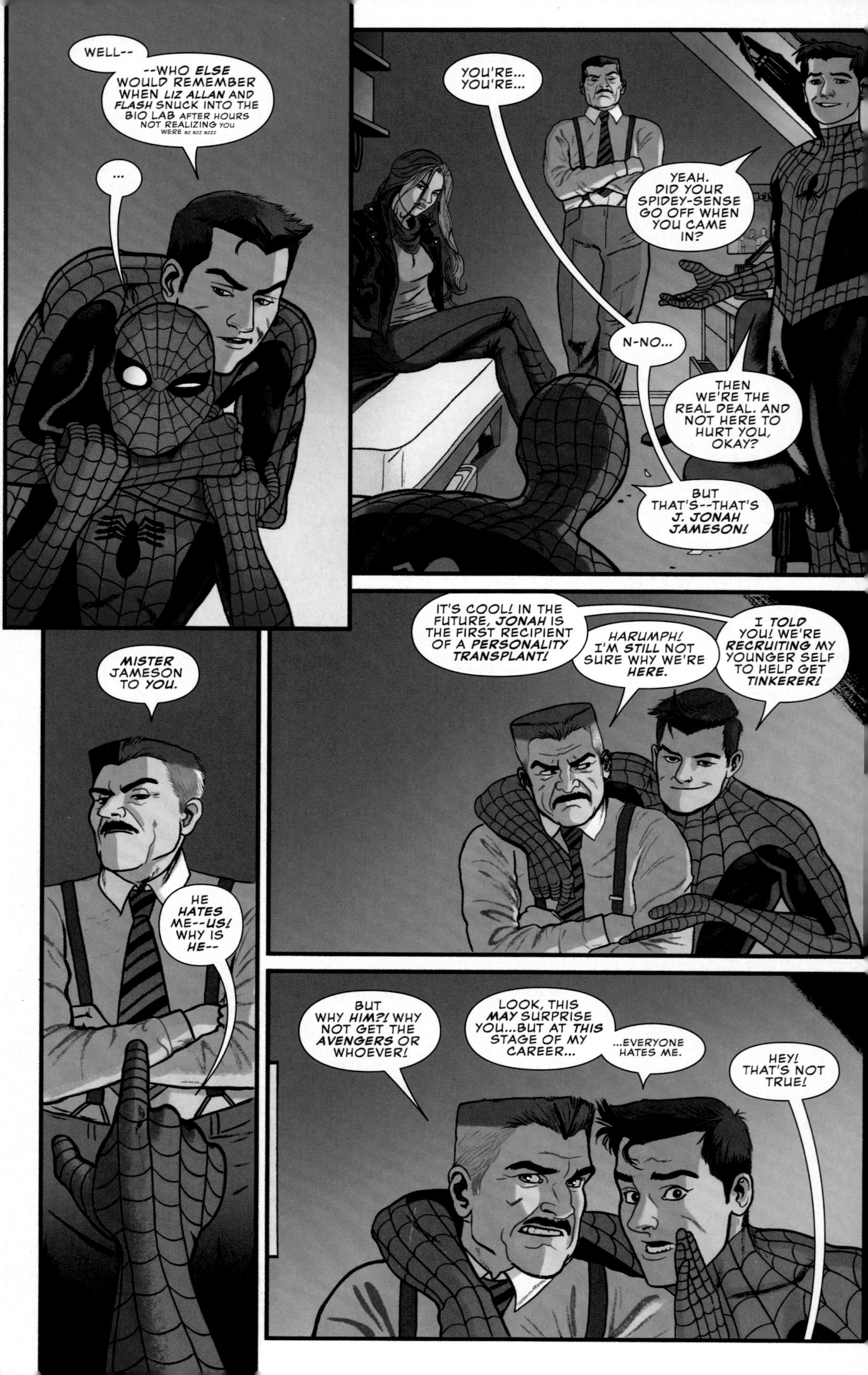
WELL--
--WHO ELSE WOULD REMEMBER WHEN LIZ ALLAN AND FLASH SNUCK INTO THE BIO LAB AFTER HOURS NOT REALIZING YOU WERE BZ BZZ BZZZ
...
YOU'RE... YOU'RE...
YEAH. DID YOUR SPIDEY-SENSE GO OFF WHEN YOU CAME IN?
N-NO...
THEN WE'RE THE REAL DEAL. AND NOT HERE TO HURT YOU, OKAY?
BUT THAT'S--THAT'S J. JONAH JAMESON!
MISTER JAMESON TO YOU.
HE HATES ME--US! WHY IS HE--
IT'S COOL! IN THE FUTURE, JONAH IS THE FIRST RECIPIENT OF A PERSONALITY TRANSPLANT!
HARUMPH! I'M STILL NOT SURE WHY WE'RE HERE.
I TOLD YOU! WE'RE RECRUITING MY YOUNGER SELF TO HELP GET TINKERER!
BUT WHY HIM?! WHY NOT GET THE AVENGERS OR WHOEVER!
LOOK, THIS MAY SURPRISE YOU...BUT AT THIS STAGE OF MY CAREER...
...EVERYONE HATES ME.
HEY! THAT'S NOT TRUE!

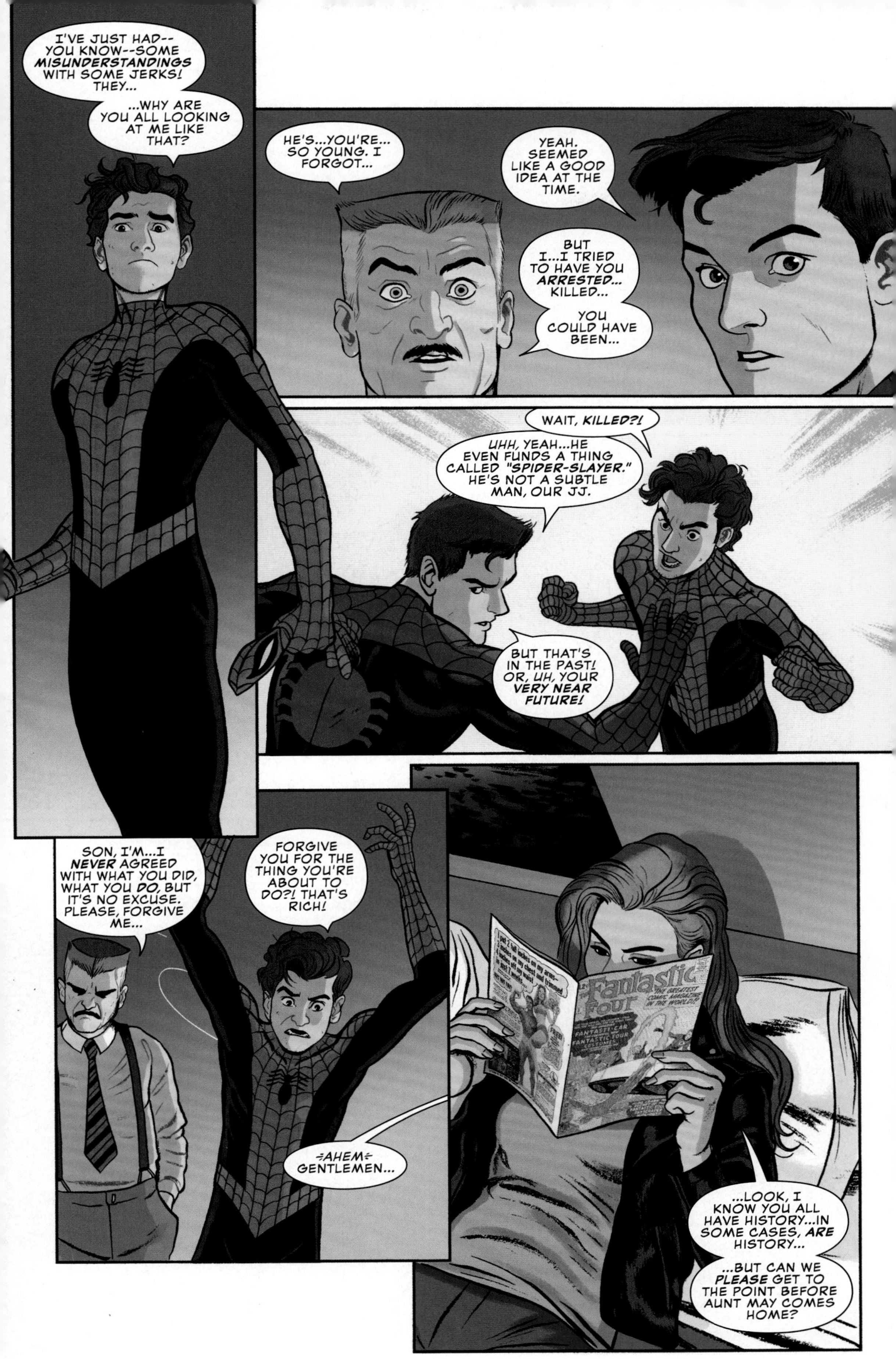

I'VE JUST HAD--
YOU KNOW--SOME MISUNDERSTANDINGS WITH SOME JERKS! THEY...
...WHY ARE YOU ALL LOOKING AT ME LIKE THAT?
HE'S...YOU'RE... SO YOUNG. I FORGOT...
YEAH. SEEMED LIKE A GOOD IDEA AT THE TIME.
BUT I...I TRIED TO HAVE YOU ARRESTED... KILLED...
YOU COULD HAVE BEEN...
WAIT, KILLED?!
UHH, YEAH...HE EVEN FUNDS A THING CALLED "SPIDER-SLAYER." HE'S NOT A SUBTLE MAN, OUR JJ.
BUT THAT'S IN THE PAST! OR, UH, YOUR VERY NEAR FUTURE!
SON, I'M...I NEVER AGREED WITH WHAT YOU DID, WHAT YOU DO, BUT IT'S NO EXCUSE. PLEASE, FORGIVE ME...
FORGIVE YOU FOR THE THING YOU'RE ABOUT TO DO?! THAT'S RICH!
AHEM GENTLEMEN...
Fantastic Four
THE GREATEST COMIC MAGAZINE IN THE WORLD!!
...LOOK, I KNOW YOU ALL HAVE HISTORY...IN SOME CASES, ARE HISTORY...
...BUT CAN WE PLEASE GET TO THE POINT BEFORE AUNT MAY COMES HOME?

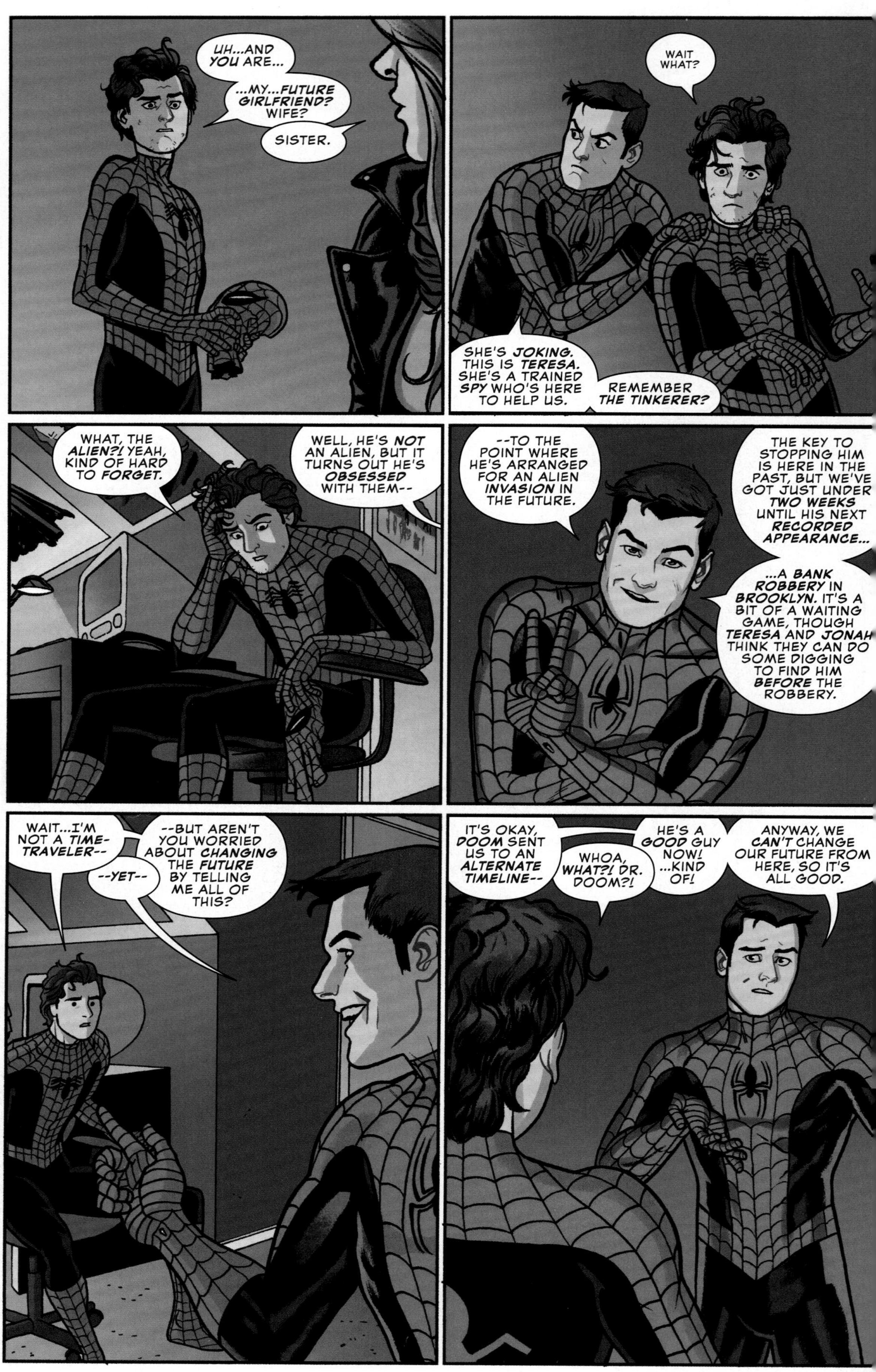

UH...AND *YOU* ARE...
...MY...*FUTURE GIRLFRIEND?* WIFE?
SISTER.
WAIT WHAT?
SHE'S *JOKING.* THIS IS *TERESA.* SHE'S A TRAINED *SPY* WHO'S HERE TO HELP US.
REMEMBER *THE TINKERER?*
WHAT, THE *ALIEN?!* YEAH, KIND OF HARD TO *FORGET.*
WELL, HE'S *NOT* AN ALIEN, BUT IT TURNS OUT HE'S *OBSESSED* WITH THEM--
--TO THE POINT WHERE HE'S ARRANGED FOR AN ALIEN *INVASION* IN THE FUTURE.
THE KEY TO STOPPING HIM IS HERE IN THE PAST, BUT WE'VE GOT JUST UNDER *TWO WEEKS* UNTIL HIS NEXT *RECORDED APPEARANCE...*
...A *BANK ROBBERY* IN *BROOKLYN.* IT'S A BIT OF A WAITING GAME, THOUGH *TERESA* AND *JONAH* THINK THEY CAN DO SOME DIGGING TO FIND HIM *BEFORE* THE ROBBERY.
WAIT...I'M NOT A *TIME-TRAVELER*--
--*YET*--
--BUT AREN'T YOU WORRIED ABOUT *CHANGING* THE *FUTURE* BY TELLING ME ALL OF THIS?
IT'S OKAY, *DOOM* SENT US TO AN *ALTERNATE TIMELINE*--
WHOA, *WHAT?!* DR. DOOM?!
HE'S A *GOOD* GUY NOW! ...KIND OF!
ANYWAY, WE *CAN'T* CHANGE OUR FUTURE FROM HERE, SO IT'S ALL GOOD.

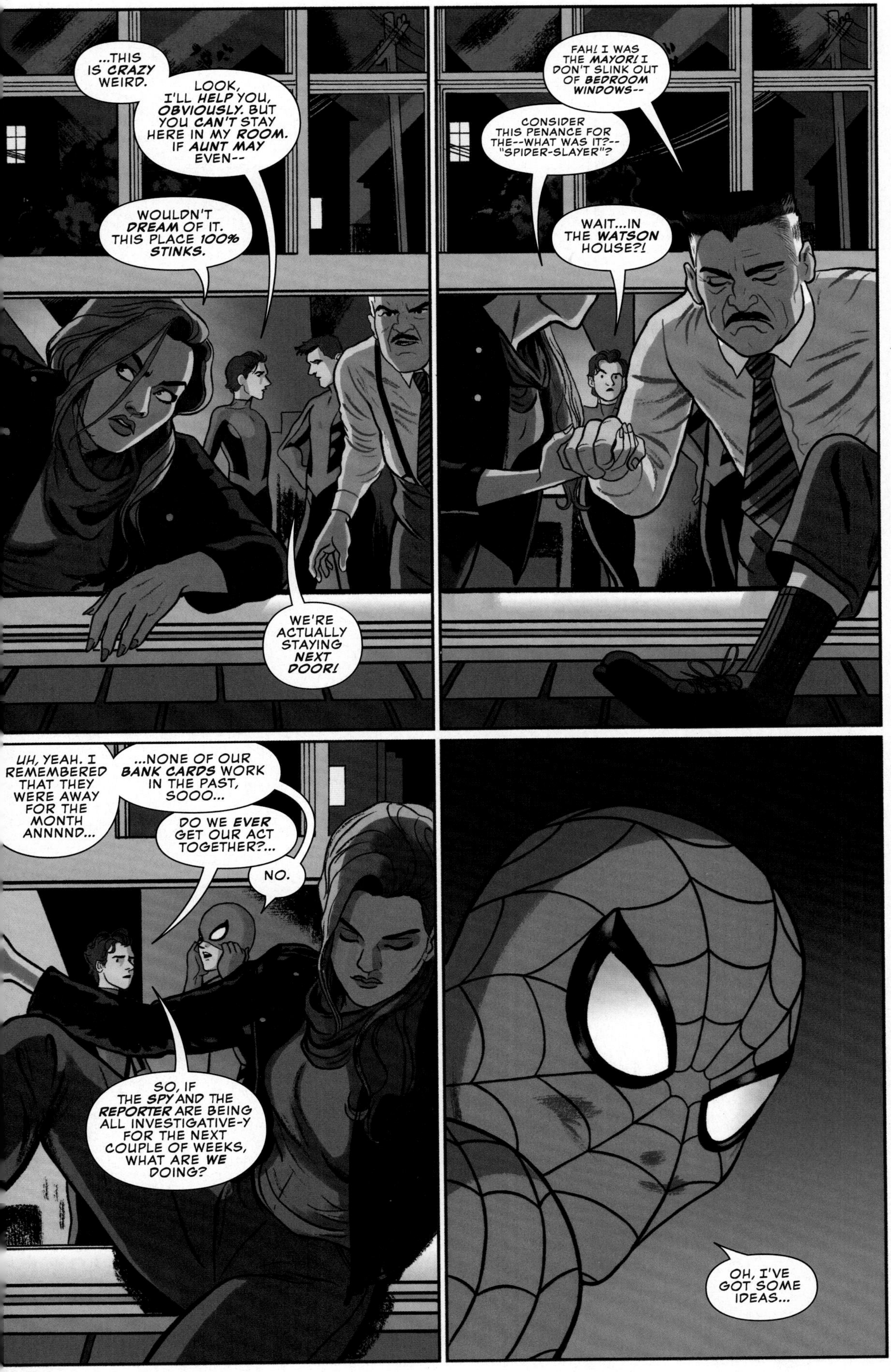
...THIS IS CRAZY WEIRD.
LOOK, I'LL HELP YOU, OBVIOUSLY. BUT YOU CAN'T STAY HERE IN MY ROOM. IF AUNT MAY EVEN--
WOULDN'T DREAM OF IT. THIS PLACE 100% STINKS.
WE'RE ACTUALLY STAYING NEXT DOOR!
FAH! I WAS THE MAYOR! I DON'T SLINK OUT OF BEDROOM WINDOWS--
CONSIDER THIS PENANCE FOR THE--WHAT WAS IT?--"SPIDER-SLAYER"?
WAIT...IN THE WATSON HOUSE?!
UH, YEAH. I REMEMBERED THAT THEY WERE AWAY FOR THE MONTH ANNNND...
...NONE OF OUR BANK CARDS WORK IN THE PAST, SOOO...
DO WE EVER GET OUR ACT TOGETHER?...
NO.
SO, IF THE SPY AND THE REPORTER ARE BEING ALL INVESTIGATIVE-Y FOR THE NEXT COUPLE OF WEEKS, WHAT ARE WE DOING?
OH, I'VE GOT SOME IDEAS...

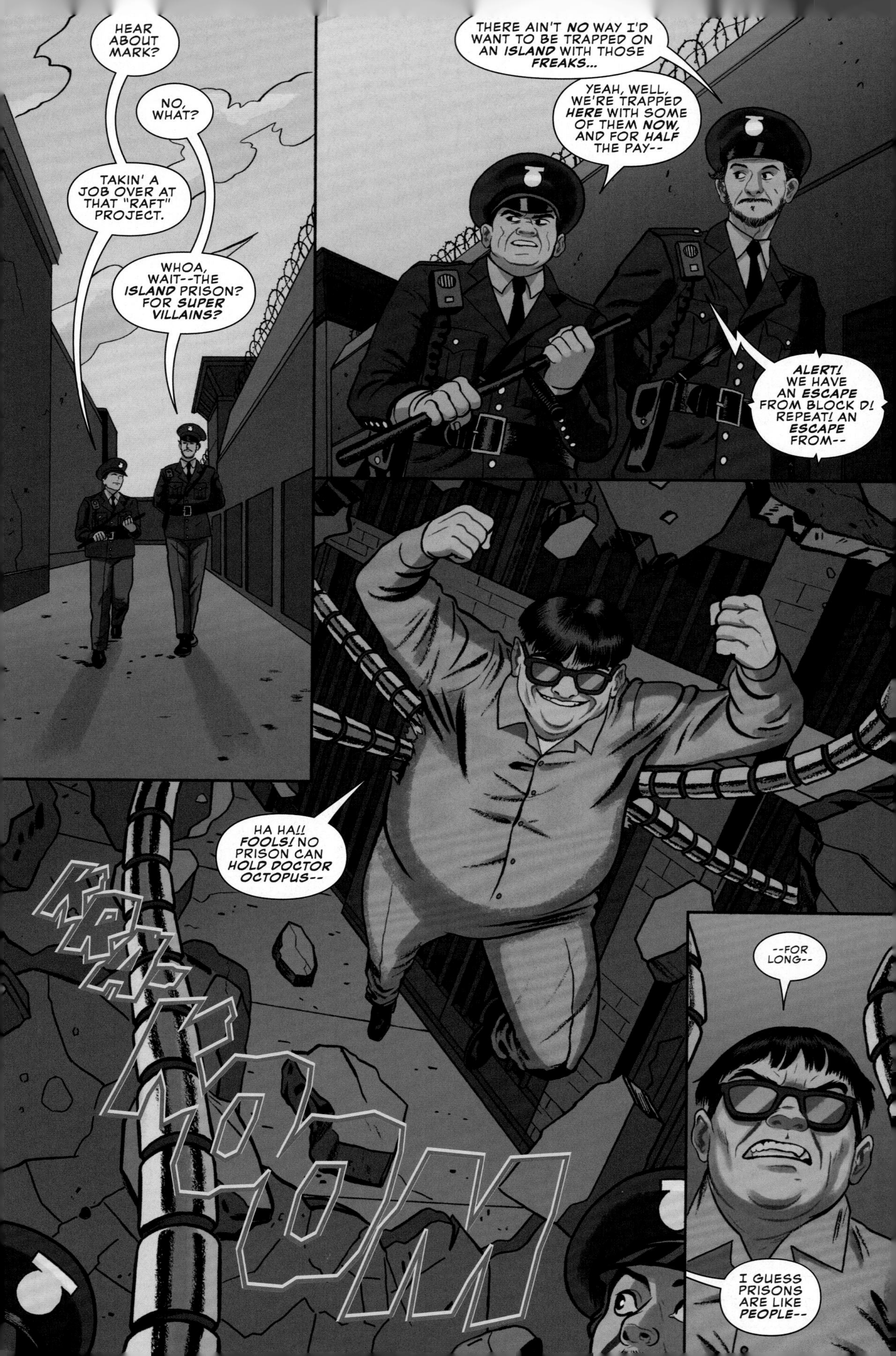
HEAR ABOUT MARK?
NO, WHAT?
TAKIN' A JOB OVER AT THAT "RAFT" PROJECT.
WHOA, WAIT--THE *ISLAND* PRISON? FOR *SUPER VILLAINS?*
THERE AIN'T *NO* WAY I'D WANT TO BE TRAPPED ON AN *ISLAND* WITH THOSE *FREAKS...*
YEAH, WELL, WE'RE TRAPPED *HERE* WITH SOME OF THEM *NOW,* AND FOR *HALF* THE PAY--
ALERT! WE HAVE AN *ESCAPE* FROM BLOCK D! REPEAT! AN *ESCAPE* FROM--
HA HA!! *FOOLS!* NO PRISON CAN *HOLD DOCTOR OCTOPUS*--
--FOR LONG--
I GUESS PRISONS ARE LIKE *PEOPLE*--

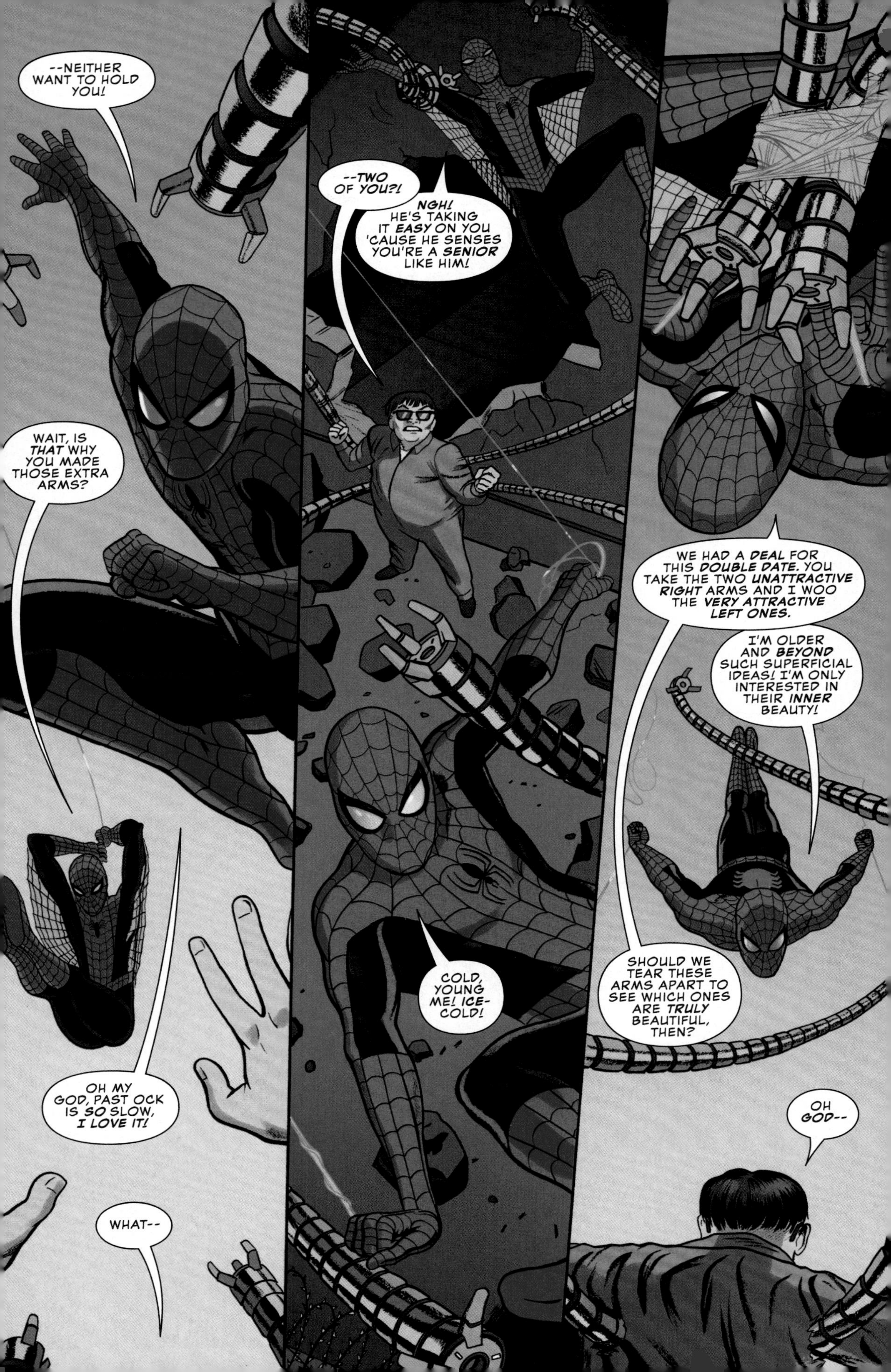
--NEITHER WANT TO HOLD YOU!
WAIT, IS THAT WHY YOU MADE THOSE EXTRA ARMS?
OH MY GOD, PAST OCK IS SO SLOW, I LOVE IT!
WHAT--
--TWO OF YOU?!
NGH! HE'S TAKING IT EASY ON YOU 'CAUSE HE SENSES YOU'RE A SENIOR LIKE HIM!
COLD, YOUNG ME! ICE-COLD!
WE HAD A DEAL FOR THIS DOUBLE DATE. YOU TAKE THE TWO UNATTRACTIVE RIGHT ARMS AND I WOO THE VERY ATTRACTIVE LEFT ONES.
I'M OLDER AND BEYOND SUCH SUPERFICIAL IDEAS! I'M ONLY INTERESTED IN THEIR INNER BEAUTY!
SHOULD WE TEAR THESE ARMS APART TO SEE WHICH ONES ARE TRULY BEAUTIFUL, THEN?
OH GOD--

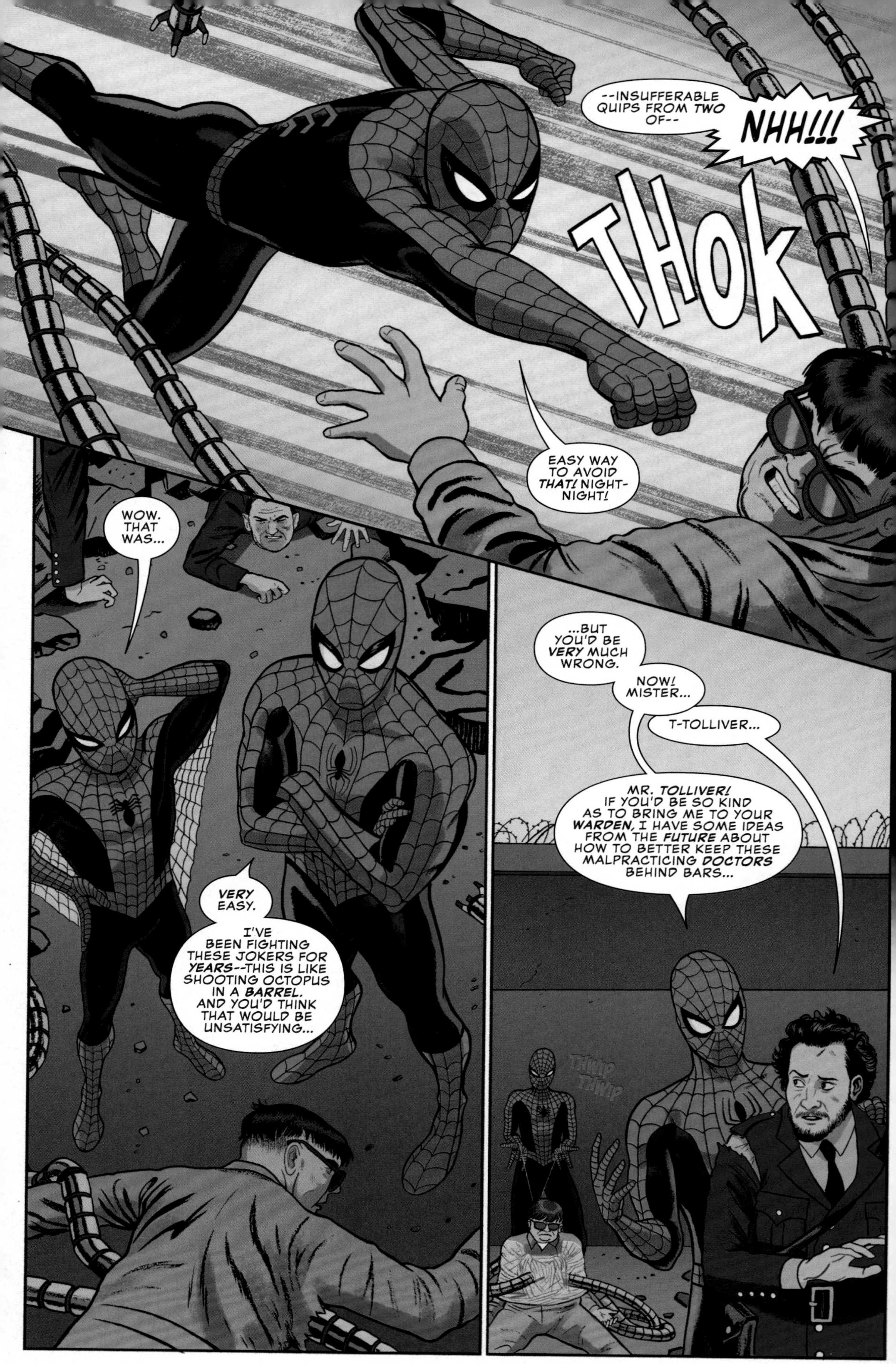
--INSUFFERABLE QUIPS FROM TWO OF--
NHH!!!
THOK
EASY WAY TO AVOID THAT! NIGHT-NIGHT!
WOW. THAT WAS...
VERY EASY.
I'VE BEEN FIGHTING THESE JOKERS FOR YEARS--THIS IS LIKE SHOOTING OCTOPUS IN A BARREL. AND YOU'D THINK THAT WOULD BE UNSATISFYING...
...BUT YOU'D BE VERY MUCH WRONG.
NOW! MISTER...
T-TOLLIVER...
MR. TOLLIVER! IF YOU'D BE SO KIND AS TO BRING ME TO YOUR WARDEN, I HAVE SOME IDEAS FROM THE FUTURE ABOUT HOW TO BETTER KEEP THESE MALPRACTICING DOCTORS BEHIND BARS...
THWIP THWIP

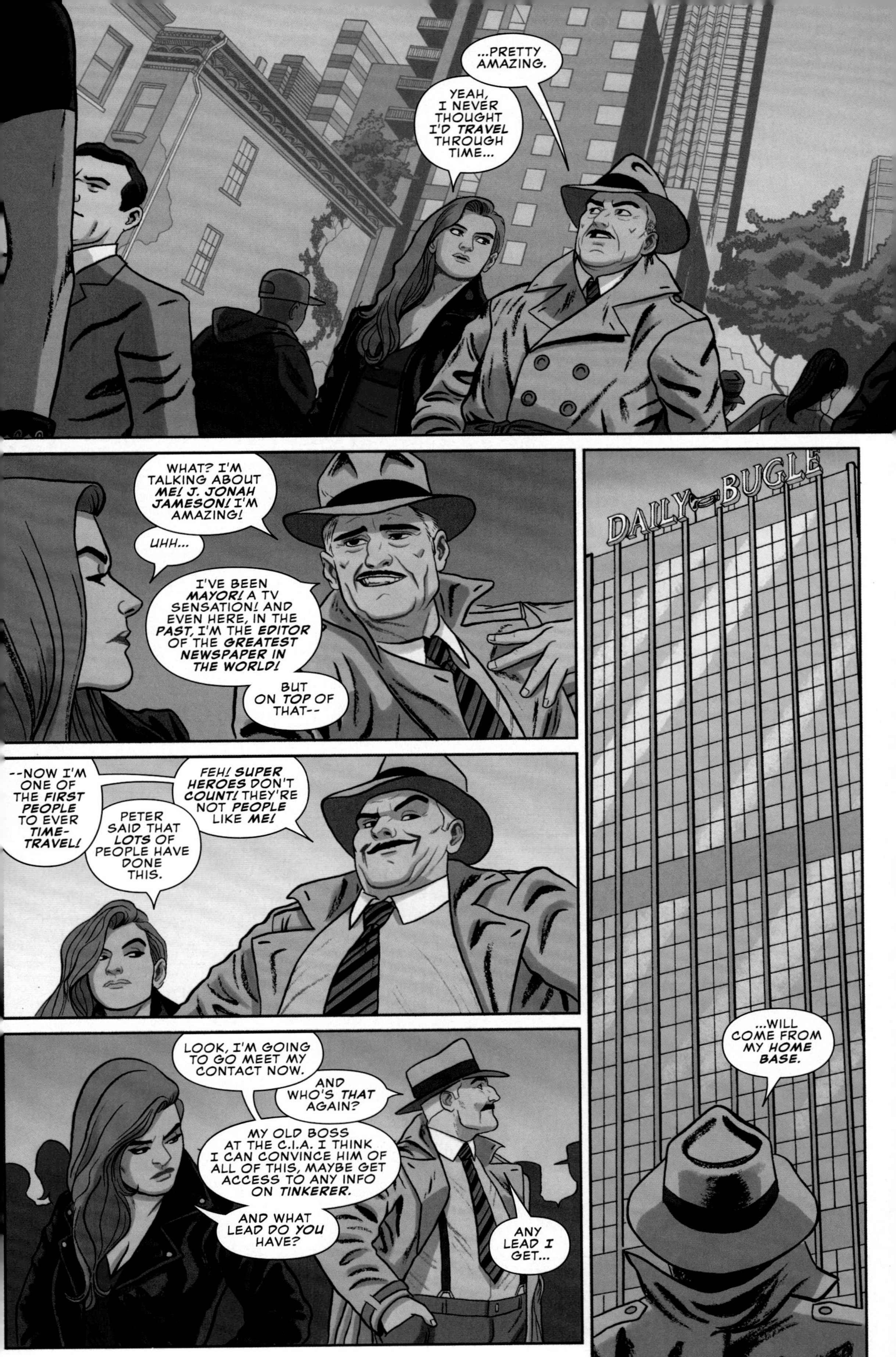
...PRETTY AMAZING.
YEAH, I NEVER THOUGHT I'D TRAVEL THROUGH TIME...
WHAT? I'M TALKING ABOUT ME! J. JONAH JAMESON! I'M AMAZING!
UHH...
I'VE BEEN MAYOR! A TV SENSATION! AND EVEN HERE, IN THE PAST, I'M THE EDITOR OF THE GREATEST NEWSPAPER IN THE WORLD!
BUT ON TOP OF THAT--
--NOW I'M ONE OF THE FIRST PEOPLE TO EVER TIME-TRAVEL!
PETER SAID THAT LOTS OF PEOPLE HAVE DONE THIS.
FEH! SUPER HEROES DON'T COUNT! THEY'RE NOT PEOPLE LIKE ME!
LOOK, I'M GOING TO GO MEET MY CONTACT NOW.
AND WHO'S THAT AGAIN?
MY OLD BOSS AT THE C.I.A. I THINK I CAN CONVINCE HIM OF ALL OF THIS, MAYBE GET ACCESS TO ANY INFO ON TINKERER.
AND WHAT LEAD DO YOU HAVE?
ANY LEAD I GET...
DAILY BUGLE
...WILL COME FROM MY HOME BASE.

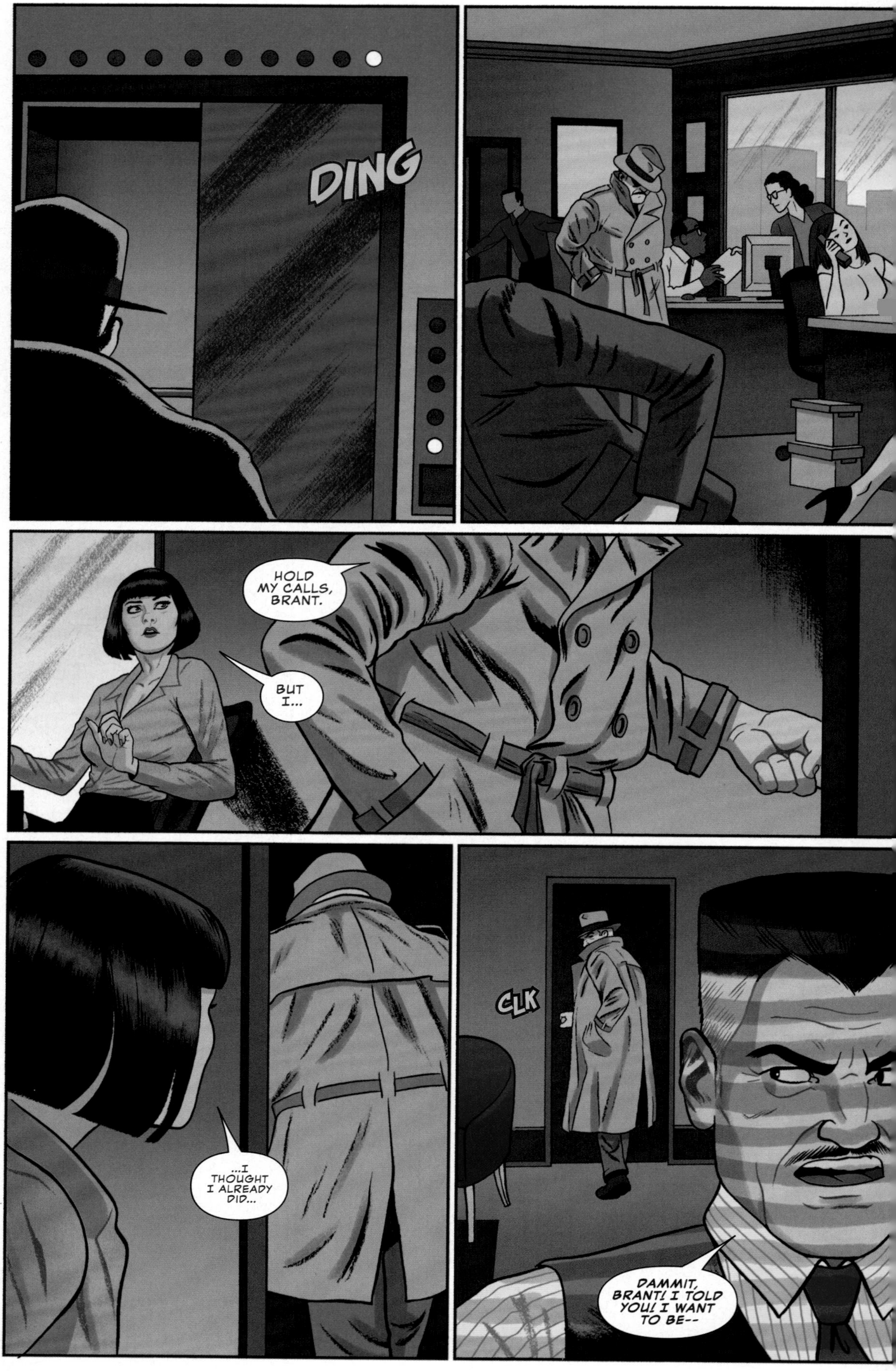
DING
HOLD MY CALLS, BRANT.
BUT I...
...I THOUGHT I ALREADY DID...
CLK
DAMMIT, BRANT! I TOLD YOU! I WANT TO BE--

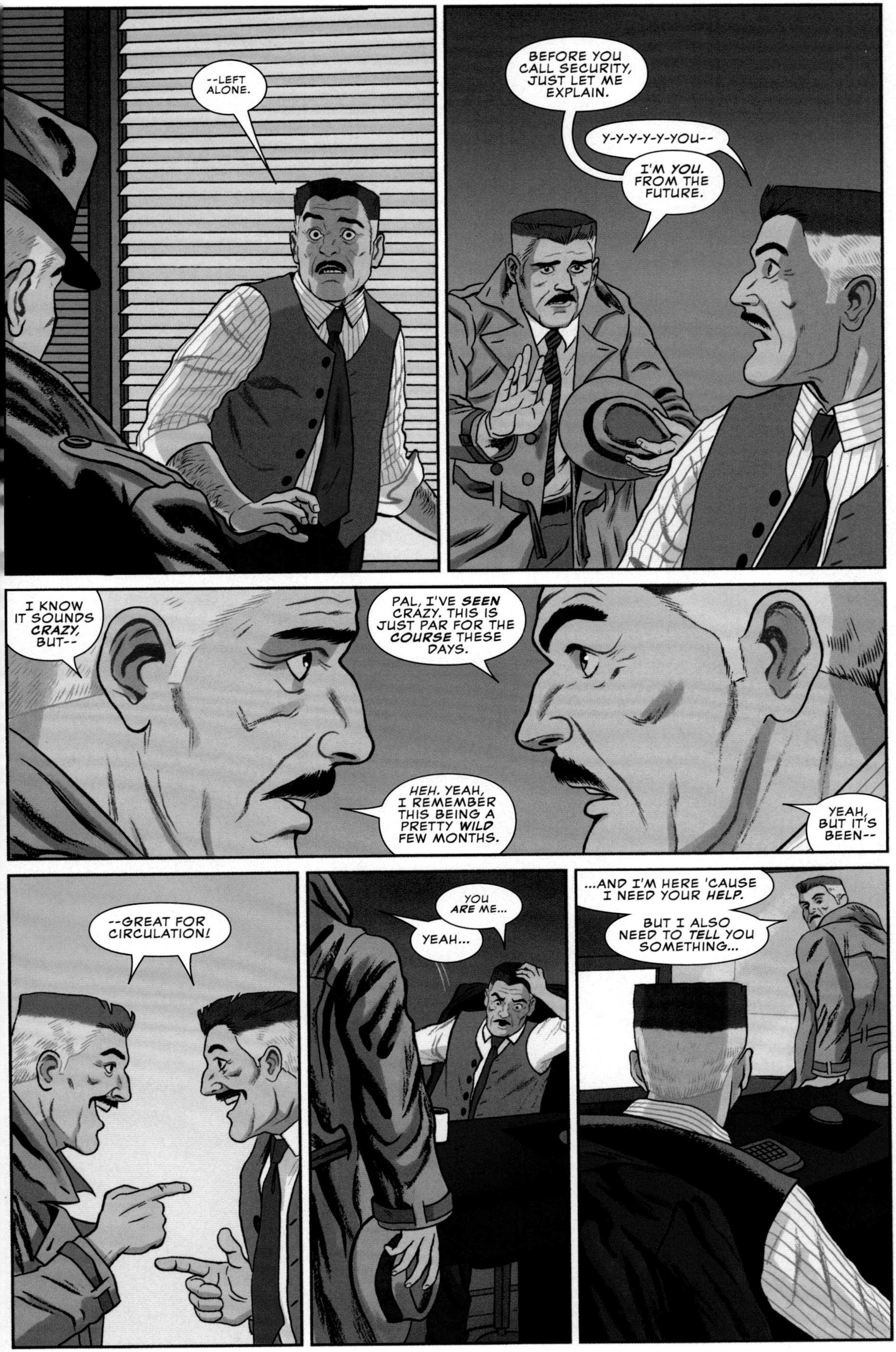
--LEFT ALONE.
BEFORE YOU CALL SECURITY, JUST LET ME EXPLAIN.
Y-Y-Y-Y-Y-YOU--
I'M *YOU*. FROM THE FUTURE.
I KNOW IT SOUNDS *CRAZY*, BUT--
PAL, I'VE *SEEN* CRAZY. THIS IS JUST PAR FOR THE *COURSE* THESE DAYS.
HEH. YEAH, I REMEMBER THIS BEING A PRETTY *WILD* FEW MONTHS.
YEAH, BUT IT'S BEEN--
--GREAT FOR CIRCULATION!
YOU *ARE* ME...
YEAH...
...AND I'M HERE 'CAUSE I NEED YOUR *HELP*.
BUT I ALSO NEED TO *TELL* YOU SOMETHING...

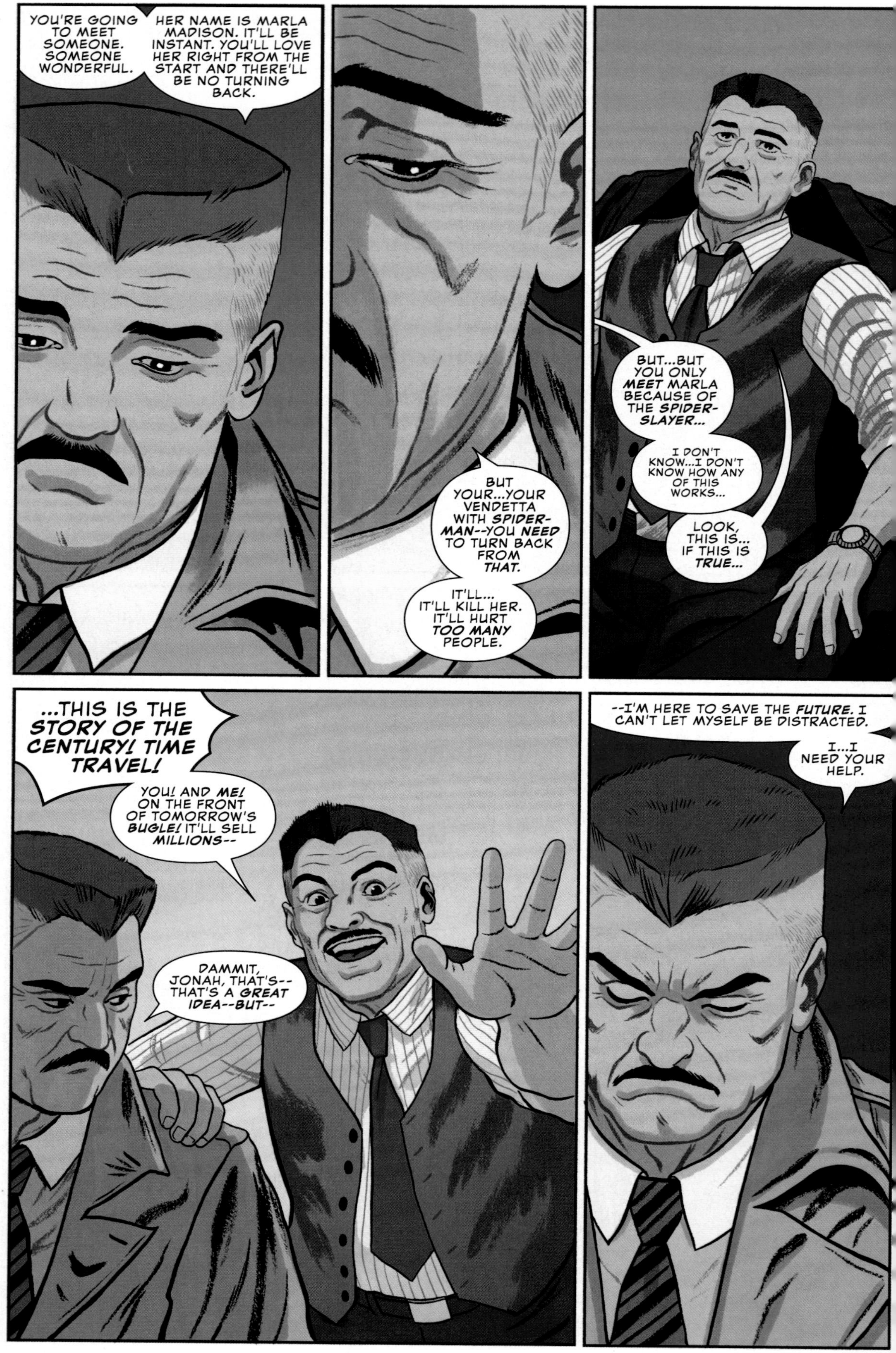
YOU'RE GOING TO MEET SOMEONE. SOMEONE WONDERFUL.
HER NAME IS MARLA MADISON. IT'LL BE INSTANT. YOU'LL LOVE HER RIGHT FROM THE START AND THERE'LL BE NO TURNING BACK.
BUT YOUR...YOUR VENDETTA WITH SPIDER-MAN--YOU NEED TO TURN BACK FROM THAT.
IT'LL... IT'LL KILL HER. IT'LL HURT TOO MANY PEOPLE.
BUT...BUT YOU ONLY MEET MARLA BECAUSE OF THE SPIDER-SLAYER...
I DON'T KNOW...I DON'T KNOW HOW ANY OF THIS WORKS...
LOOK, THIS IS... IF THIS IS TRUE...
...THIS IS THE STORY OF THE CENTURY! TIME TRAVEL!
YOU! AND ME! ON THE FRONT OF TOMORROW'S BUGLE! IT'LL SELL MILLIONS--
DAMMIT, JONAH, THAT'S-- THAT'S A GREAT IDEA--BUT--
--I'M HERE TO SAVE THE FUTURE. I CAN'T LET MYSELF BE DISTRACTED.
I...I NEED YOUR HELP.

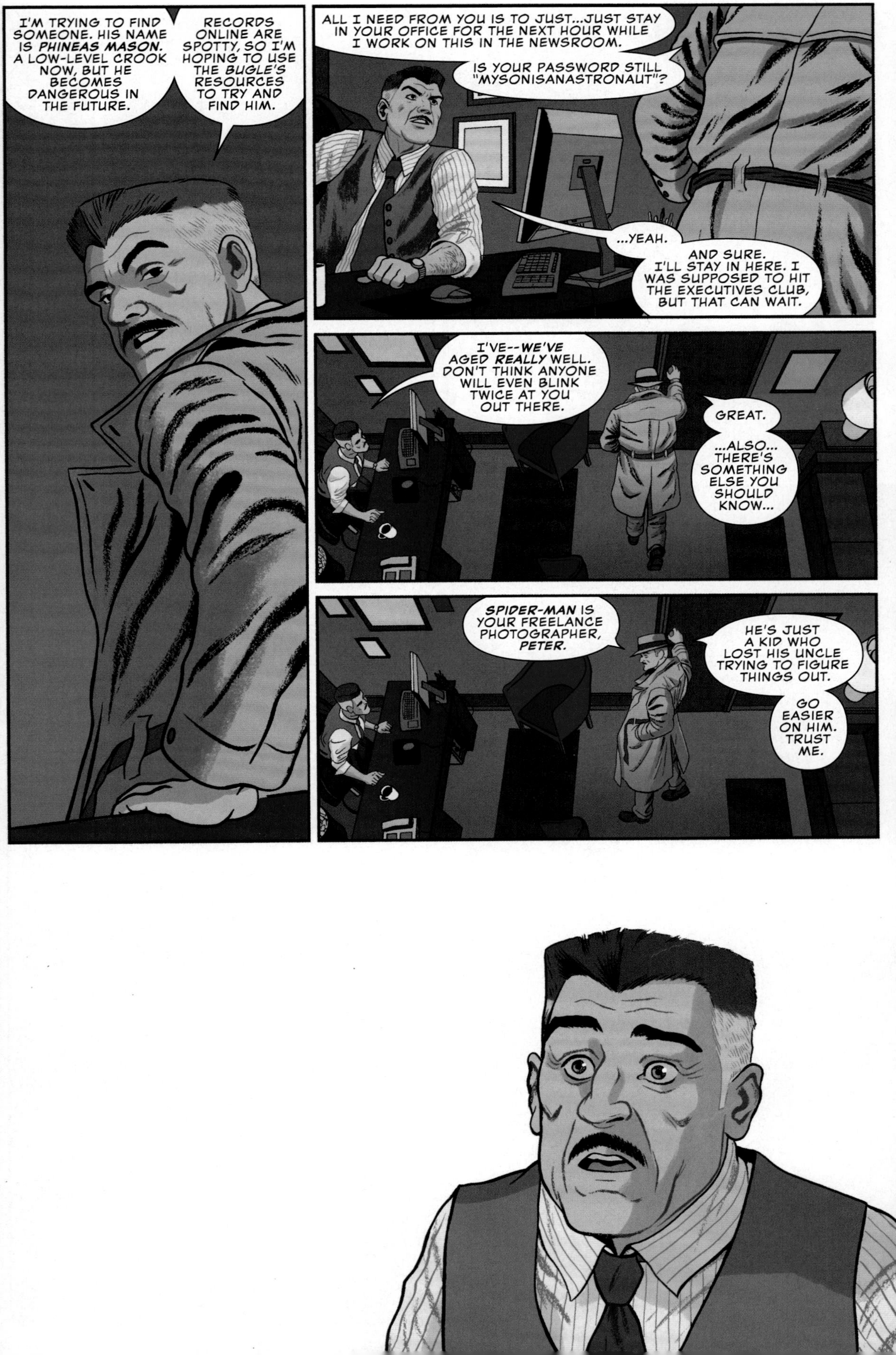
I'M TRYING TO FIND SOMEONE. HIS NAME IS PHINEAS MASON. A LOW-LEVEL CROOK NOW, BUT HE BECOMES DANGEROUS IN THE FUTURE.
RECORDS ONLINE ARE SPOTTY, SO I'M HOPING TO USE THE BUGLE'S RESOURCES TO TRY AND FIND HIM.
ALL I NEED FROM YOU IS TO JUST...JUST STAY IN YOUR OFFICE FOR THE NEXT HOUR WHILE I WORK ON THIS IN THE NEWSROOM.
IS YOUR PASSWORD STILL "MYSONISANASTRONAUT"?
...YEAH.
AND SURE. I'LL STAY IN HERE. I WAS SUPPOSED TO HIT THE EXECUTIVES CLUB, BUT THAT CAN WAIT.
I'VE--WE'VE AGED REALLY WELL. DON'T THINK ANYONE WILL EVEN BLINK TWICE AT YOU OUT THERE.
GREAT.
...ALSO... THERE'S SOMETHING ELSE YOU SHOULD KNOW...
SPIDER-MAN IS YOUR FREELANCE PHOTOGRAPHER, PETER.
HE'S JUST A KID WHO LOST HIS UNCLE TRYING TO FIGURE THINGS OUT.
GO EASIER ON HIM. TRUST ME.

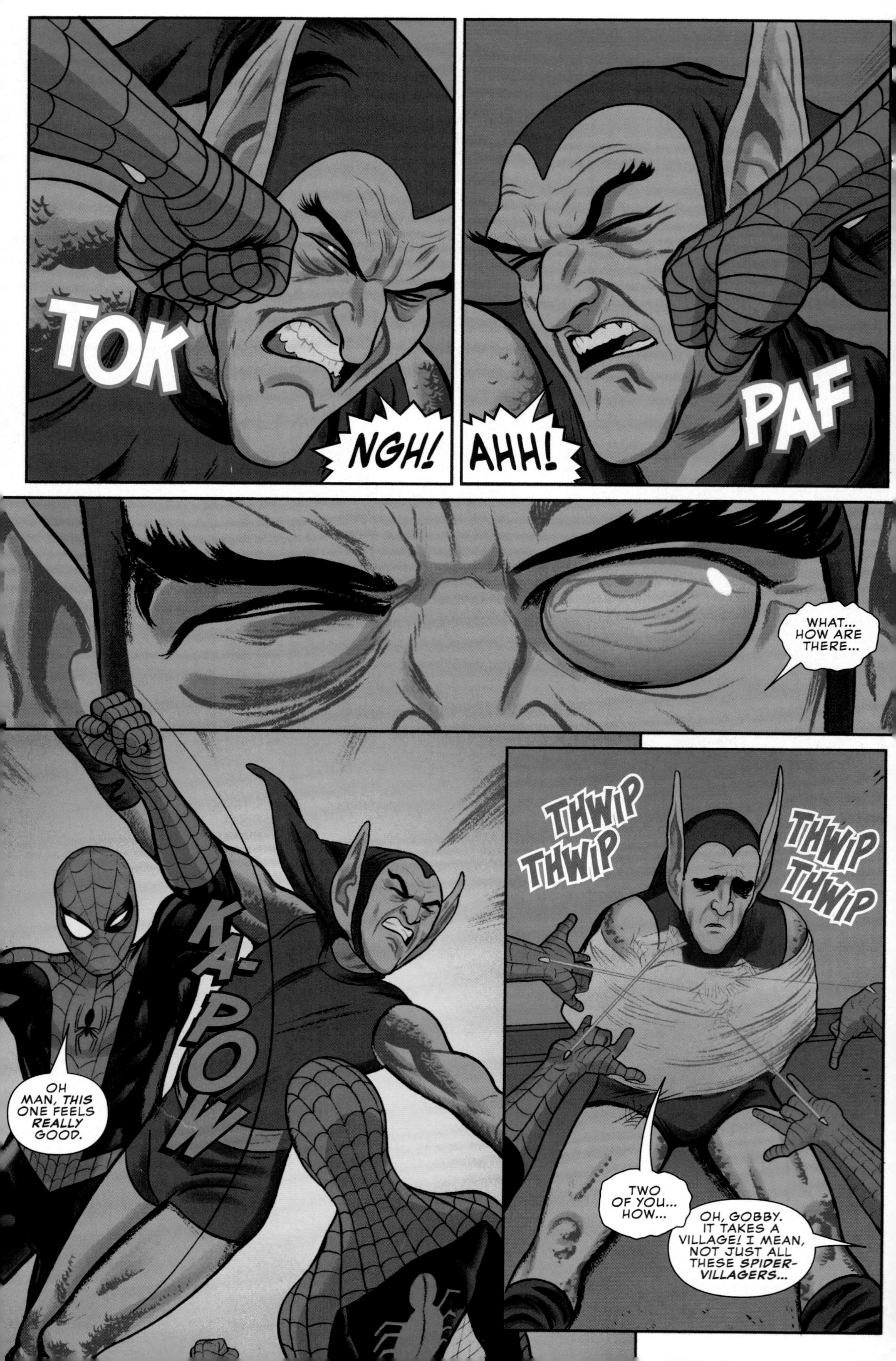
TOK
NGH!
AHH!
PAF
WHAT... HOW ARE THERE...
KA-POW
OH MAN, THIS ONE FEELS REALLY GOOD.
THWIP THWIP
THWIP THWIP
TWO OF YOU... HOW...
OH, GOBBY. IT TAKES A VILLAGE! I MEAN, NOT JUST ALL THESE SPIDER-VILLAGERS...

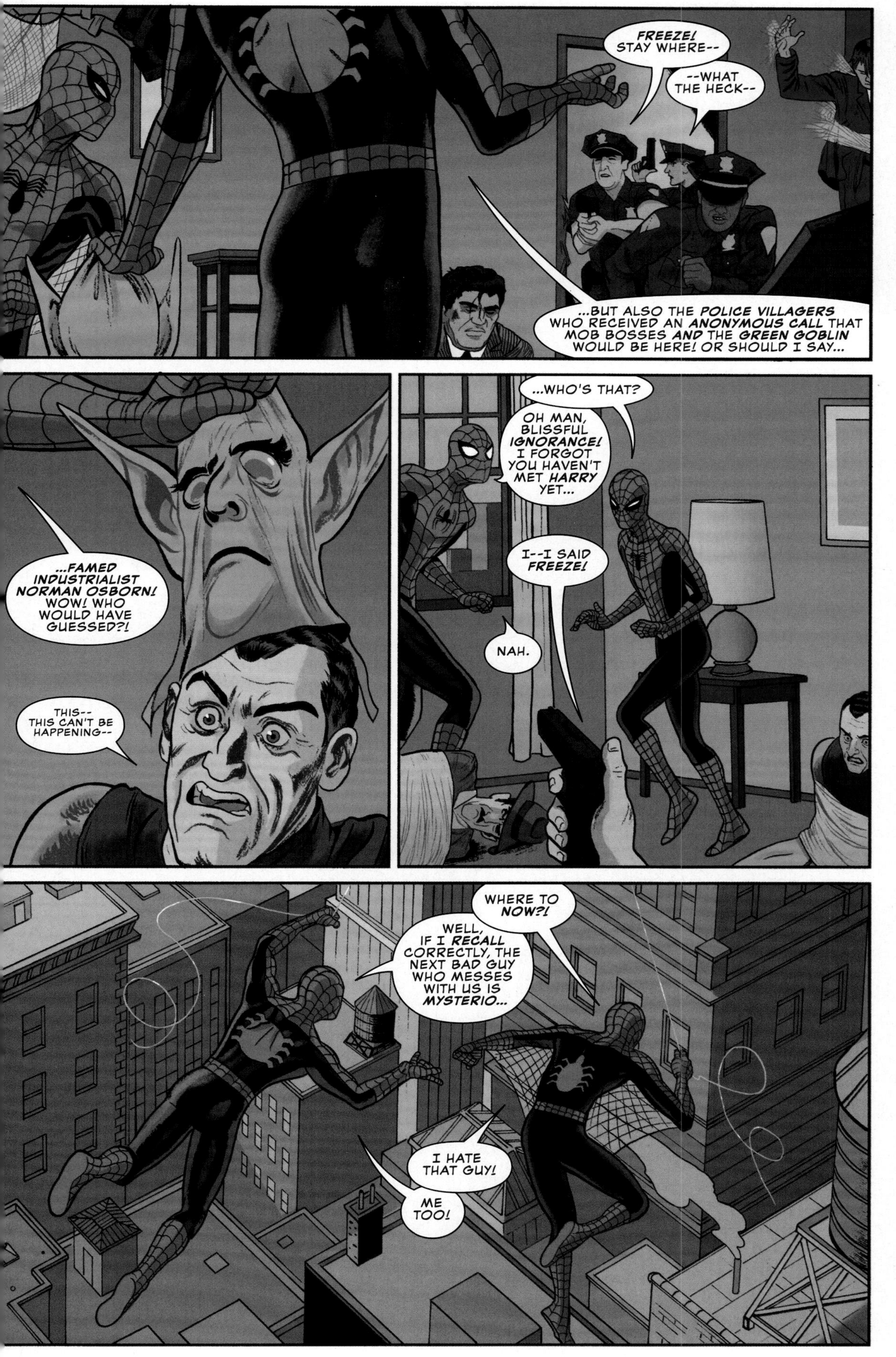
FREEZE! STAY WHERE--
--WHAT THE HECK--
...BUT ALSO THE POLICE VILLAGERS WHO RECEIVED AN ANONYMOUS CALL THAT MOB BOSSES AND THE GREEN GOBLIN WOULD BE HERE! OR SHOULD I SAY...
...FAMED INDUSTRIALIST NORMAN OSBORN! WOW! WHO WOULD HAVE GUESSED?!
THIS-- THIS CAN'T BE HAPPENING--
...WHO'S THAT?
OH MAN, BLISSFUL IGNORANCE! I FORGOT YOU HAVEN'T MET HARRY YET...
I--I SAID FREEZE!
NAH.
WHERE TO NOW?!
WELL, IF I RECALL CORRECTLY, THE NEXT BAD GUY WHO MESSES WITH US IS MYSTERIO...
I HATE THAT GUY!
ME TOO!

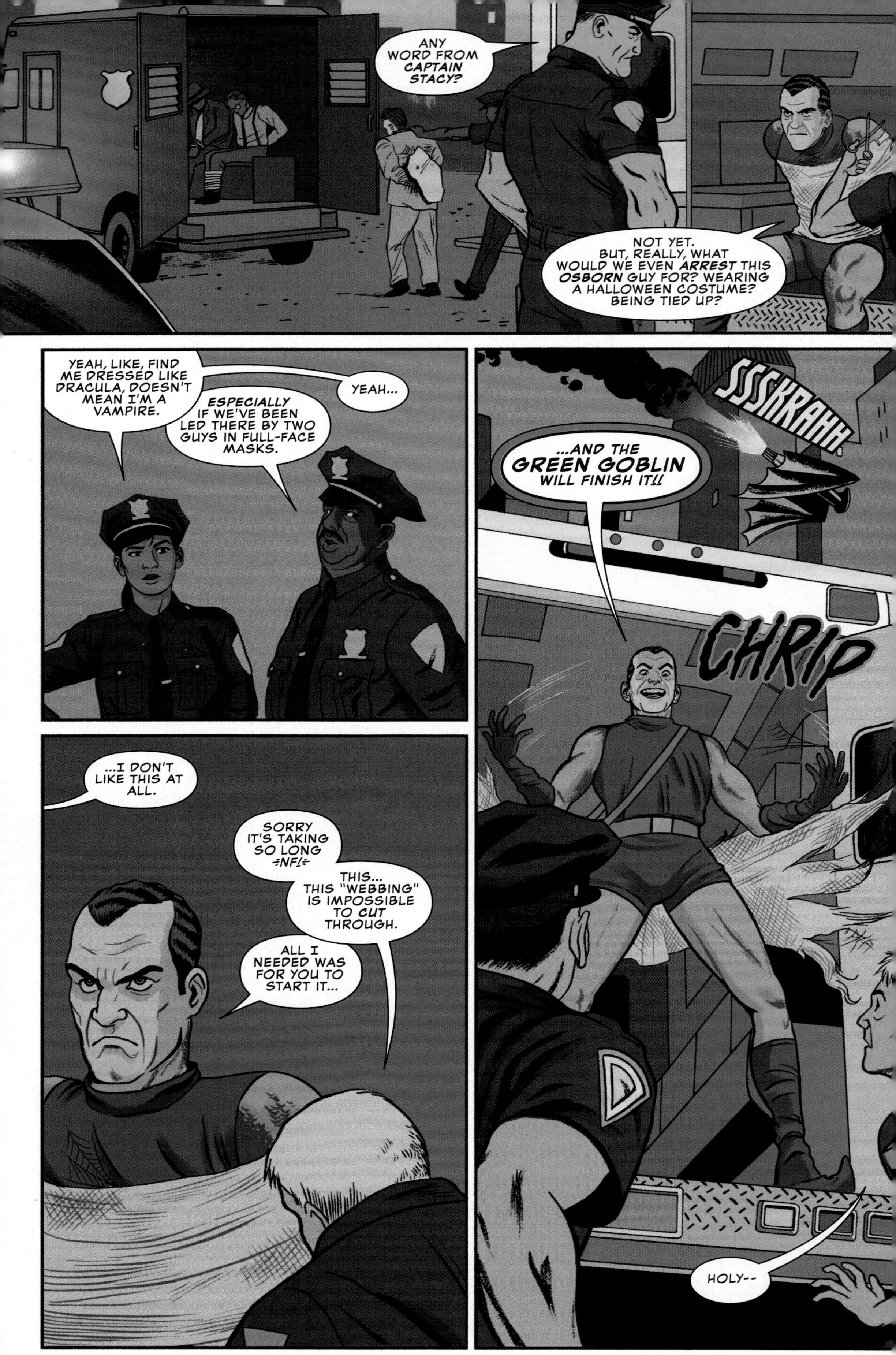
ANY WORD FROM CAPTAIN STACY?
NOT YET. BUT, REALLY, WHAT WOULD WE EVEN ARREST THIS OSBORN GUY FOR? WEARING A HALLOWEEN COSTUME? BEING TIED UP?
YEAH, LIKE, FIND ME DRESSED LIKE DRACULA, DOESN'T MEAN I'M A VAMPIRE.
YEAH...
ESPECIALLY IF WE'VE BEEN LED THERE BY TWO GUYS IN FULL-FACE MASKS.
...I DON'T LIKE THIS AT ALL.
SORRY IT'S TAKING SO LONG =NF!=
THIS... THIS "WEBBING" IS IMPOSSIBLE TO CUT THROUGH.
ALL I NEEDED WAS FOR YOU TO START IT...
SSSKRAHH
...AND THE GREEN GOBLIN WILL FINISH IT!!
CHRIP
HOLY--

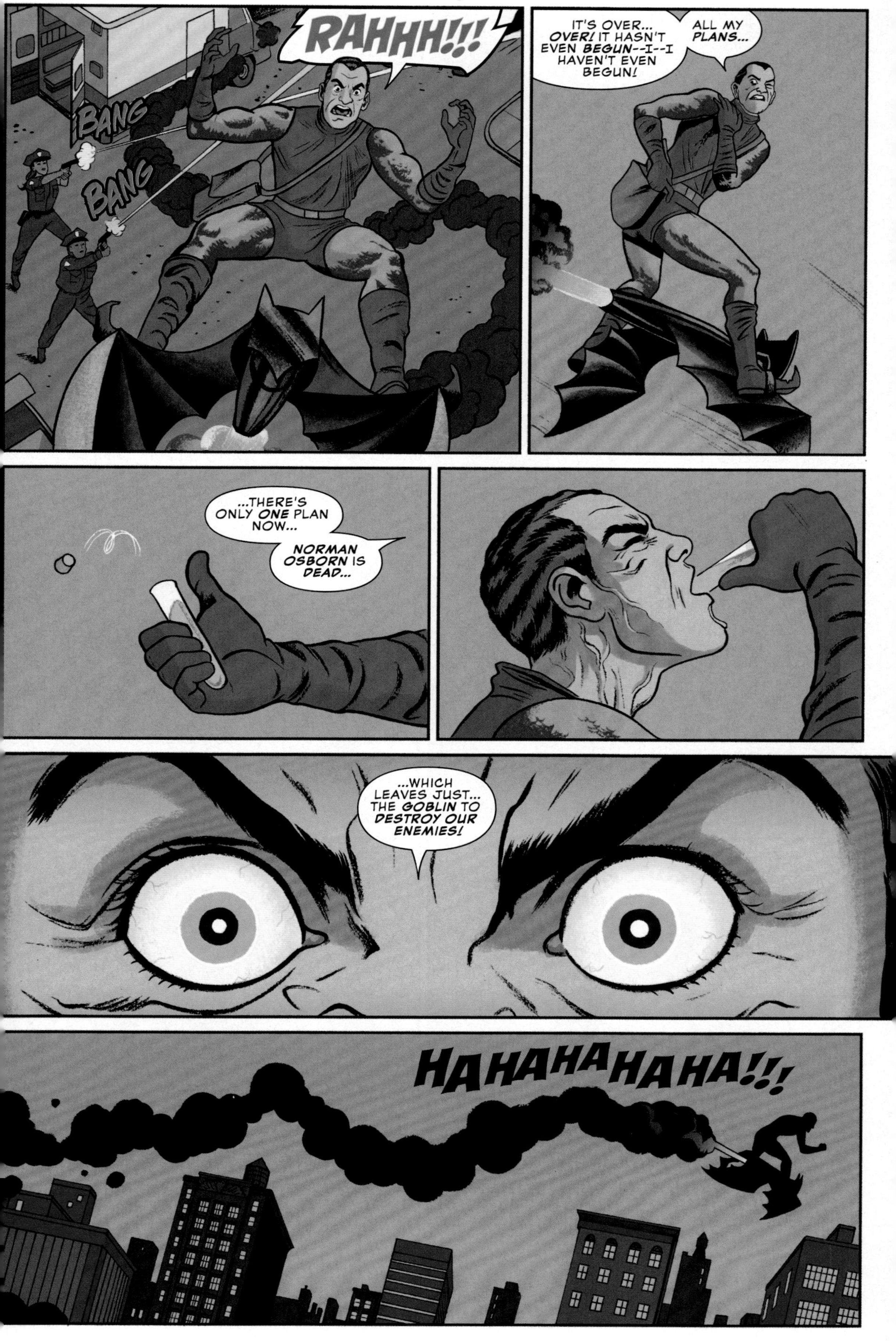
RAHHH!!!
BANG
BANG
IT'S OVER... OVER! IT HASN'T EVEN BEGUN--I--I HAVEN'T EVEN BEGUN!
ALL MY PLANS...
...THERE'S ONLY ONE PLAN NOW...
NORMAN OSBORN IS DEAD...
...WHICH LEAVES JUST... THE GOBLIN TO DESTROY OUR ENEMIES!
HAHAHAHAHAHA!!!

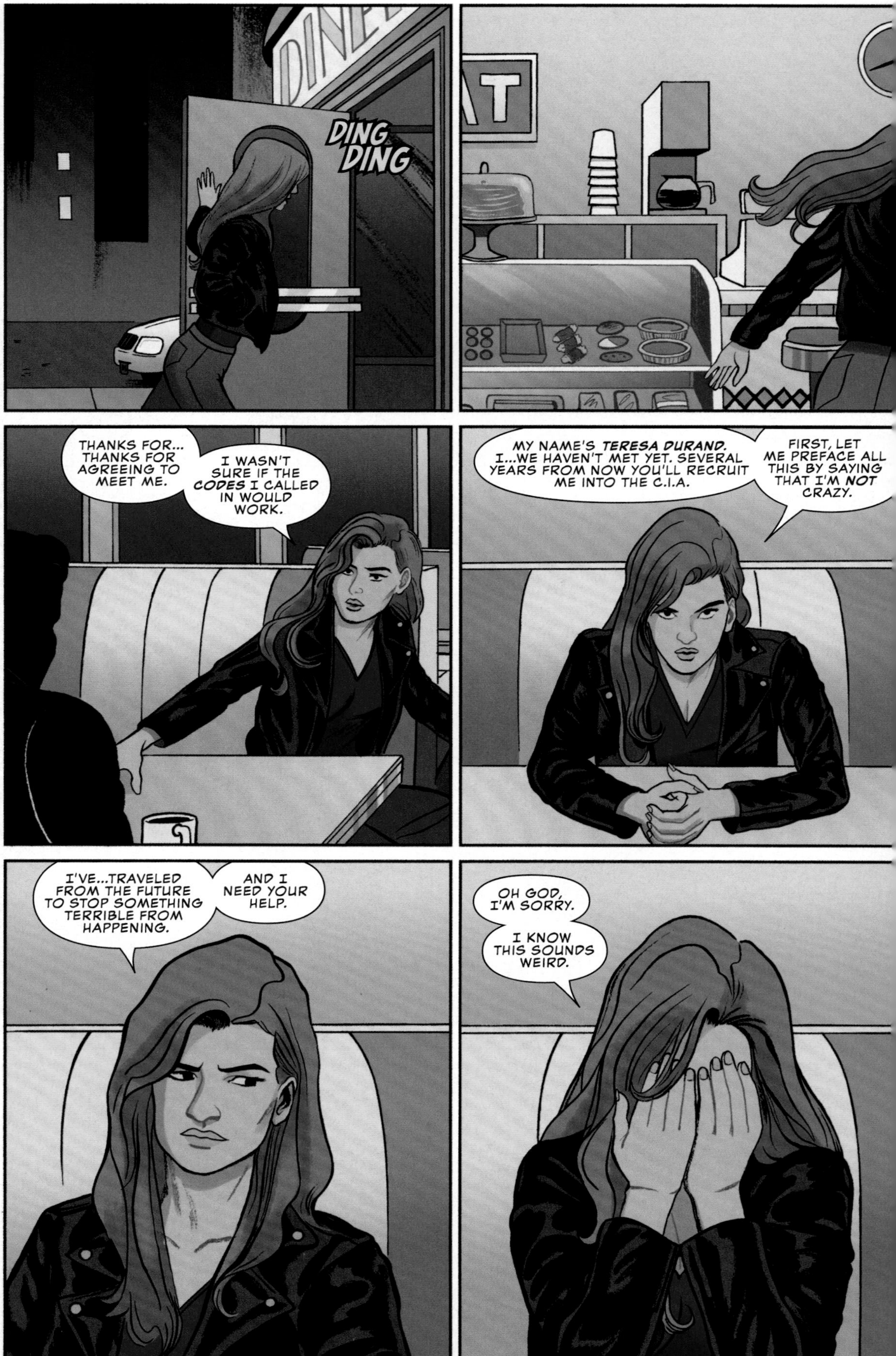

DING DING
THANKS FOR... THANKS FOR AGREEING TO MEET ME.
I WASN'T SURE IF THE CODES I CALLED IN WOULD WORK.
MY NAME'S TERESA DURAND. I...WE HAVEN'T MET YET. SEVERAL YEARS FROM NOW YOU'LL RECRUIT ME INTO THE C.I.A.
FIRST, LET ME PREFACE ALL THIS BY SAYING THAT I'M NOT CRAZY.
I'VE...TRAVELED FROM THE FUTURE TO STOP SOMETHING TERRIBLE FROM HAPPENING.
AND I NEED YOUR HELP.
OH GOD, I'M SORRY.
I KNOW THIS SOUNDS WEIRD.

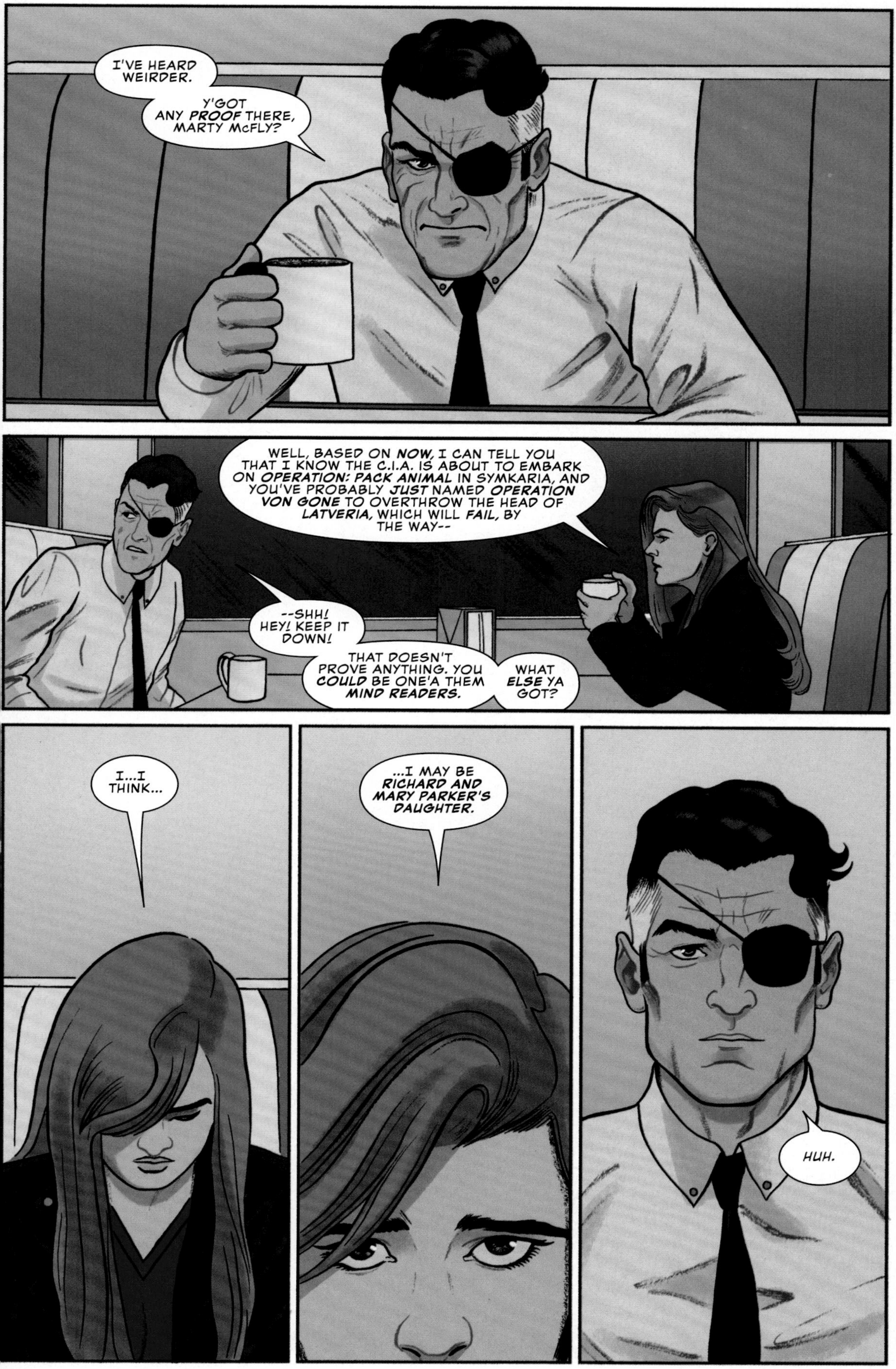
I'VE HEARD WEIRDER.
Y'GOT ANY PROOF THERE, MARTY McFLY?
WELL, BASED ON NOW, I CAN TELL YOU THAT I KNOW THE C.I.A. IS ABOUT TO EMBARK ON OPERATION: PACK ANIMAL IN SYMKARIA, AND YOU'VE PROBABLY JUST NAMED OPERATION VON GONE TO OVERTHROW THE HEAD OF LATVERIA, WHICH WILL FAIL, BY THE WAY--
--SHH! HEY! KEEP IT DOWN!
THAT DOESN'T PROVE ANYTHING. YOU COULD BE ONE'A THEM MIND READERS.
WHAT ELSE YA GOT?
I...I THINK...
...I MAY BE RICHARD AND MARY PARKER'S DAUGHTER.
HUH.

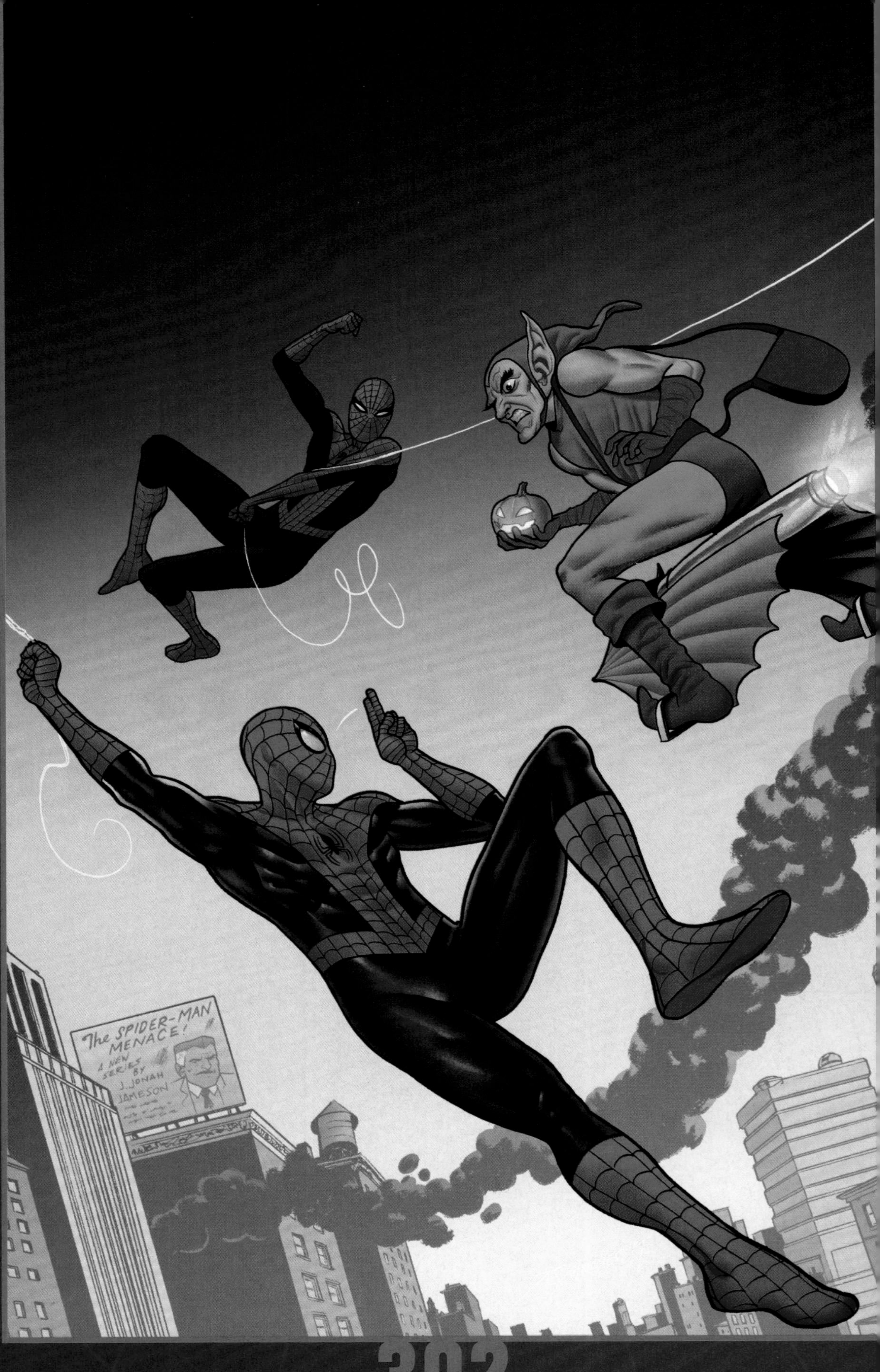

The SPIDER-MAN MENACE!
A NEW SERIES BY J. JONAH JAMESON

302

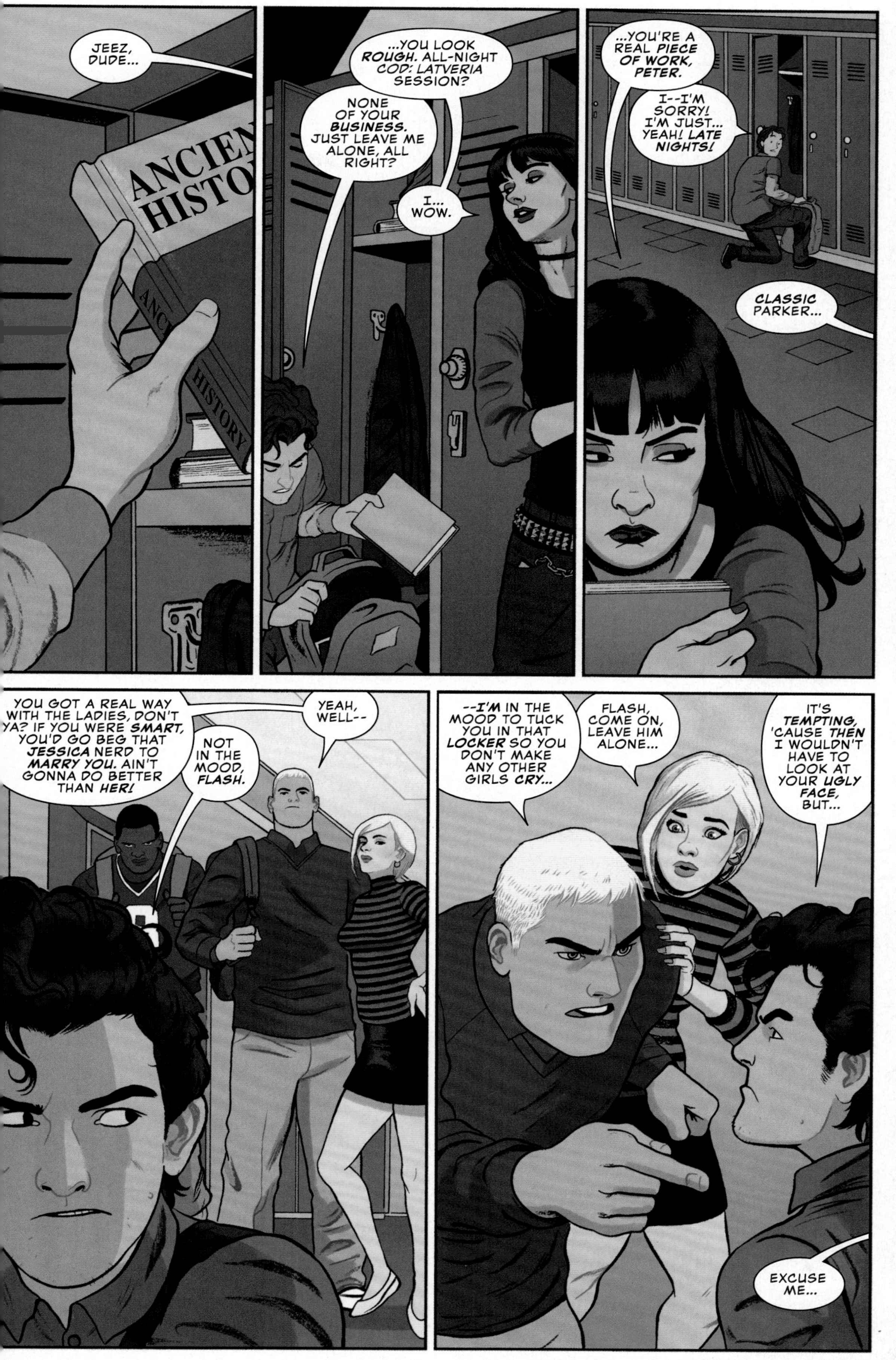
JEEZ, DUDE...
ANCIENT HISTORY
...YOU LOOK ROUGH. ALL-NIGHT COD: LATVERIA SESSION?
NONE OF YOUR BUSINESS. JUST LEAVE ME ALONE, ALL RIGHT?
I... WOW.
...YOU'RE A REAL PIECE OF WORK, PETER.
I--I'M SORRY! I'M JUST... YEAH! LATE NIGHTS!
CLASSIC PARKER...
YOU GOT A REAL WAY WITH THE LADIES, DON'T YA? IF YOU WERE SMART, YOU'D GO BEG THAT JESSICA NERD TO MARRY YOU. AIN'T GONNA DO BETTER THAN HER!
YEAH, WELL--
NOT IN THE MOOD, FLASH.
--I'M IN THE MOOD TO TUCK YOU IN THAT LOCKER SO YOU DON'T MAKE ANY OTHER GIRLS CRY...
FLASH, COME ON, LEAVE HIM ALONE...
IT'S TEMPTING, 'CAUSE THEN I WOULDN'T HAVE TO LOOK AT YOUR UGLY FACE, BUT...
EXCUSE ME...

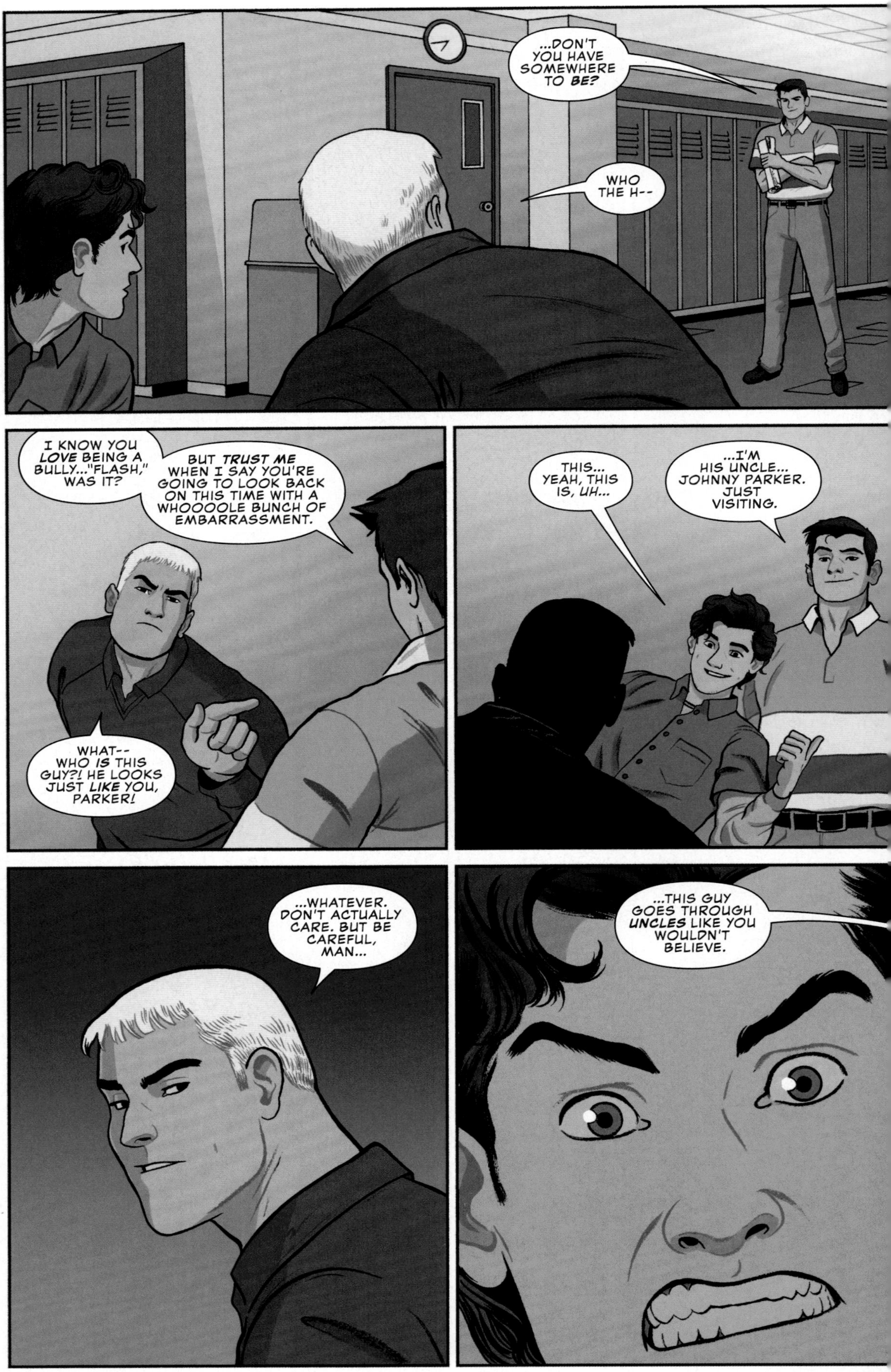
...DON'T YOU HAVE SOMEWHERE TO BE?
WHO THE H--
I KNOW YOU LOVE BEING A BULLY..."FLASH," WAS IT?
BUT TRUST ME WHEN I SAY YOU'RE GOING TO LOOK BACK ON THIS TIME WITH A WHOOOOLE BUNCH OF EMBARRASSMENT.
WHAT-- WHO IS THIS GUY?! HE LOOKS JUST LIKE YOU, PARKER!
THIS... YEAH, THIS IS, UH...
...I'M HIS UNCLE... JOHNNY PARKER. JUST VISITING.
...WHATEVER. DON'T ACTUALLY CARE. BUT BE CAREFUL, MAN...
...THIS GUY GOES THROUGH UNCLES LIKE YOU WOULDN'T BELIEVE.

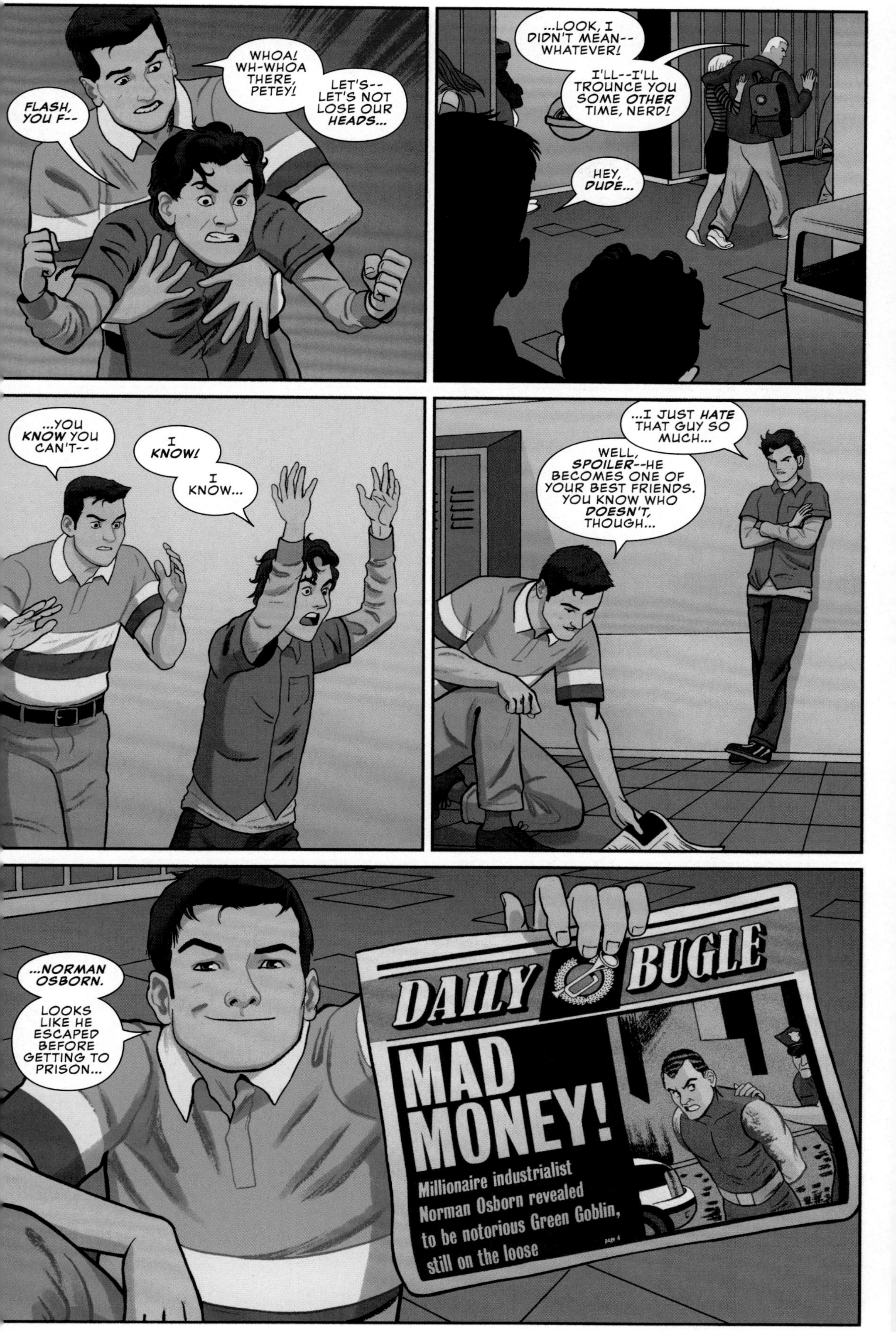
FLASH, YOU F--
WHOA! WH-WHOA THERE, PETEY!
LET'S--LET'S NOT LOSE OUR HEADS...
...LOOK, I DIDN'T MEAN--WHATEVER!
I'LL--I'LL TROUNCE YOU SOME OTHER TIME, NERD!
HEY, DUDE...
...YOU KNOW YOU CAN'T--
I KNOW!
I KNOW...
...I JUST HATE THAT GUY SO MUCH...
WELL, SPOILER--HE BECOMES ONE OF YOUR BEST FRIENDS. YOU KNOW WHO DOESN'T, THOUGH...
...NORMAN OSBORN.
LOOKS LIKE HE ESCAPED BEFORE GETTING TO PRISON...
DAILY BUGLE
MAD MONEY!
Millionaire industrialist Norman Osborn revealed to be notorious Green Goblin, still on the loose
page 4

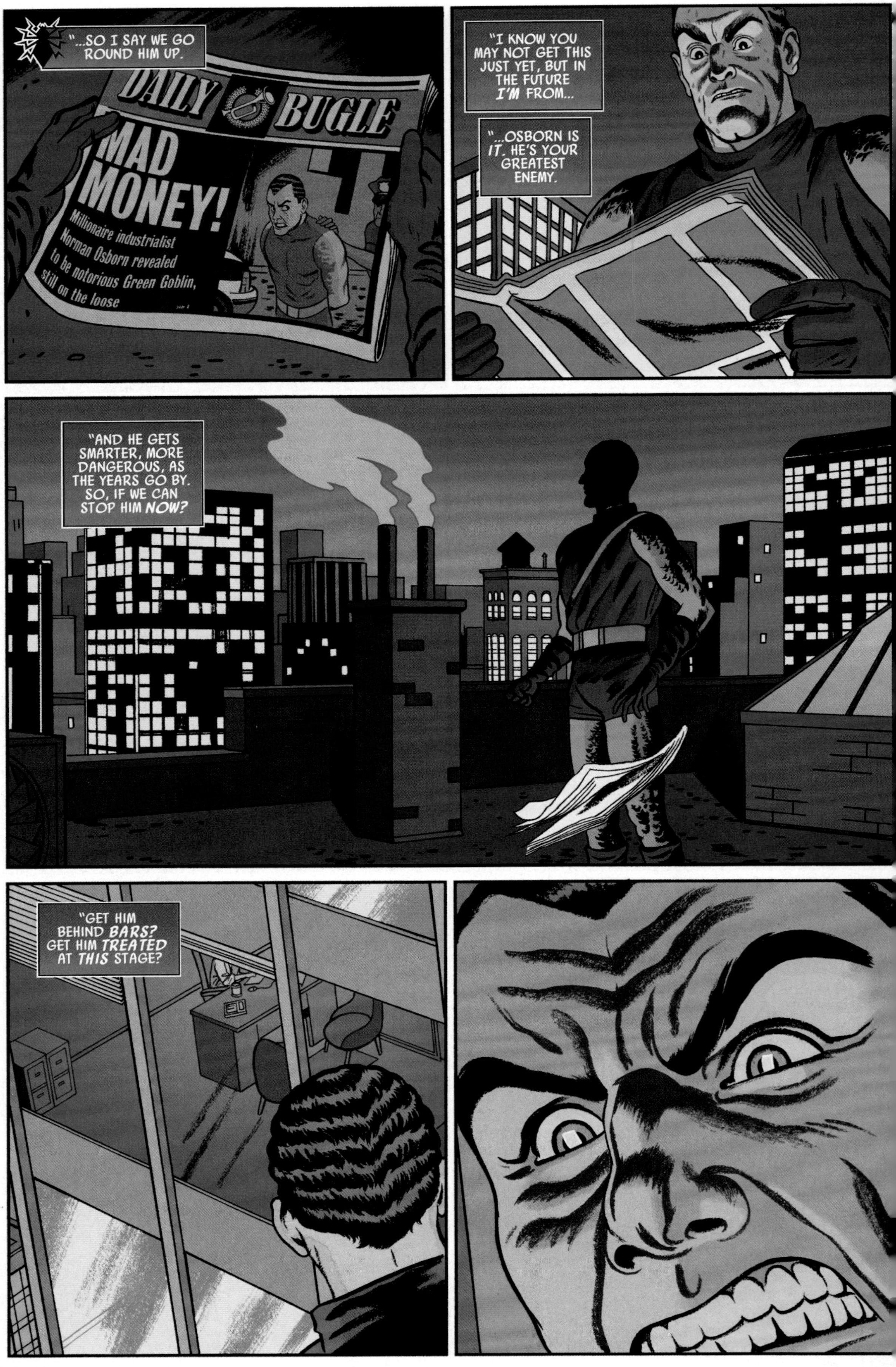
"...SO I SAY WE GO ROUND HIM UP.
DAILY BUGLE
MAD MONEY!
Millionaire industrialist Norman Osborn revealed to be notorious Green Goblin, still on the loose
"I KNOW YOU MAY NOT GET THIS JUST YET, BUT IN THE FUTURE I'M FROM...
"...OSBORN IS IT. HE'S YOUR GREATEST ENEMY.
"AND HE GETS SMARTER, MORE DANGEROUS, AS THE YEARS GO BY. SO, IF WE CAN STOP HIM NOW?
"GET HIM BEHIND BARS? GET HIM TREATED AT THIS STAGE?

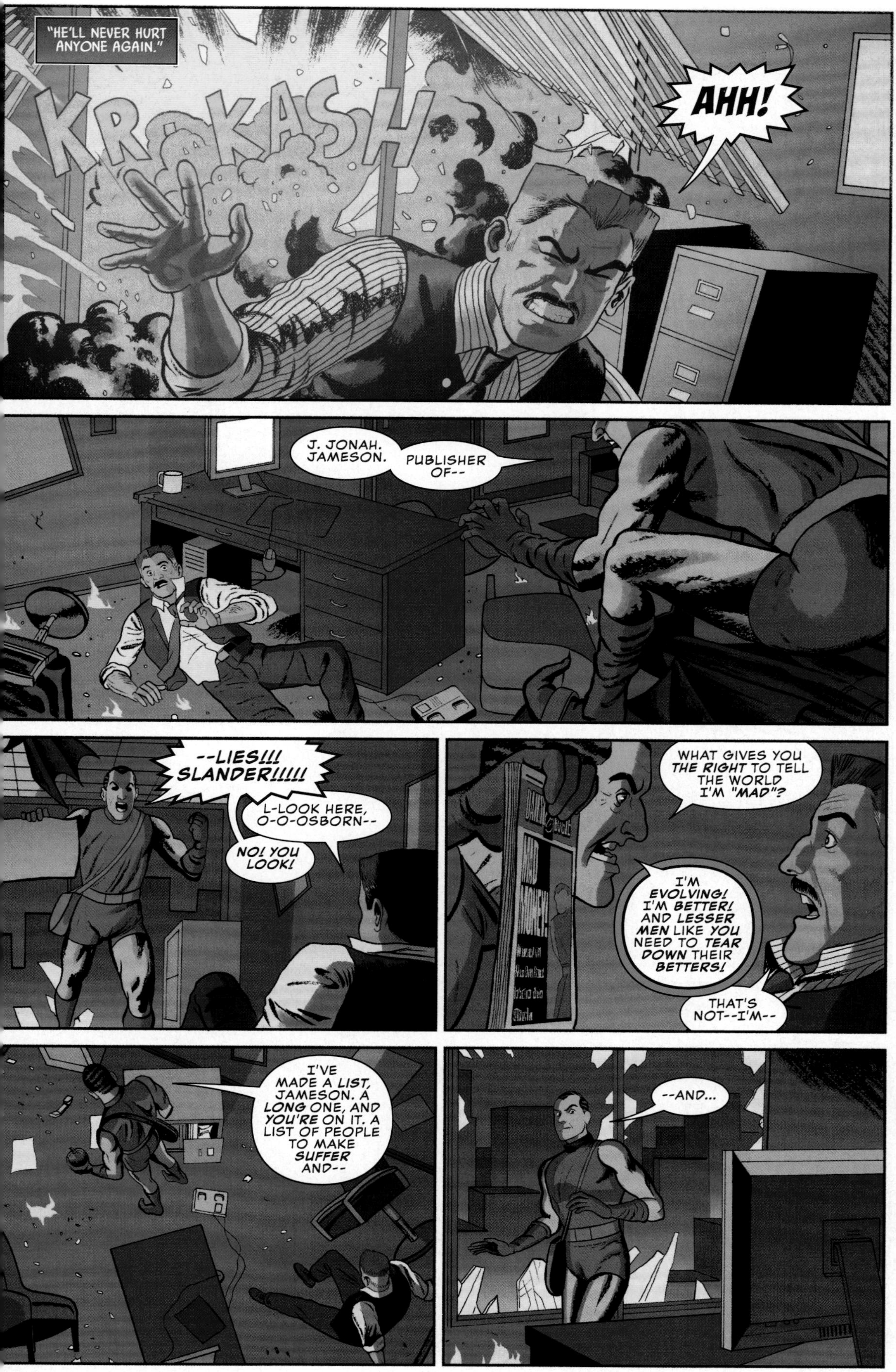
"HE'LL NEVER HURT ANYONE AGAIN."
KRAKASH
AHH!
J. JONAH. JAMESON.
PUBLISHER OF--
--LIES!!! SLANDER!!!!!
L-LOOK HERE, O-O-OSBORN--
NO! YOU LOOK!
WHAT GIVES YOU THE RIGHT TO TELL THE WORLD I'M "MAD"?
I'M EVOLVING! I'M BETTER! AND LESSER MEN LIKE YOU NEED TO TEAR DOWN THEIR BETTERS!
THAT'S NOT--I'M--
I'VE MADE A LIST, JAMESON. A LONG ONE, AND YOU'RE ON IT. A LIST OF PEOPLE TO MAKE SUFFER AND--
--AND...

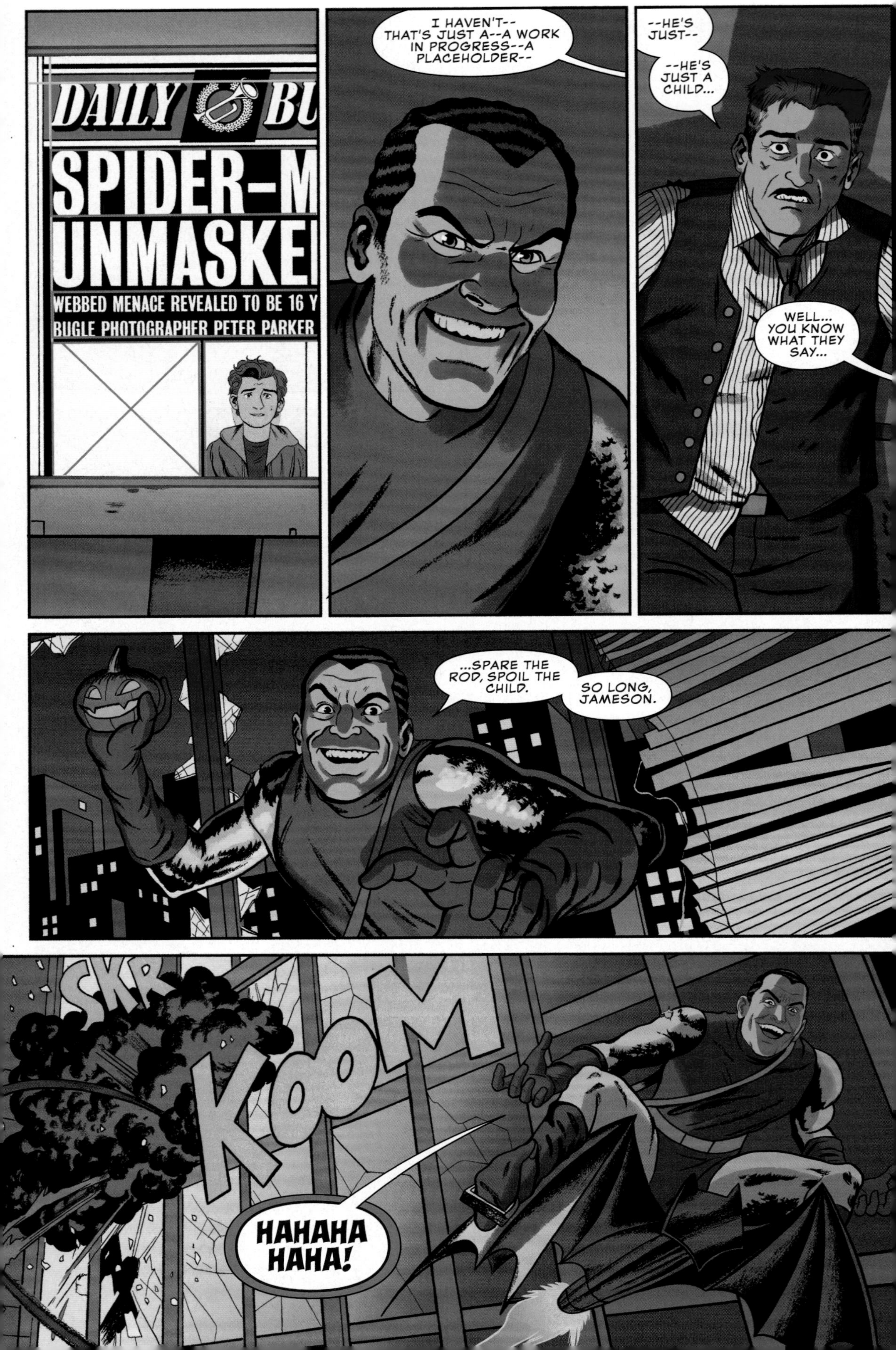
DAILY BU
SPIDER-M
UNMASKE
WEBBED MENACE REVEALED TO BE 16 Y
BUGLE PHOTOGRAPHER PETER PARKER
I HAVEN'T-- THAT'S JUST A--A WORK IN PROGRESS--A PLACEHOLDER--
--HE'S JUST--
--HE'S JUST A CHILD...
WELL... YOU KNOW WHAT THEY SAY...
...SPARE THE ROD, SPOIL THE CHILD.
SO LONG, JAMESON.
SKR
KOOM
HAHAHA HAHA!

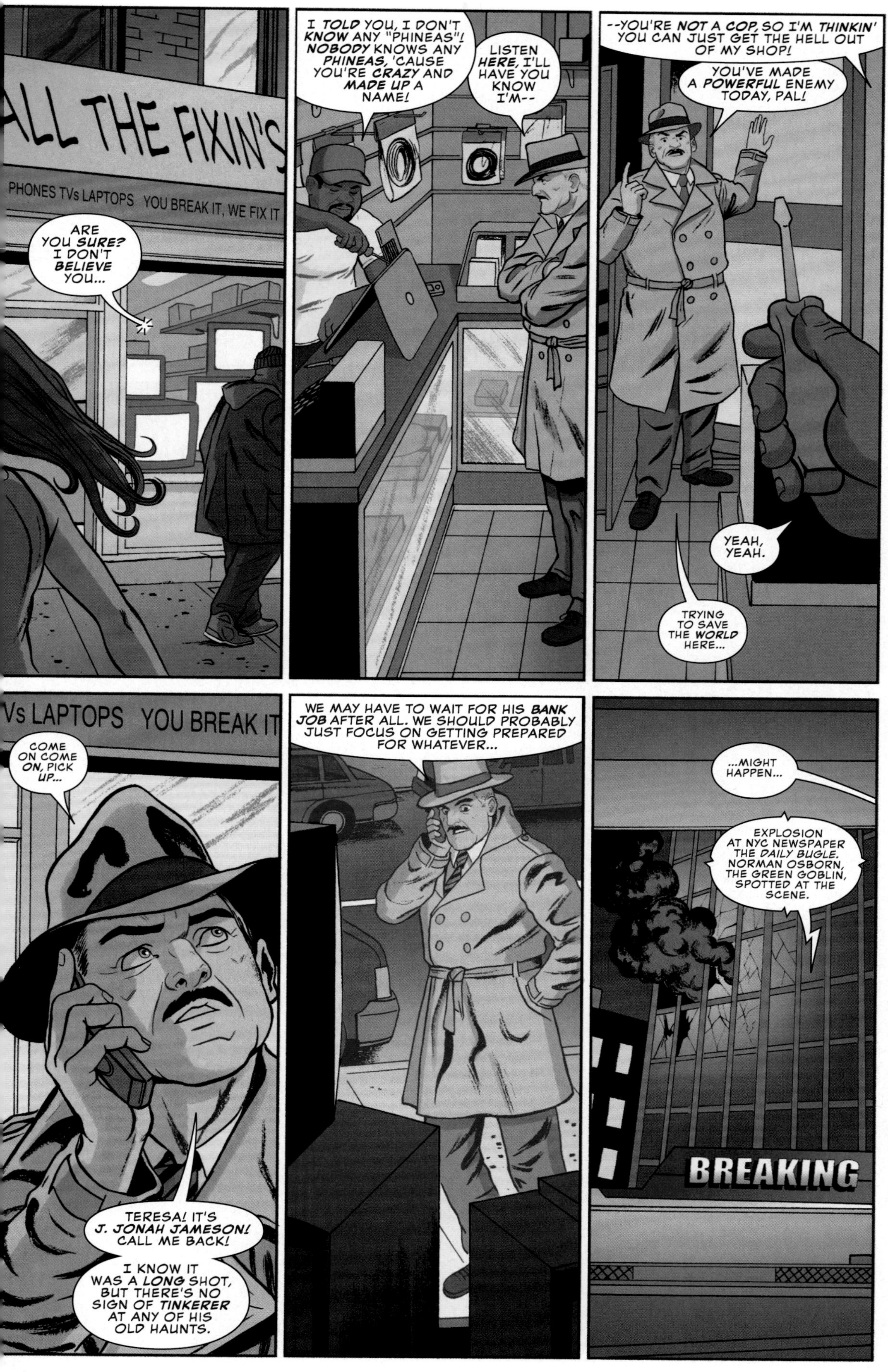
ALL THE FIXIN'S
PHONES TVs LAPTOPS YOU BREAK IT, WE FIX IT
ARE YOU SURE? I DON'T BELIEVE YOU...
I TOLD YOU, I DON'T KNOW ANY "PHINEAS"! NOBODY KNOWS ANY PHINEAS, 'CAUSE YOU'RE CRAZY AND MADE UP A NAME!
LISTEN HERE, I'LL HAVE YOU KNOW I'M--
--YOU'RE NOT A COP, SO I'M THINKIN' YOU CAN JUST GET THE HELL OUT OF MY SHOP!
YOU'VE MADE A POWERFUL ENEMY TODAY, PAL!
YEAH, YEAH.
TRYING TO SAVE THE WORLD HERE...
Vs LAPTOPS YOU BREAK IT
COME ON COME ON, PICK UP...
TERESA! IT'S J. JONAH JAMESON! CALL ME BACK!
I KNOW IT WAS A LONG SHOT, BUT THERE'S NO SIGN OF TINKERER AT ANY OF HIS OLD HAUNTS.
WE MAY HAVE TO WAIT FOR HIS BANK JOB AFTER ALL. WE SHOULD PROBABLY JUST FOCUS ON GETTING PREPARED FOR WHATEVER...
...MIGHT HAPPEN...
EXPLOSION AT NYC NEWSPAPER THE DAILY BUGLE. NORMAN OSBORN, THE GREEN GOBLIN, SPOTTED AT THE SCENE.
BREAKING

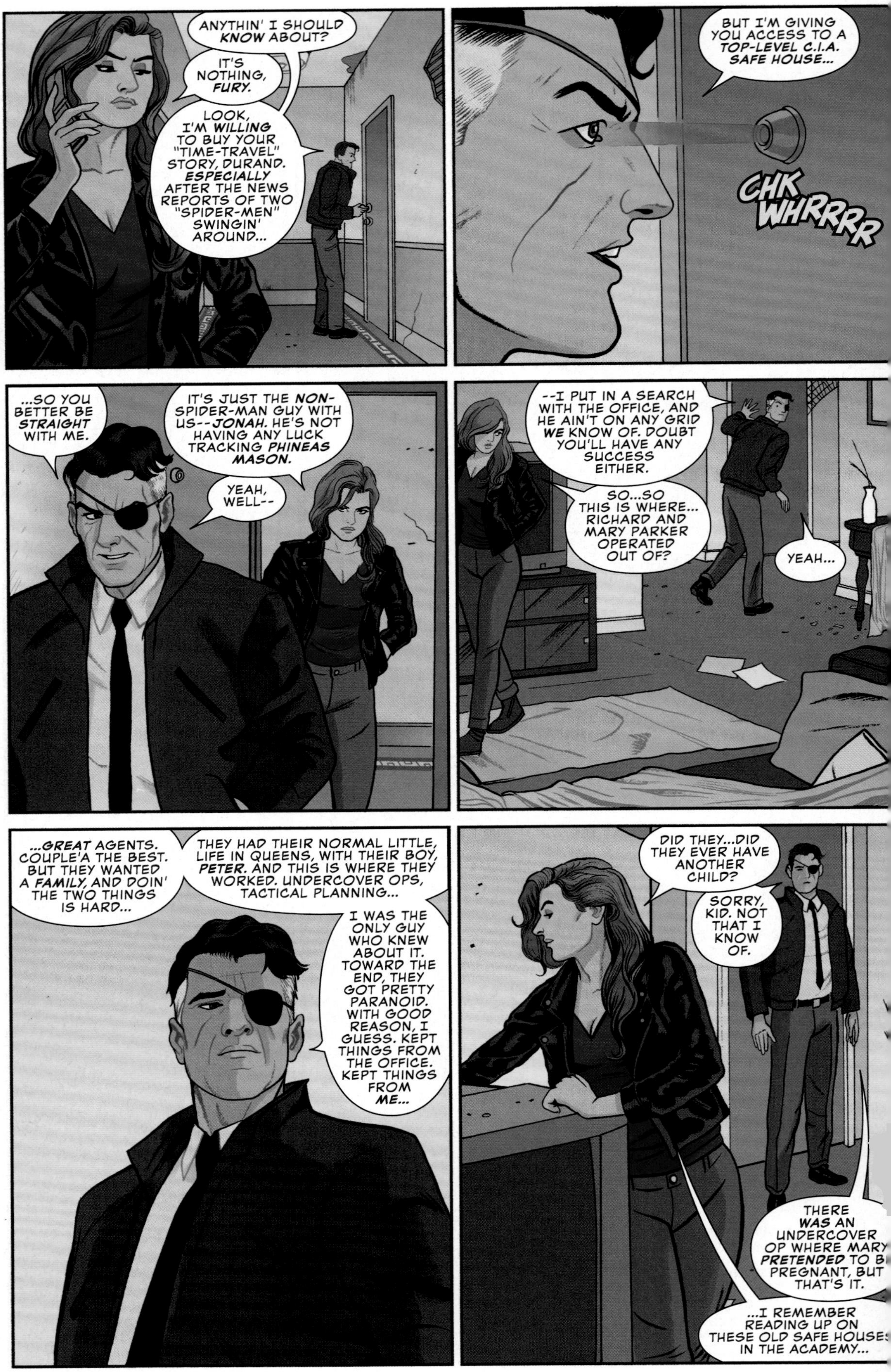
ANYTHIN' I SHOULD KNOW ABOUT?
IT'S NOTHING, FURY.
LOOK, I'M WILLING TO BUY YOUR "TIME-TRAVEL" STORY, DURAND. ESPECIALLY AFTER THE NEWS REPORTS OF TWO "SPIDER-MEN" SWINGIN' AROUND...
BUT I'M GIVING YOU ACCESS TO A TOP-LEVEL C.I.A. SAFE HOUSE...
CHK WHRRRR
...SO YOU BETTER BE STRAIGHT WITH ME.
IT'S JUST THE NON-SPIDER-MAN GUY WITH US--JONAH. HE'S NOT HAVING ANY LUCK TRACKING PHINEAS MASON.
YEAH, WELL--
--I PUT IN A SEARCH WITH THE OFFICE, AND HE AIN'T ON ANY GRID WE KNOW OF. DOUBT YOU'LL HAVE ANY SUCCESS EITHER.
SO...SO THIS IS WHERE... RICHARD AND MARY PARKER OPERATED OUT OF?
YEAH...
...GREAT AGENTS. COUPLE'A THE BEST. BUT THEY WANTED A FAMILY, AND DOIN' THE TWO THINGS IS HARD...
THEY HAD THEIR NORMAL LITTLE, LIFE IN QUEENS, WITH THEIR BOY, PETER. AND THIS IS WHERE THEY WORKED. UNDERCOVER OPS, TACTICAL PLANNING...
I WAS THE ONLY GUY WHO KNEW ABOUT IT. TOWARD THE END, THEY GOT PRETTY PARANOID. WITH GOOD REASON, I GUESS. KEPT THINGS FROM THE OFFICE. KEPT THINGS FROM ME...
DID THEY...DID THEY EVER HAVE ANOTHER CHILD?
SORRY, KID. NOT THAT I KNOW OF.
THERE WAS AN UNDERCOVER OP WHERE MARY PRETENDED TO B PREGNANT, BUT THAT'S IT.
...I REMEMBER READING UP ON THESE OLD SAFE HOUSES IN THE ACADEMY...

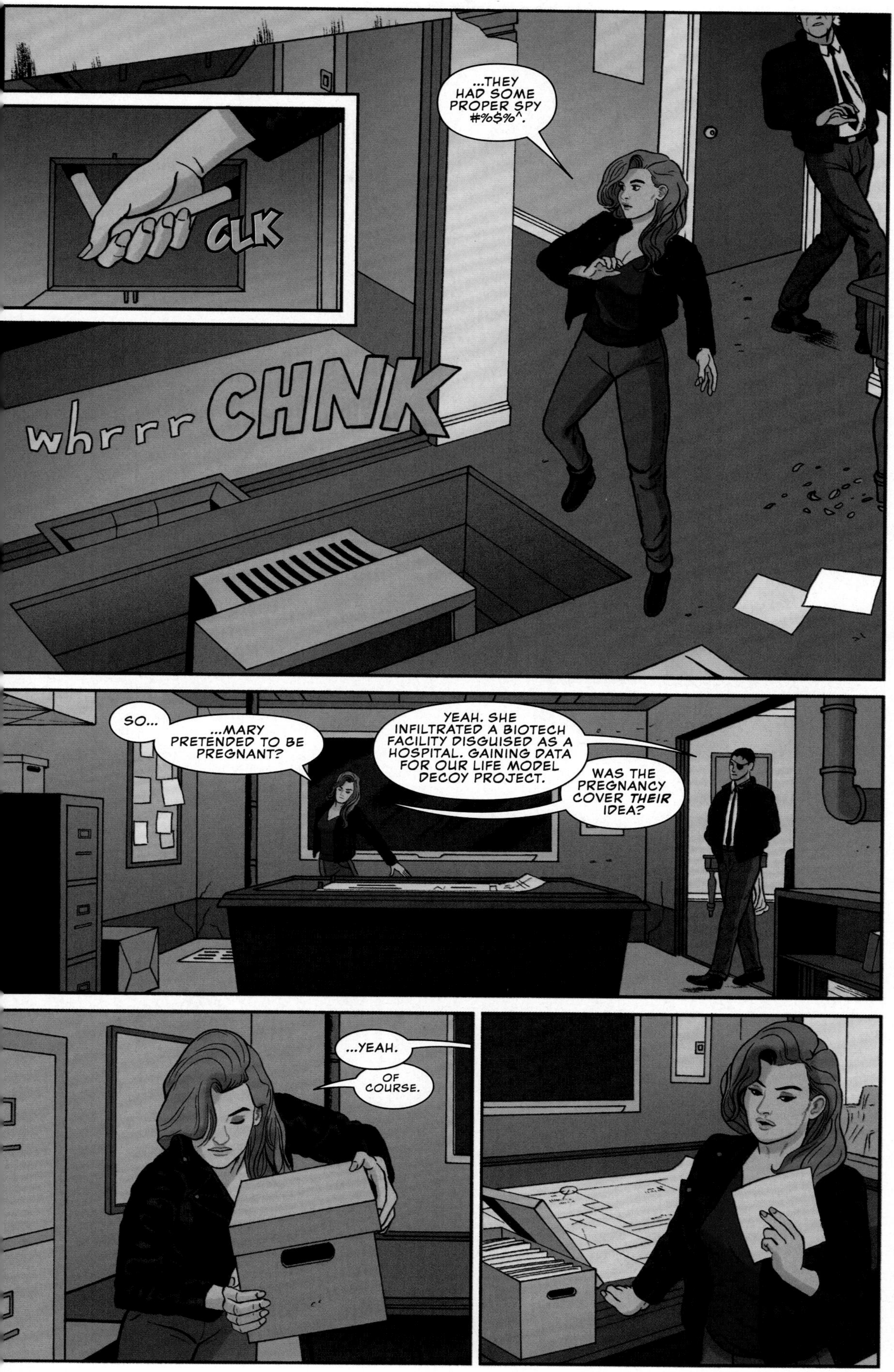
CLK
whrrr CHNK
...THEY HAD SOME PROPER SPY #%$%^.
SO...
...MARY PRETENDED TO BE PREGNANT?
YEAH. SHE INFILTRATED A BIOTECH FACILITY DISGUISED AS A HOSPITAL. GAINING DATA FOR OUR LIFE MODEL DECOY PROJECT.
WAS THE PREGNANCY COVER THEIR IDEA?
...YEAH.
OF COURSE.

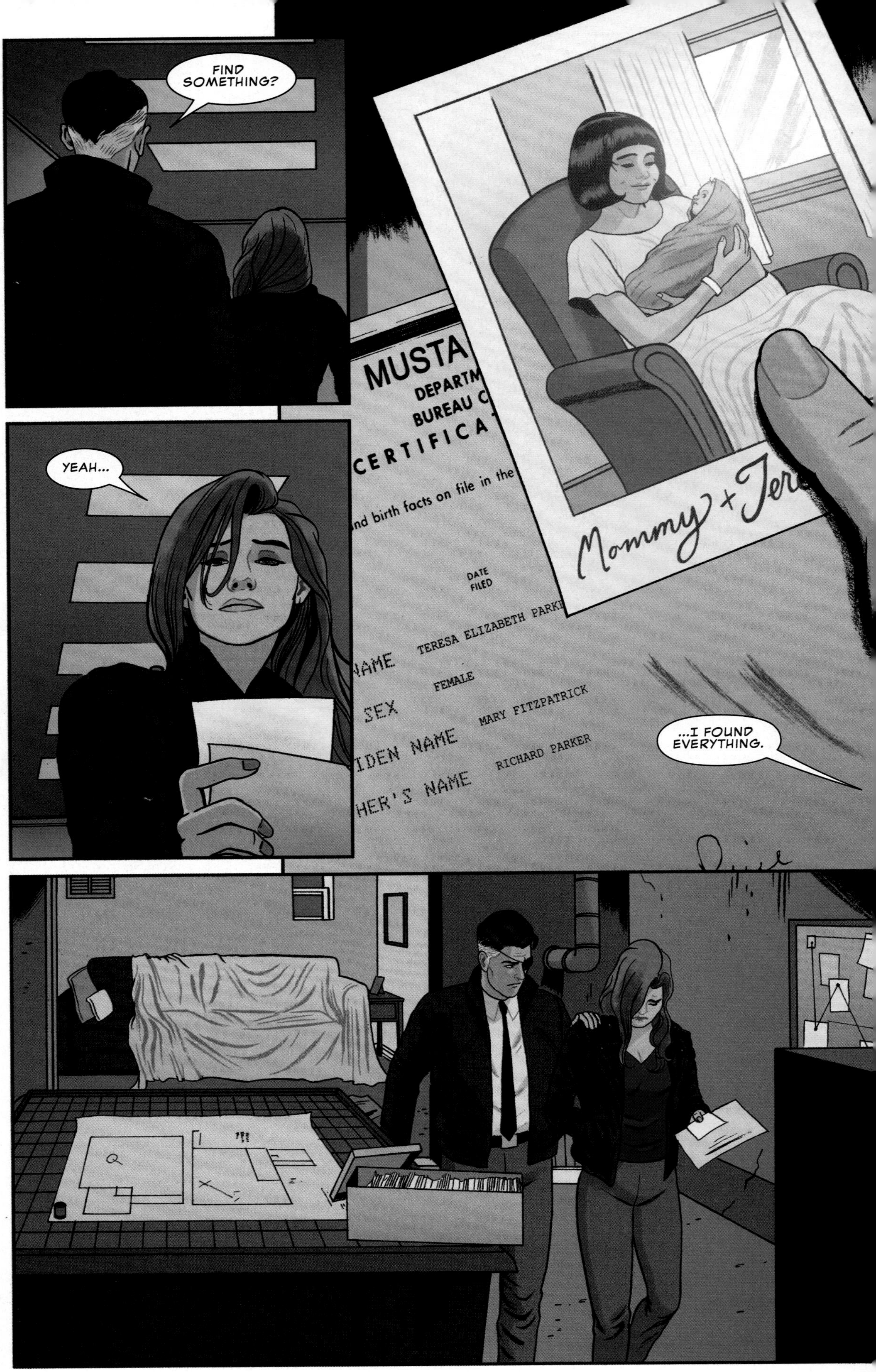
FIND SOMETHING?
YEAH...
MUSTA
DEPARTM
BUREAU C
CERTIFICA
nd birth facts on file in the
DATE FILED
NAME TERESA ELIZABETH PARKE
SEX FEMALE
IDEN NAME MARY FITZPATRICK
HER'S NAME RICHARD PARKER
Mommy + Ter
...I FOUND EVERYTHING.

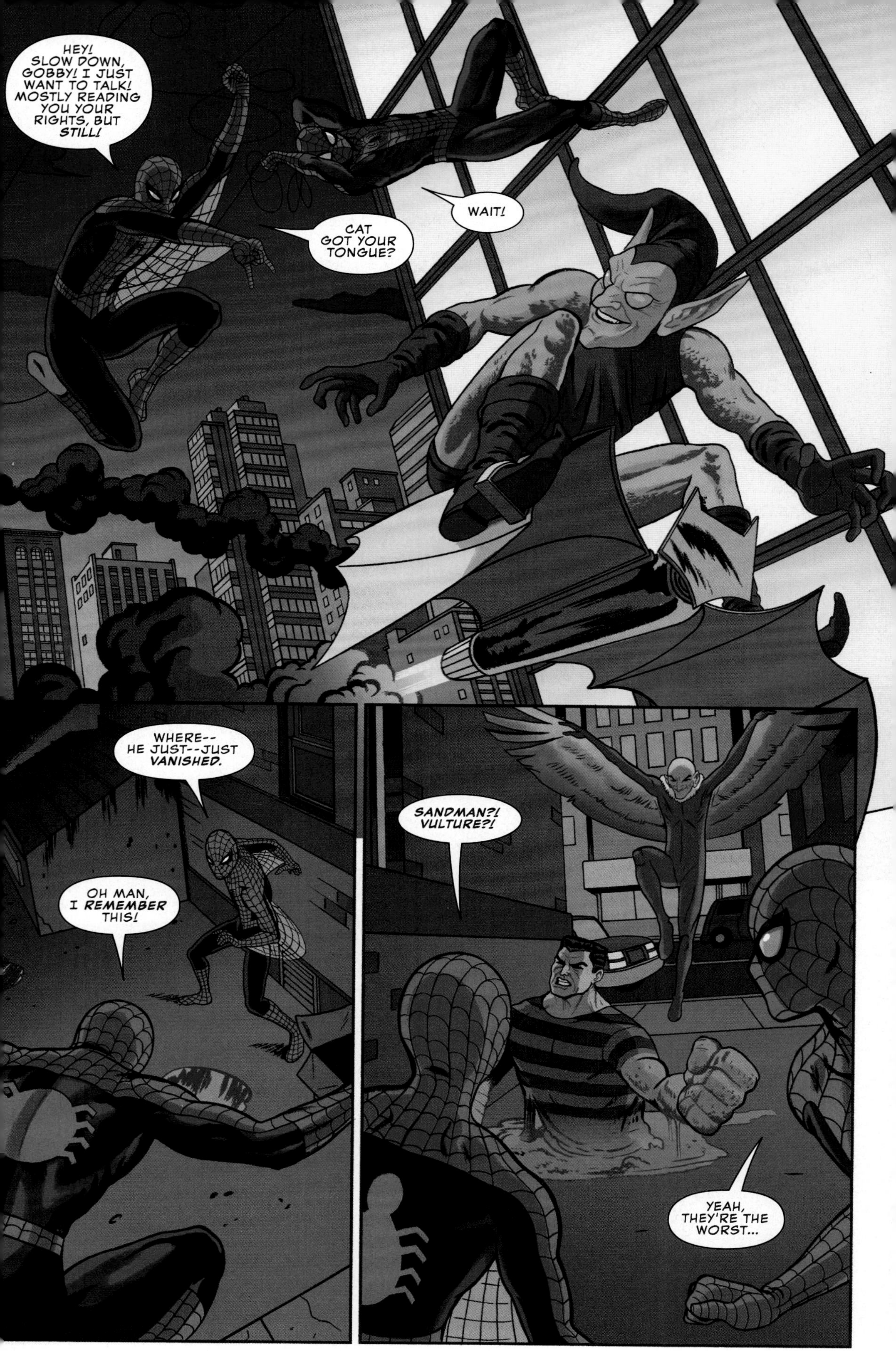
HEY! SLOW DOWN, GOBBY! I JUST WANT TO TALK! MOSTLY READING YOU YOUR RIGHTS, BUT STILL!
CAT GOT YOUR TONGUE?
WAIT!
WHERE-- HE JUST--JUST VANISHED.
OH MAN, I REMEMBER THIS!
SANDMAN?! VULTURE?!
YEAH, THEY'RE THE WORST...

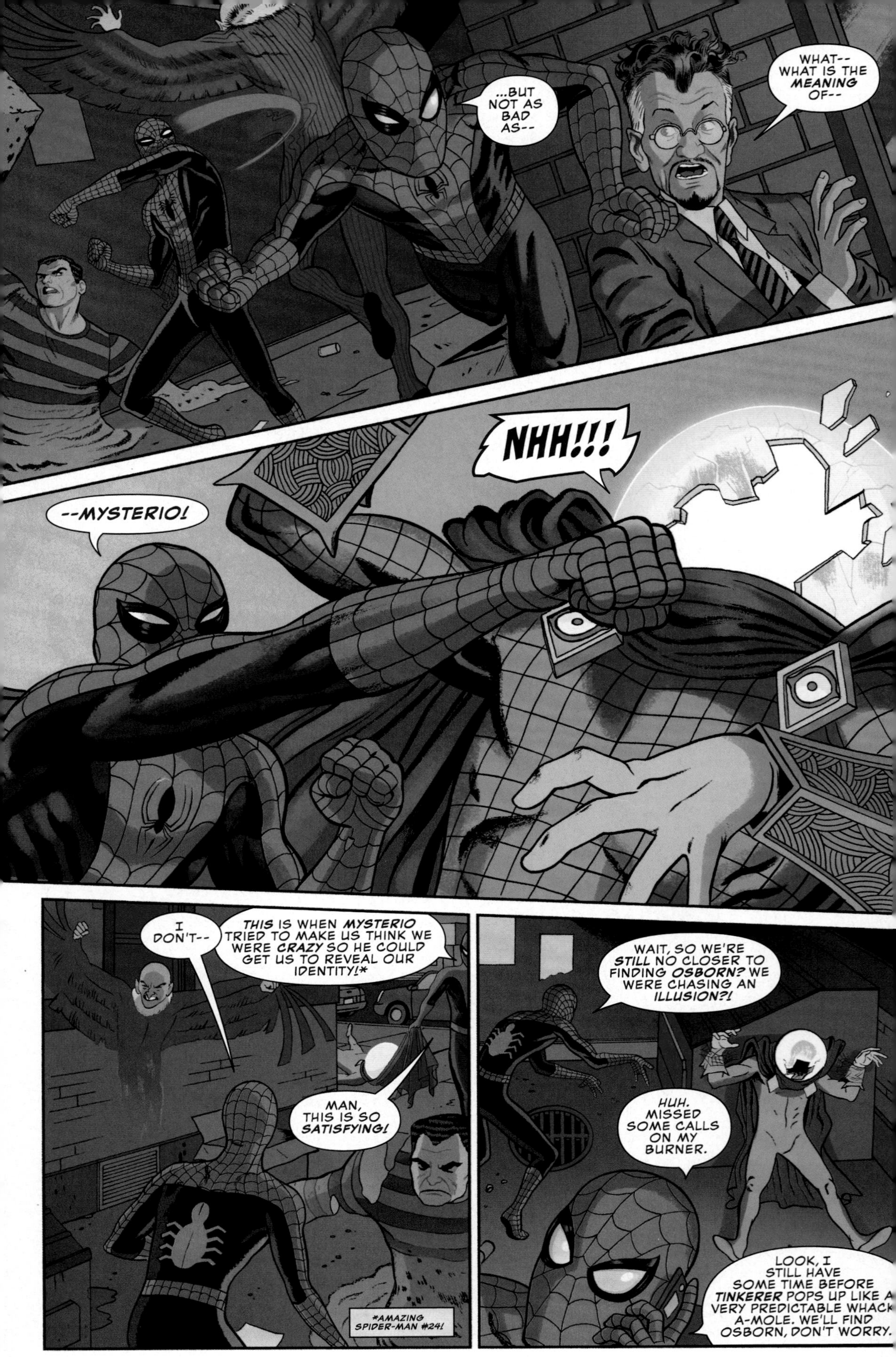
...BUT NOT AS BAD AS--
WHAT-- WHAT IS THE MEANING OF--
NHH!!!
--MYSTERIO!
I DON'T--
THIS IS WHEN MYSTERIO TRIED TO MAKE US THINK WE WERE CRAZY SO HE COULD GET US TO REVEAL OUR IDENTITY!*
MAN, THIS IS SO SATISFYING!
*AMAZING SPIDER-MAN #24!
WAIT, SO WE'RE STILL NO CLOSER TO FINDING OSBORN? WE WERE CHASING AN ILLUSION?!
HUH. MISSED SOME CALLS ON MY BURNER.
LOOK, I STILL HAVE SOME TIME BEFORE TINKERER POPS UP LIKE A VERY PREDICTABLE WHACK-A-MOLE. WE'LL FIND OSBORN, DON'T WORRY.

UH, WHAT'S A "BURNER"?

OH MAN, YOU STILL HAVE *THE WIRE* AHEAD OF YOU! I'M WEIRDLY JEALOUS!

HUH...

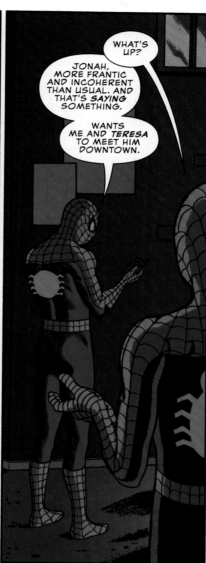

WHAT'S *UP*?

JONAH, MORE FRANTIC AND INCOHERENT THAN USUAL. AND THAT'S *SAYING* SOMETHING.

WANTS ME AND *TERESA* TO MEET HIM DOWNTOWN.

IT'S GETTING LATE! *YOU* CHECK IN WITH *AUNT MAY*, WHO, IF I RECALL, IS *CONSTANTLY* ON THE VERGE OF A HEART ATTACK WHEN YOU'RE NOT HOME BEFORE SUNDOWN.

I'LL CHECK IN WITH THE GUYS AND WE'LL RECONVENE IN THE MORNING. COOL?

THWIP

...COOL.

JONAH! I'M HEADED TO YOU NOW! WHAT'S THE EMERGENCY?

NAH, I SENT HIM HOME. TEENS NEED THEIR SLEEP! AND BETWEEN YOU AND ME--

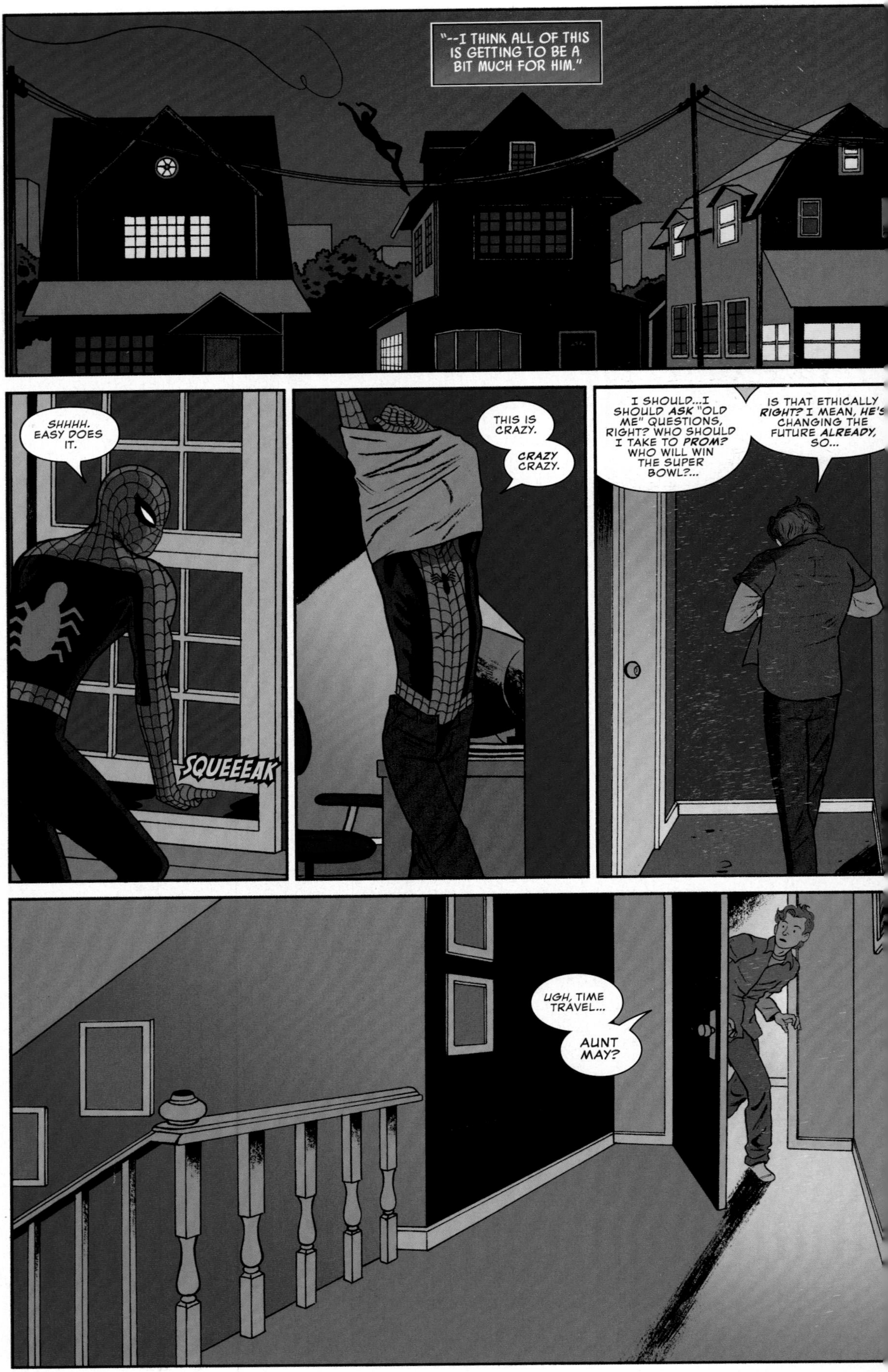
"--I THINK ALL OF THIS IS GETTING TO BE A BIT MUCH FOR HIM."
SHHHH. EASY DOES IT.
SQUEEEAK
THIS IS CRAZY.
CRAZY CRAZY.
I SHOULD...I SHOULD ASK "OLD ME" QUESTIONS, RIGHT? WHO SHOULD I TAKE TO PROM? WHO WILL WIN THE SUPER BOWL?...
IS THAT ETHICALLY RIGHT? I MEAN, HE'S CHANGING THE FUTURE ALREADY, SO...
UGH, TIME TRAVEL...
AUNT MAY?

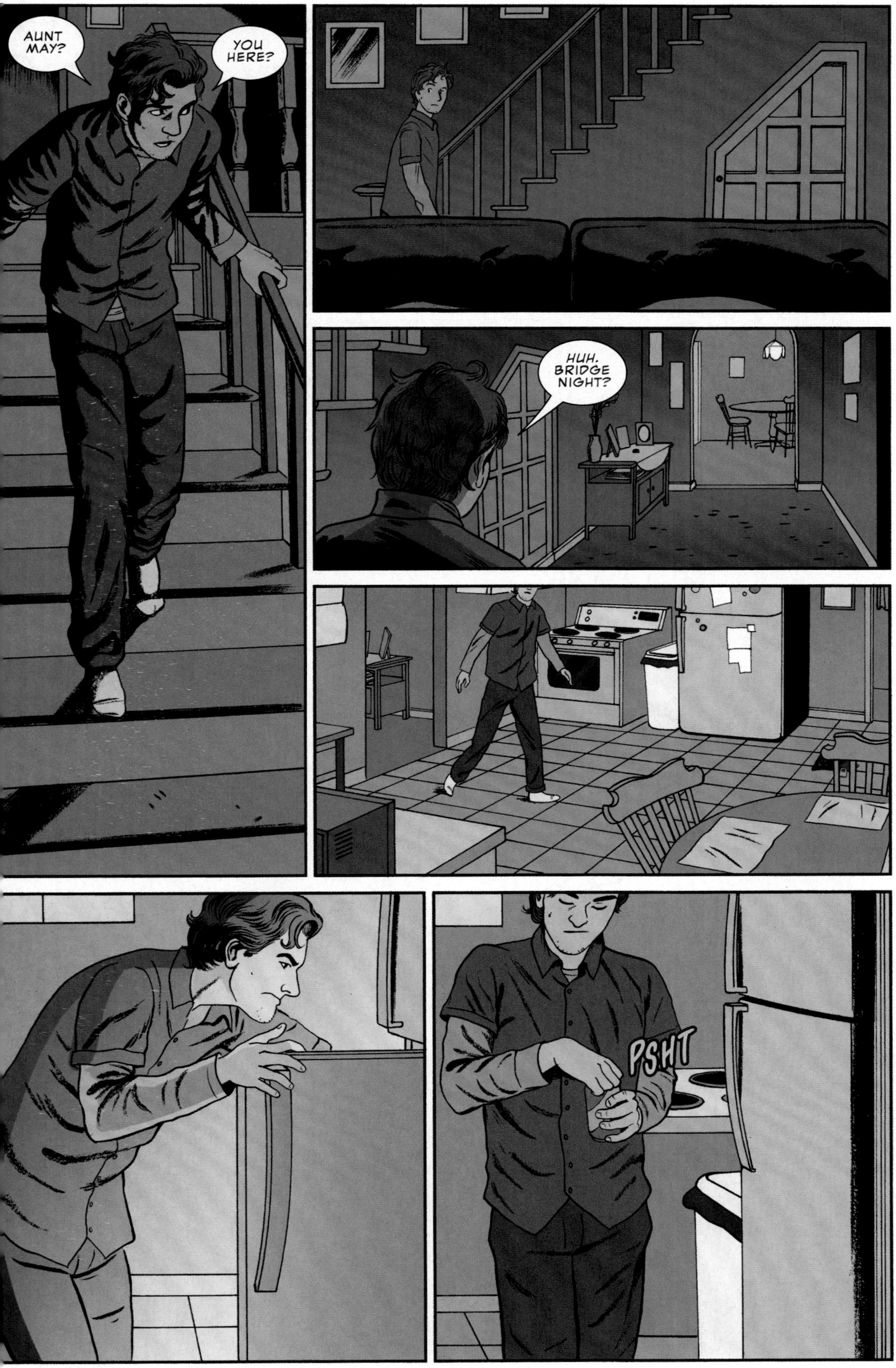
AUNT MAY?
YOU HERE?
HUH. BRIDGE NIGHT?
PSHT

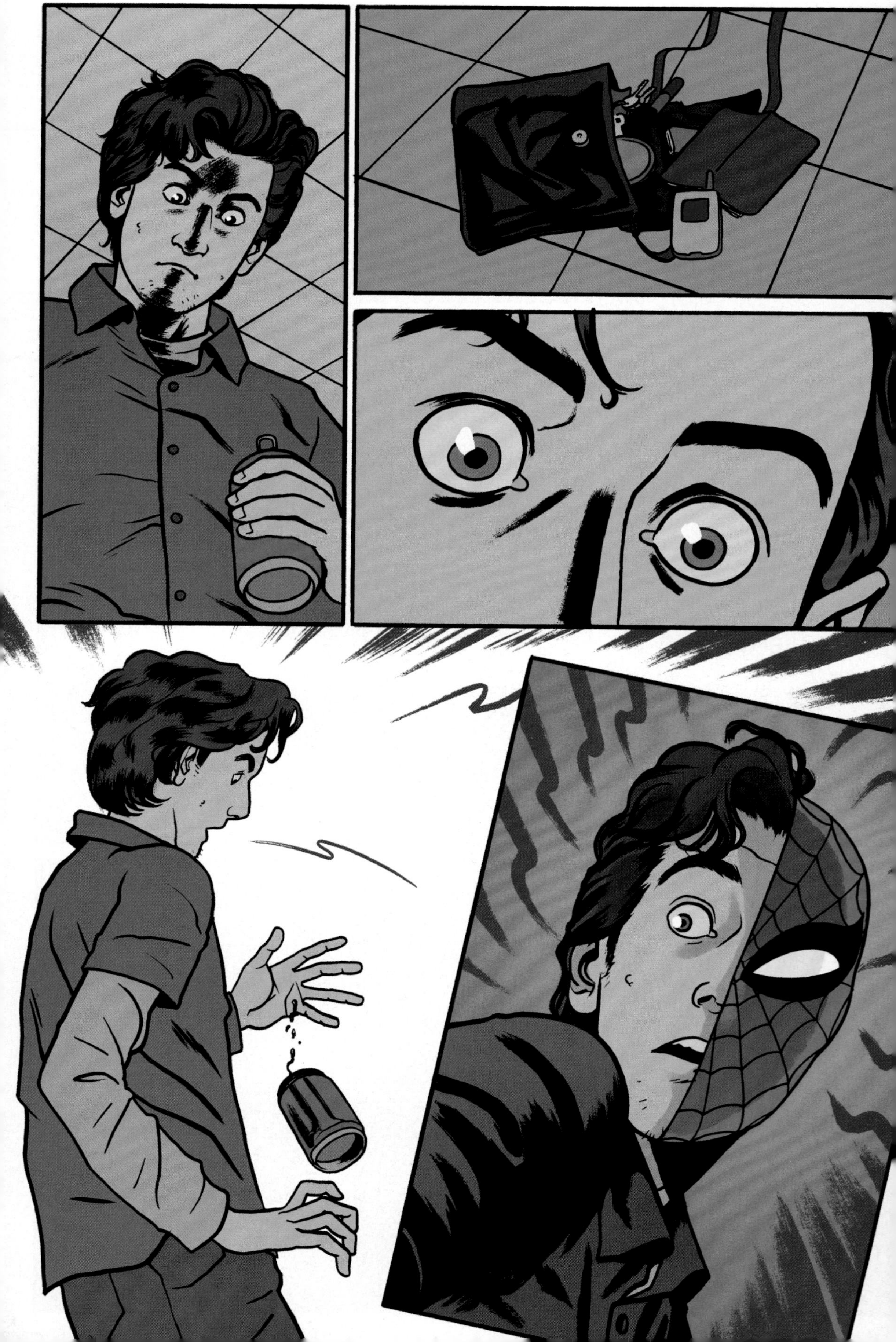

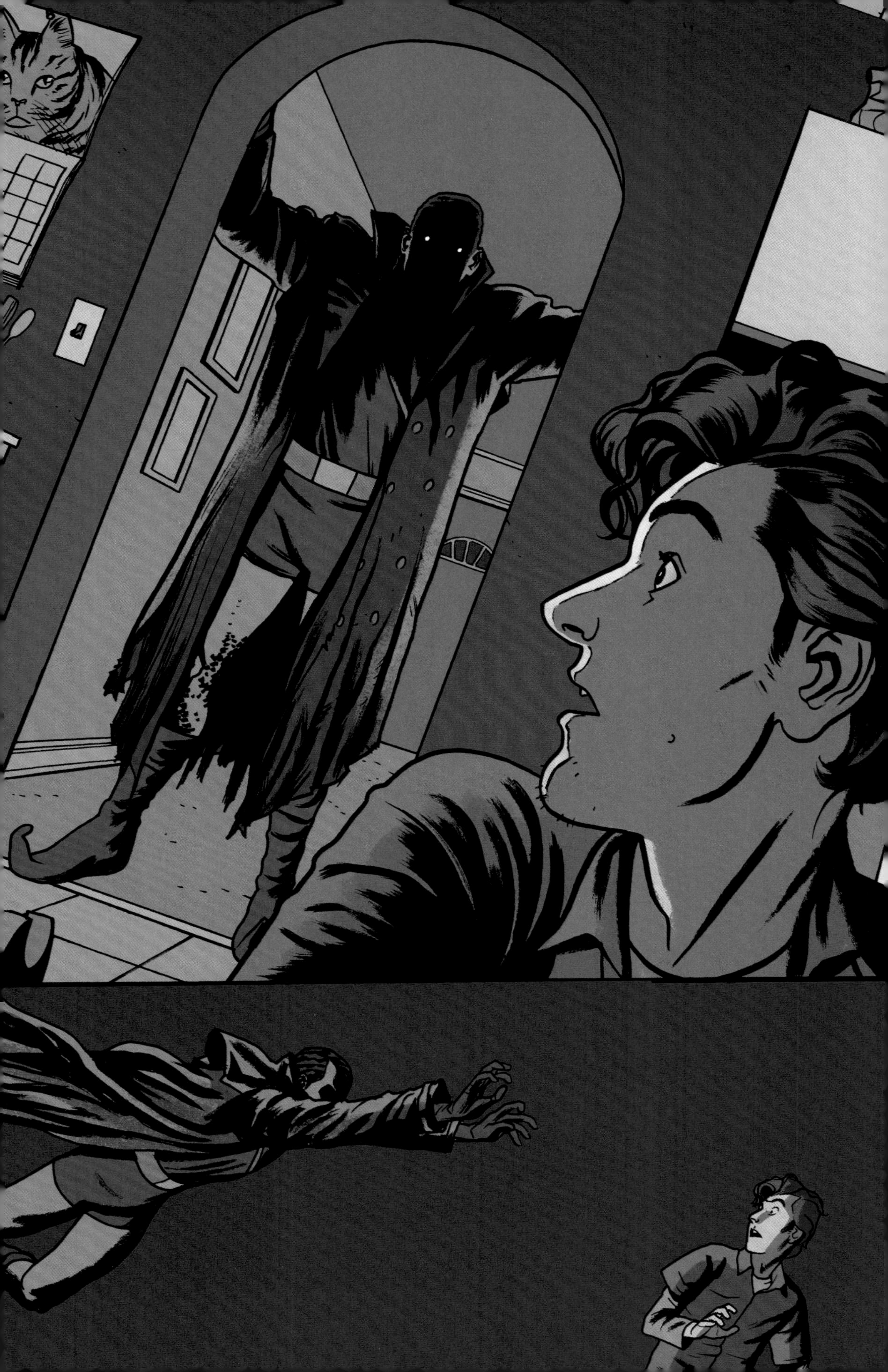

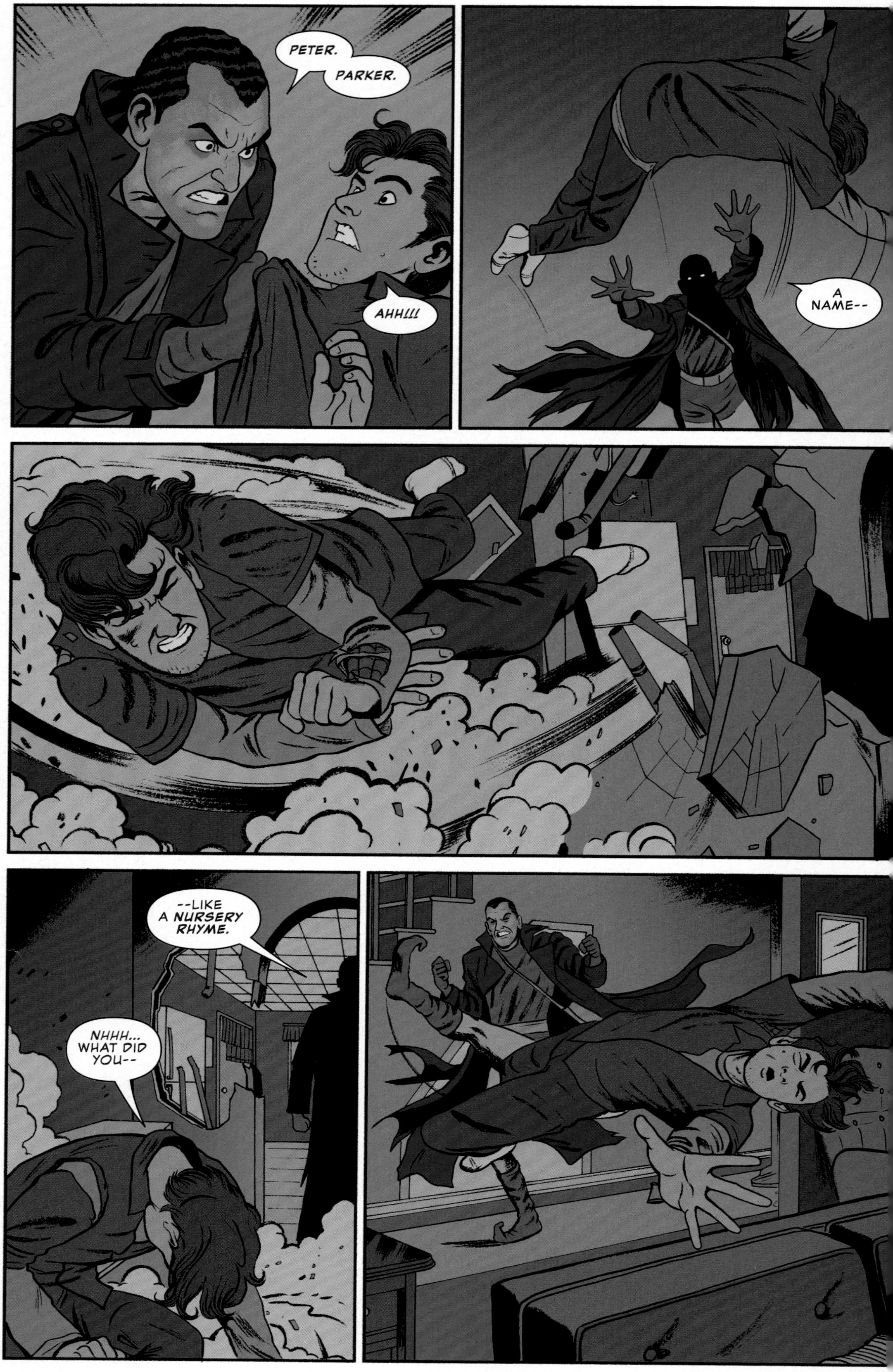
PETER.
PARKER.
AHH!!!
A NAME--
--LIKE A NURSERY RHYME.
NHHH... WHAT DID YOU--

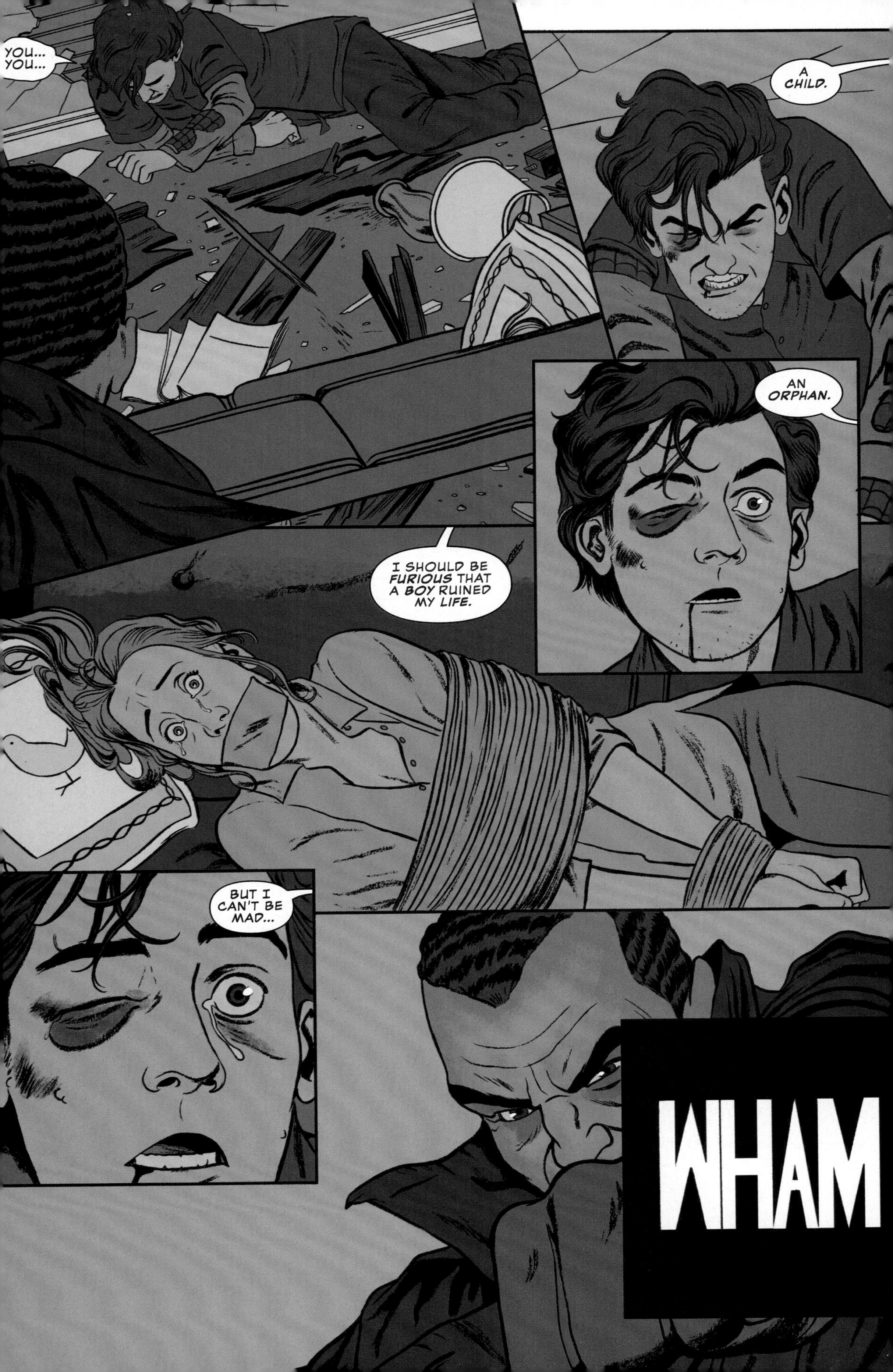
YOU... YOU...
A CHILD.
AN ORPHAN.
I SHOULD BE *FURIOUS* THAT A *BOY* RUINED MY *LIFE.*
BUT I CAN'T BE MAD...
WHAM

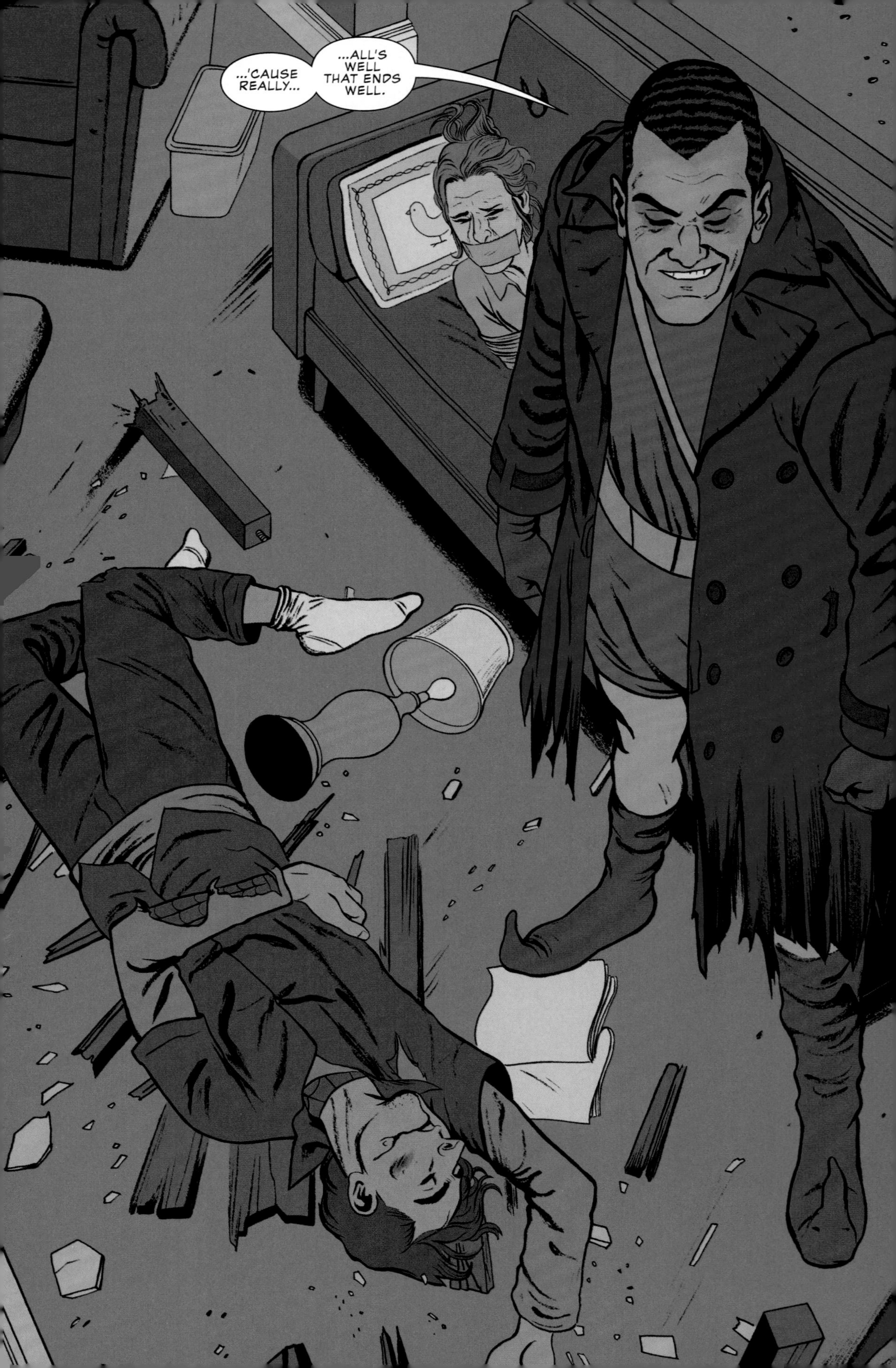
...'CAUSE REALLY...
...ALL'S WELL THAT ENDS WELL.

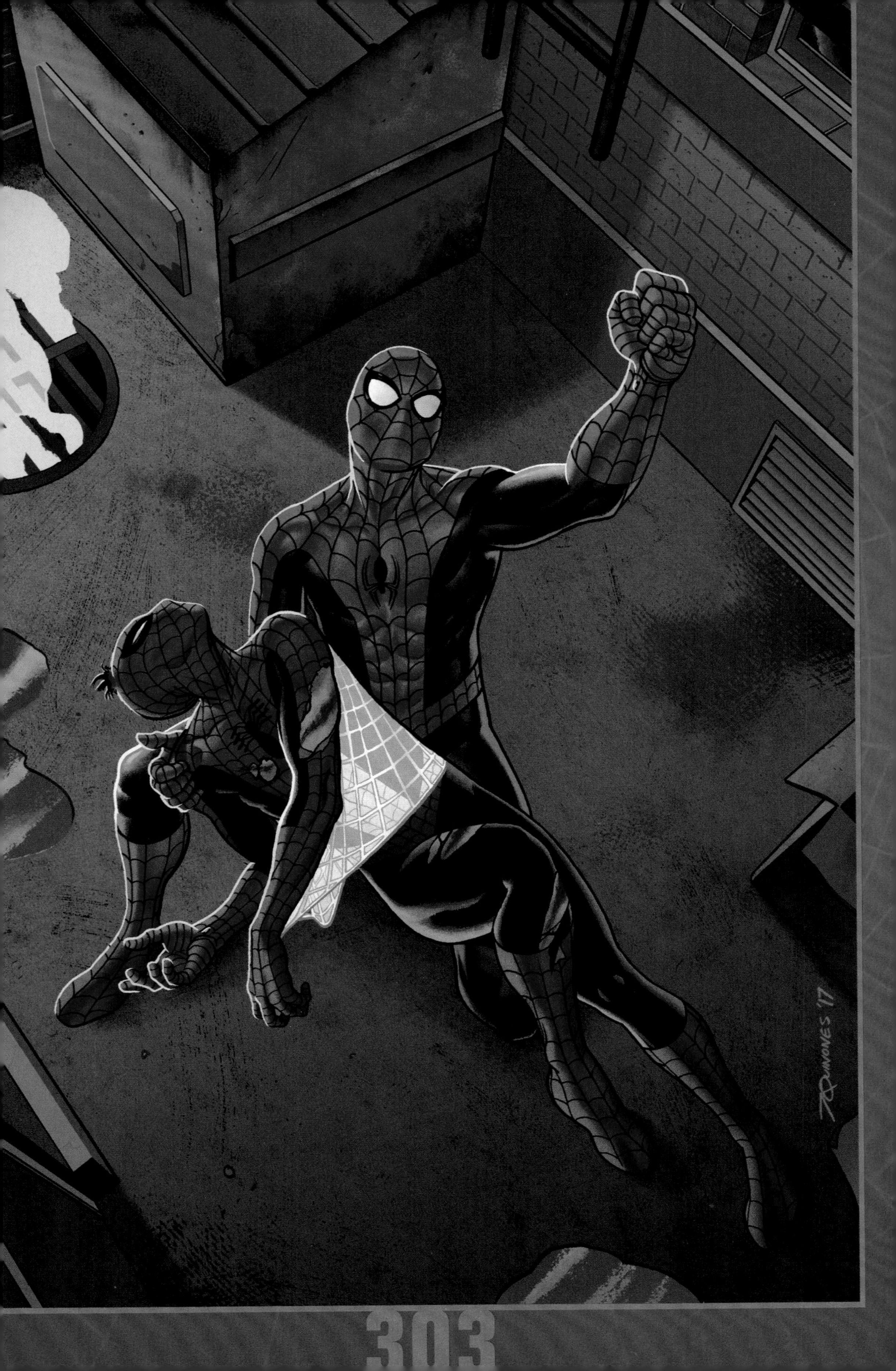
303

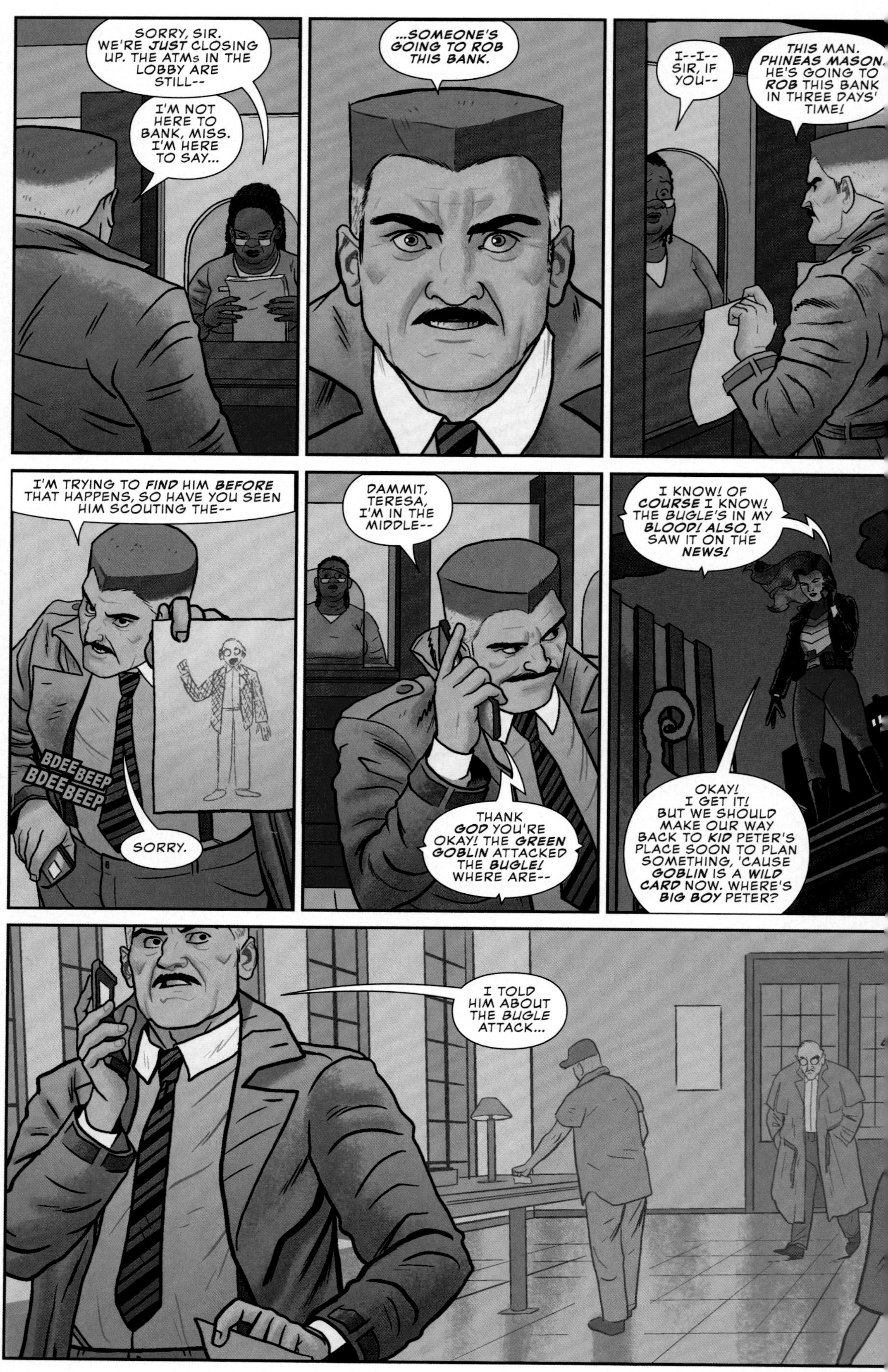

SORRY, SIR. WE'RE JUST CLOSING UP. THE ATMs IN THE LOBBY ARE STILL--
I'M NOT HERE TO BANK, MISS. I'M HERE TO SAY...
...SOMEONE'S GOING TO ROB THIS BANK.
I--I-- SIR, IF YOU--
THIS MAN. PHINEAS MASON. HE'S GOING TO ROB THIS BANK IN THREE DAYS' TIME!
I'M TRYING TO FIND HIM BEFORE THAT HAPPENS, SO HAVE YOU SEEN HIM SCOUTING THE--
BDEEBEEP BDEEBEEP
SORRY.
DAMMIT, TERESA, I'M IN THE MIDDLE--
THANK GOD YOU'RE OKAY! THE GREEN GOBLIN ATTACKED THE BUGLE! WHERE ARE--
I KNOW! OF COURSE I KNOW! THE BUGLE'S IN MY BLOOD! ALSO, I SAW IT ON THE NEWS!
OKAY! I GET IT! BUT WE SHOULD MAKE OUR WAY BACK TO KID PETER'S PLACE SOON TO PLAN SOMETHING, 'CAUSE GOBLIN IS A WILD CARD NOW. WHERE'S BIG BOY PETER?
I TOLD HIM ABOUT THE BUGLE ATTACK...

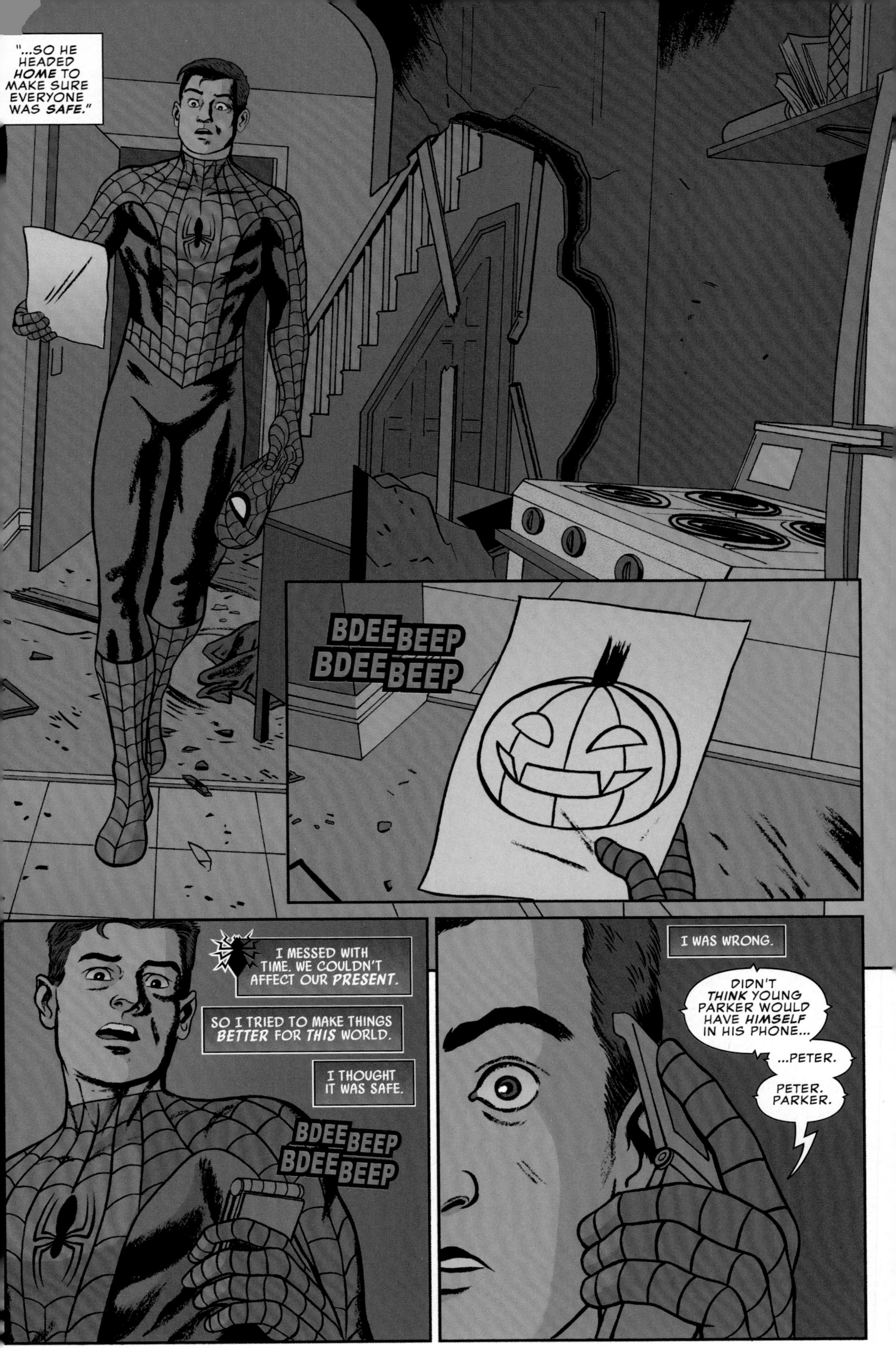
"...SO HE HEADED *HOME* TO MAKE SURE EVERYONE WAS *SAFE.*"
BDEE BEEP
BDEE BEEP
I MESSED WITH TIME. WE COULDN'T AFFECT OUR *PRESENT.*
SO I TRIED TO MAKE THINGS *BETTER* FOR *THIS* WORLD.
I THOUGHT IT WAS SAFE.
BDEE BEEP
BDEE BEEP
I WAS WRONG.
DIDN'T *THINK* YOUNG PARKER WOULD HAVE *HIMSELF* IN HIS PHONE...
...PETER.
PETER. PARKER.

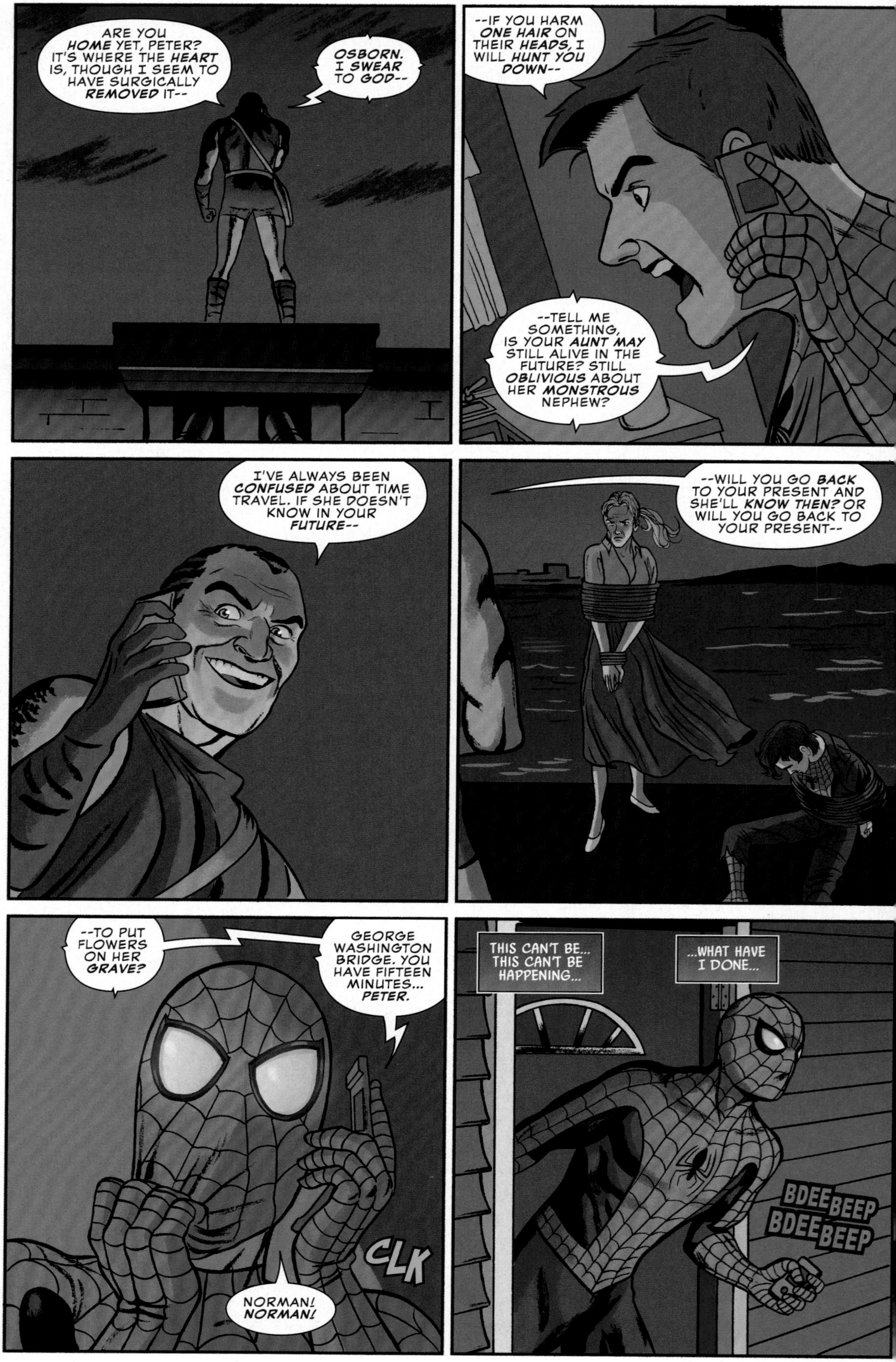
ARE YOU HOME YET, PETER? IT'S WHERE THE HEART IS, THOUGH I SEEM TO HAVE SURGICALLY REMOVED IT--
OSBORN. I SWEAR TO GOD--
--IF YOU HARM ONE HAIR ON THEIR HEADS, I WILL HUNT YOU DOWN--
--TELL ME SOMETHING, IS YOUR AUNT MAY STILL ALIVE IN THE FUTURE? STILL OBLIVIOUS ABOUT HER MONSTROUS NEPHEW?
I'VE ALWAYS BEEN CONFUSED ABOUT TIME TRAVEL. IF SHE DOESN'T KNOW IN YOUR FUTURE--
--WILL YOU GO BACK TO YOUR PRESENT AND SHE'LL KNOW THEN? OR WILL YOU GO BACK TO YOUR PRESENT--
--TO PUT FLOWERS ON HER GRAVE?
GEORGE WASHINGTON BRIDGE. YOU HAVE FIFTEEN MINUTES... PETER.
CLK
NORMAN! NORMAN!
THIS CAN'T BE... THIS CAN'T BE HAPPENING...
...WHAT HAVE I DONE...
BDEEBEEP
BDEEBEEP

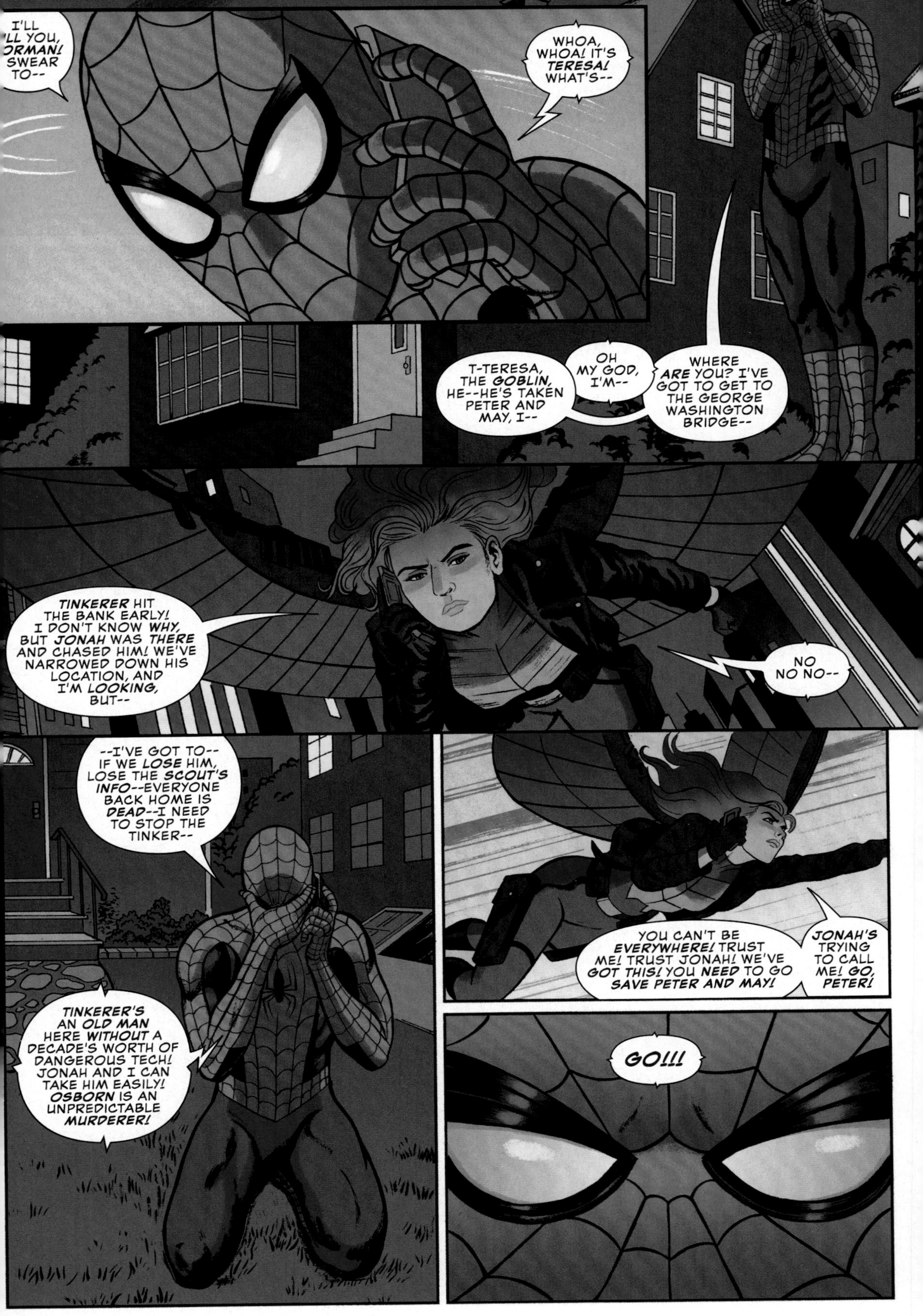
I'LL LL YOU, ORMAN! SWEAR TO--
WHOA, WHOA! IT'S TERESA! WHAT'S--
T-TERESA, THE GOBLIN, HE--HE'S TAKEN PETER AND MAY, I--
OH MY GOD, I'M--
WHERE ARE YOU? I'VE GOT TO GET TO THE GEORGE WASHINGTON BRIDGE--
TINKERER HIT THE BANK EARLY! I DON'T KNOW WHY, BUT JONAH WAS THERE AND CHASED HIM! WE'VE NARROWED DOWN HIS LOCATION, AND I'M LOOKING, BUT--
NO NO NO--
--I'VE GOT TO-- IF WE LOSE HIM, LOSE THE SCOUT'S INFO--EVERYONE BACK HOME IS DEAD--I NEED TO STOP THE TINKER--
TINKERER'S AN OLD MAN HERE WITHOUT A DECADE'S WORTH OF DANGEROUS TECH! JONAH AND I CAN TAKE HIM EASILY! OSBORN IS AN UNPREDICTABLE MURDERER!
YOU CAN'T BE EVERYWHERE! TRUST ME! TRUST JONAH! WE'VE GOT THIS! YOU NEED TO GO SAVE PETER AND MAY!
JONAH'S TRYING TO CALL ME! GO, PETER!
GO!!!

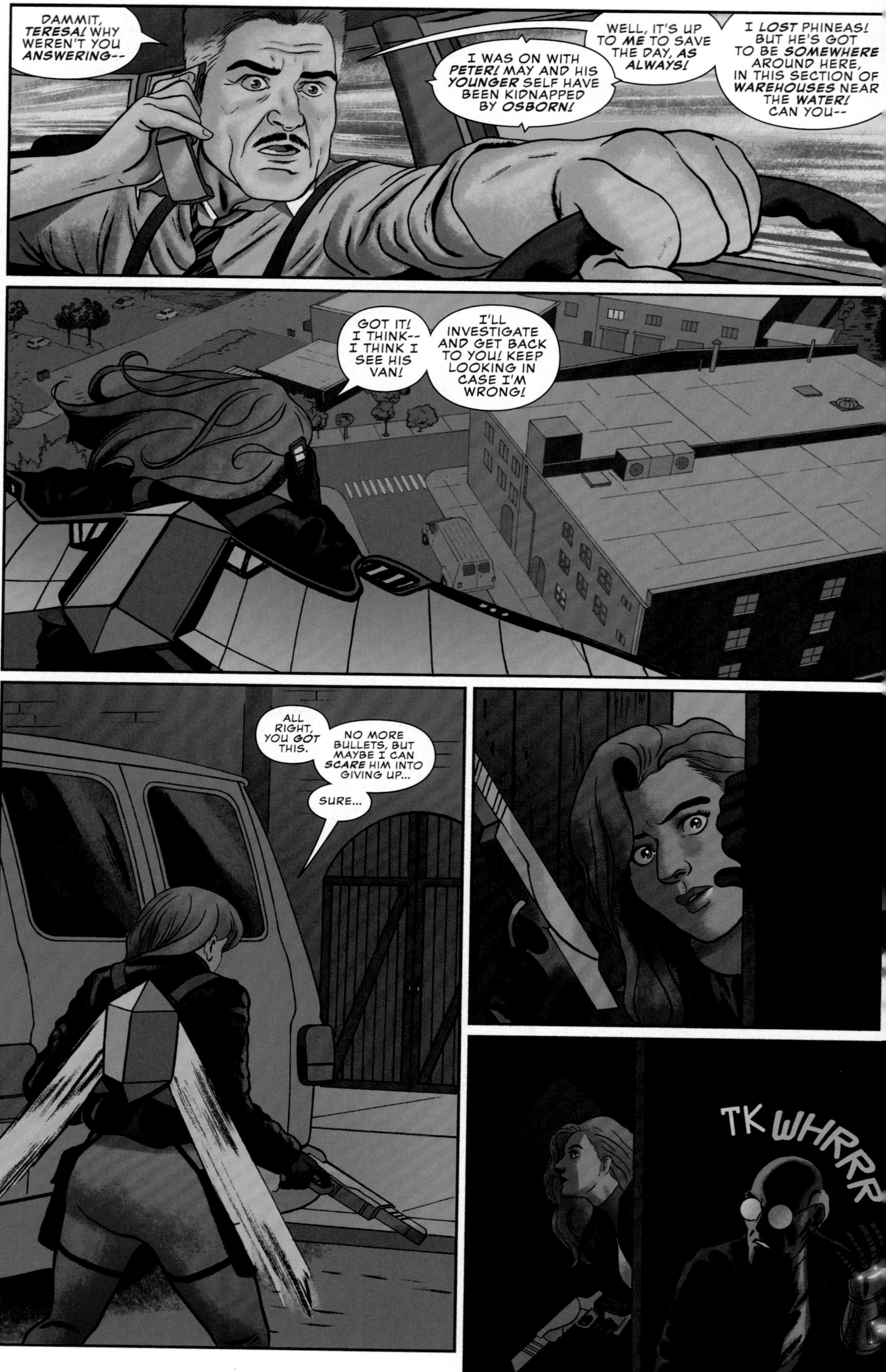

DAMMIT, TERESA! WHY WEREN'T YOU ANSWERING--
I WAS ON WITH PETER! MAY AND HIS YOUNGER SELF HAVE BEEN KIDNAPPED BY OSBORN!
WELL, IT'S UP TO ME TO SAVE THE DAY, AS ALWAYS!
I LOST PHINEAS! BUT HE'S GOT TO BE SOMEWHERE AROUND HERE, IN THIS SECTION OF WAREHOUSES NEAR THE WATER! CAN YOU--
GOT IT! I THINK-- I THINK I SEE HIS VAN!
I'LL INVESTIGATE AND GET BACK TO YOU! KEEP LOOKING IN CASE I'M WRONG!
ALL RIGHT, YOU GOT THIS.
NO MORE BULLETS, BUT MAYBE I CAN SCARE HIM INTO GIVING UP...
SURE...
TK WHRRR

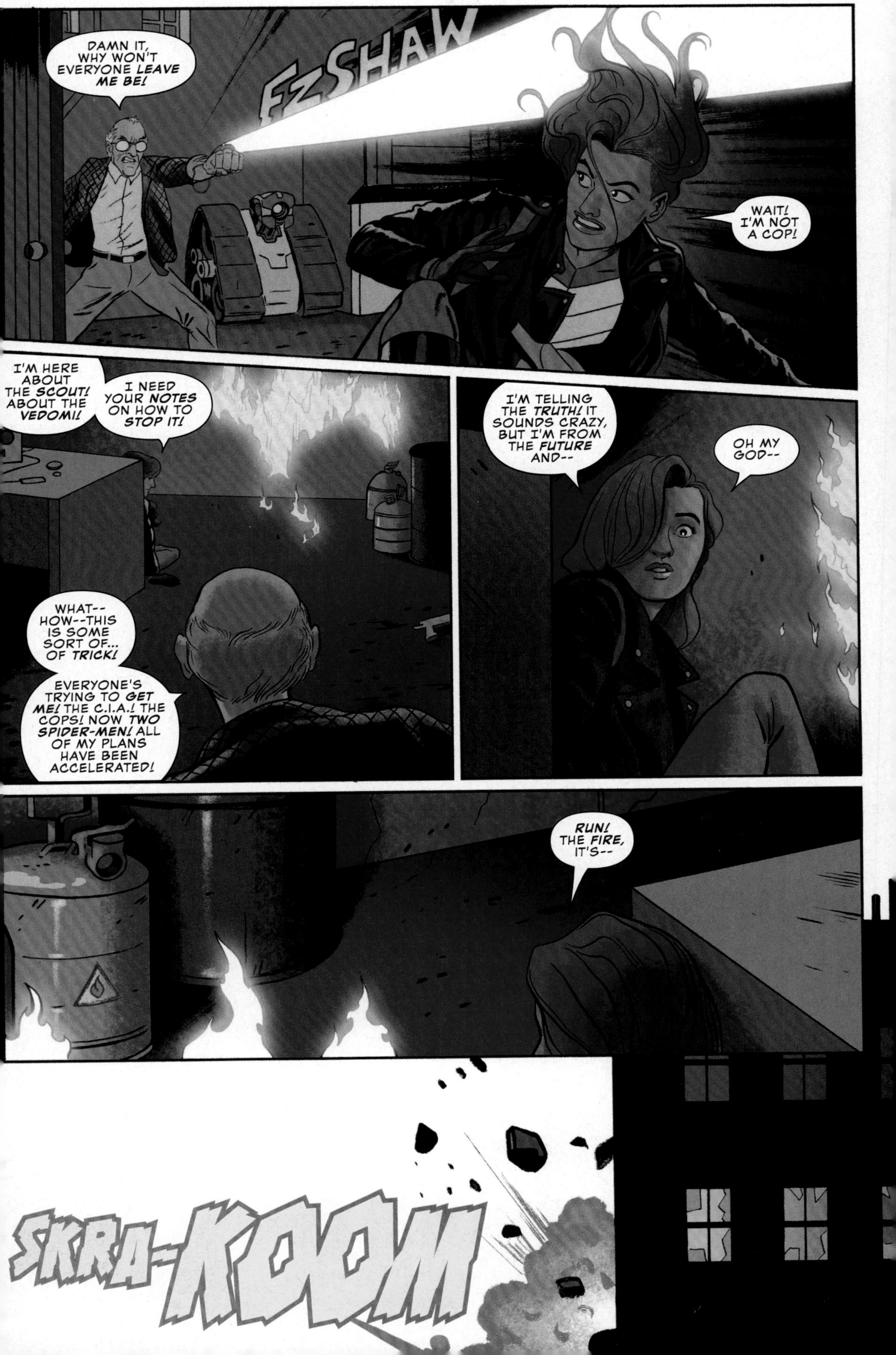

DAMN IT, WHY WON'T EVERYONE LEAVE ME BE!
FZSHAW
WAIT! I'M NOT A COP!
I'M HERE ABOUT THE SCOUT! ABOUT THE VEDOMI!
I NEED YOUR NOTES ON HOW TO STOP IT!
WHAT--HOW--THIS IS SOME SORT OF... OF TRICK!
EVERYONE'S TRYING TO GET ME! THE C.I.A.! THE COPS! NOW TWO SPIDER-MEN! ALL OF MY PLANS HAVE BEEN ACCELERATED!
I'M TELLING THE TRUTH! IT SOUNDS CRAZY, BUT I'M FROM THE FUTURE AND--
OH MY GOD--
RUN! THE FIRE, IT'S--
SKRA-KOOM

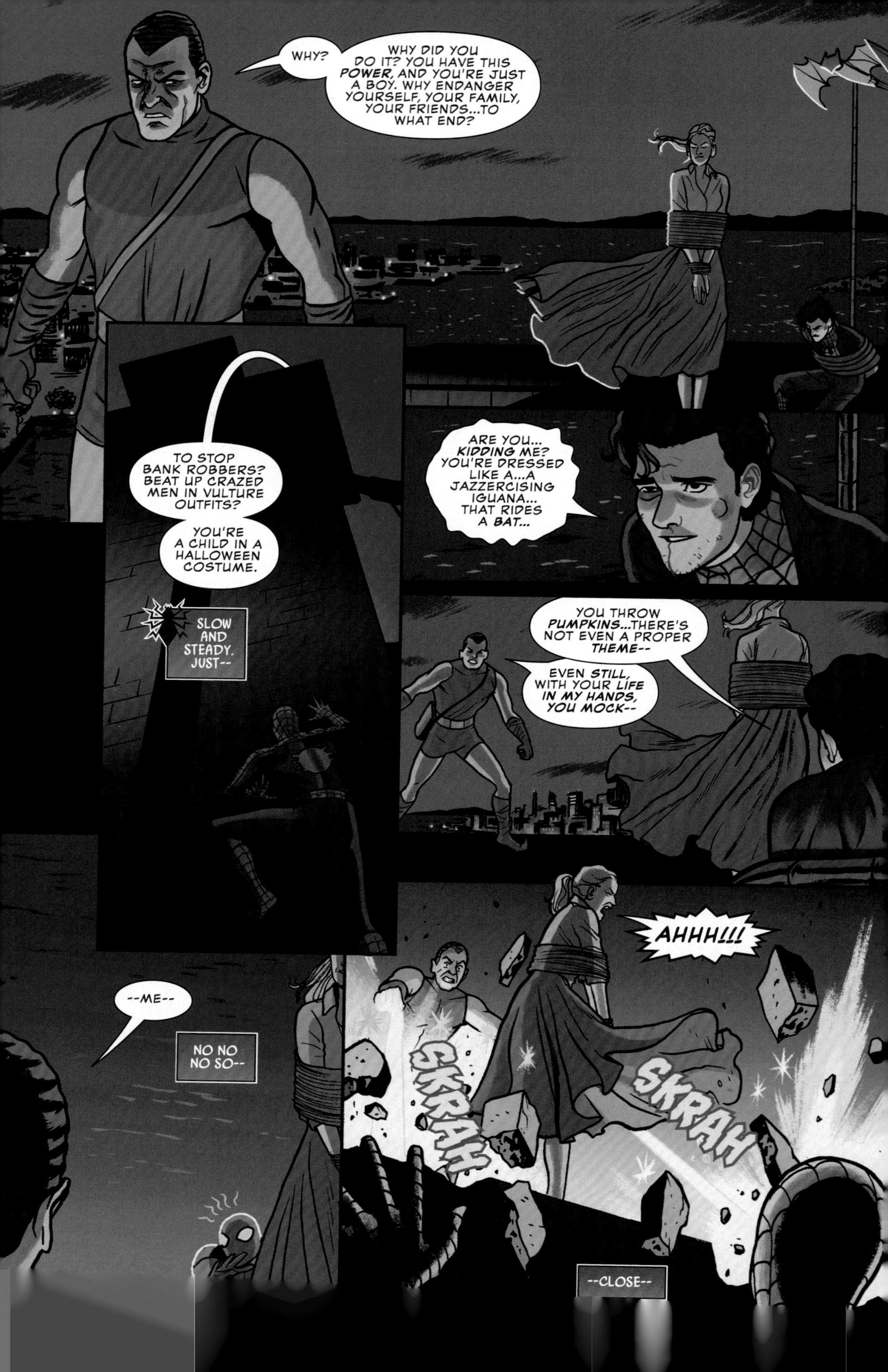
WHY?
WHY DID YOU DO IT? YOU HAVE THIS POWER, AND YOU'RE JUST A BOY. WHY ENDANGER YOURSELF, YOUR FAMILY, YOUR FRIENDS...TO WHAT END?
TO STOP BANK ROBBERS? BEAT UP CRAZED MEN IN VULTURE OUTFITS?
YOU'RE A CHILD IN A HALLOWEEN COSTUME.
SLOW AND STEADY. JUST--
ARE YOU... KIDDING ME? YOU'RE DRESSED LIKE A...A JAZZERCISING IGUANA... THAT RIDES A BAT...
YOU THROW PUMPKINS...THERE'S NOT EVEN A PROPER THEME--
EVEN STILL, WITH YOUR LIFE IN MY HANDS, YOU MOCK--
--ME--
NO NO NO SO--
AHHH!!!
SKRAH
SKRAH
--CLOSE--

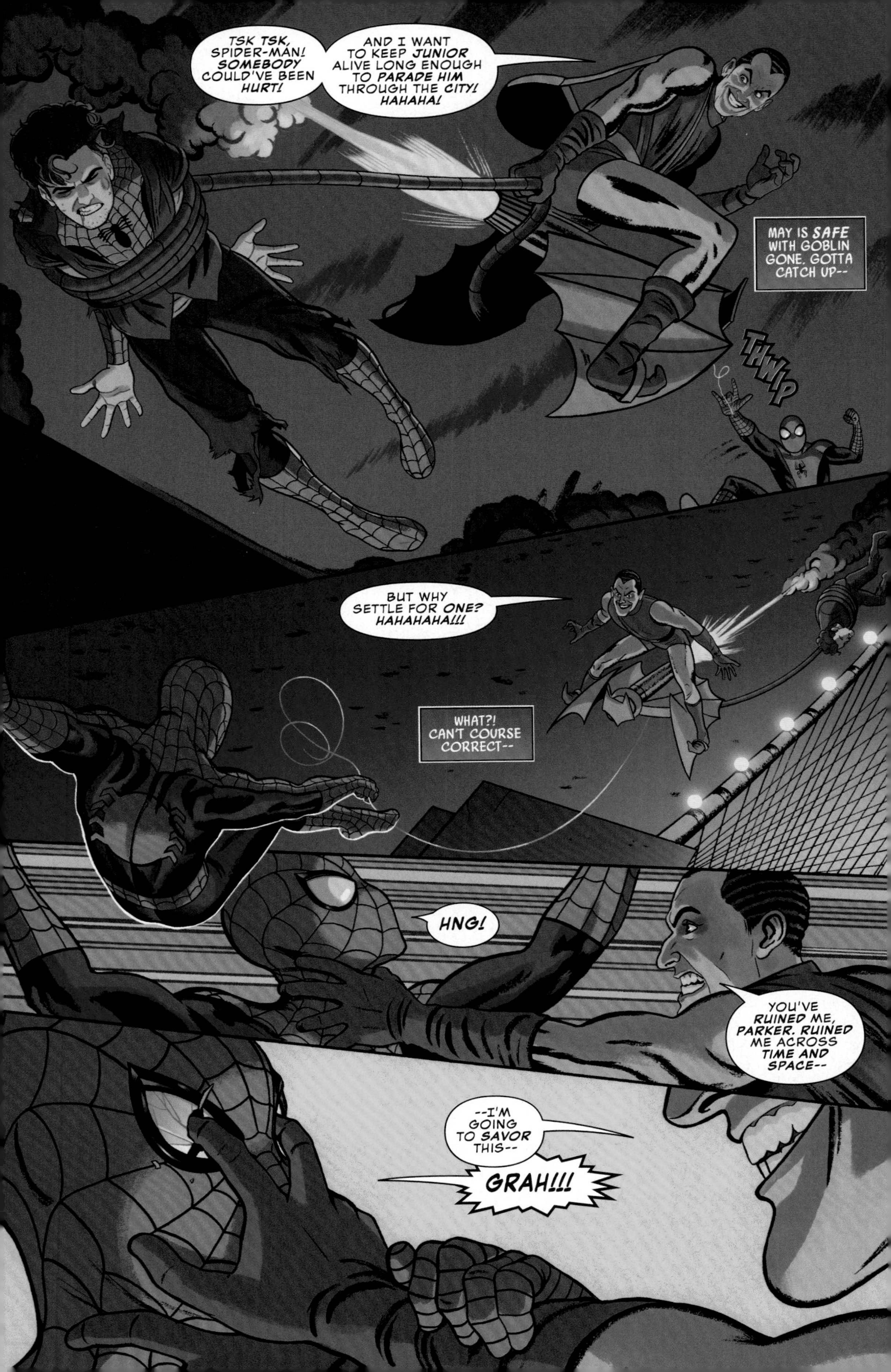

TSK TSK, SPIDER-MAN! SOMEBODY COULD'VE BEEN HURT!
AND I WANT TO KEEP JUNIOR ALIVE LONG ENOUGH TO PARADE HIM THROUGH THE CITY! HAHAHA!
MAY IS SAFE WITH GOBLIN GONE. GOTTA CATCH UP--
THWIP
BUT WHY SETTLE FOR ONE? HAHAHAHA!!!
WHAT?! CAN'T COURSE CORRECT--
HNG!
YOU'VE RUINED ME, PARKER. RUINED ME ACROSS TIME AND SPACE--
--I'M GOING TO SAVOR THIS--
GRAH!!!

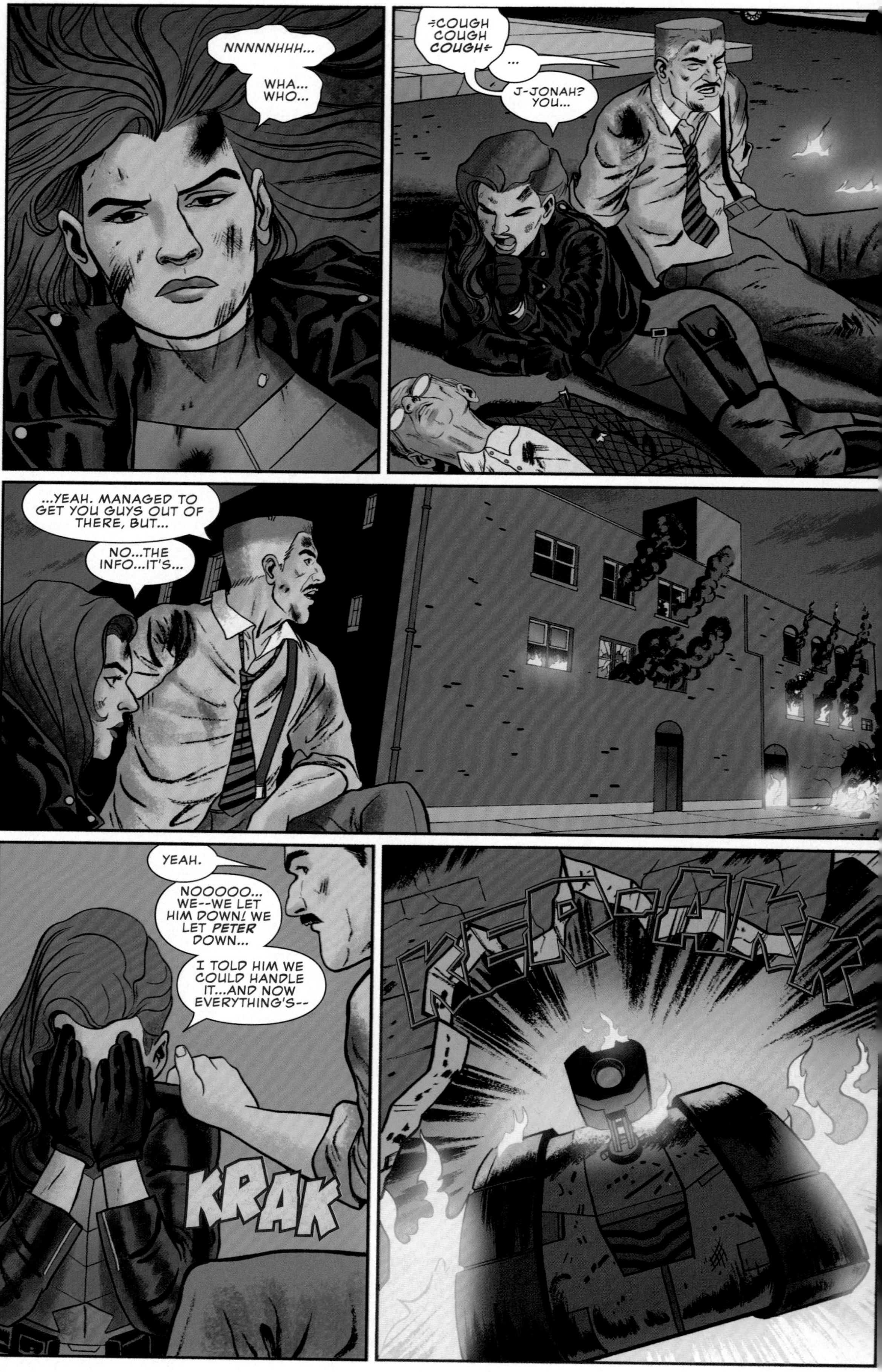
NNNNNHHH...
WHA... WHO...
=COUGH COUGH COUGH=
...
J-JONAH? YOU...
...YEAH. MANAGED TO GET YOU GUYS OUT OF THERE, BUT...
NO...THE INFO...IT'S...
YEAH.
NOOOOO... WE--WE LET HIM DOWN! WE LET PETER DOWN...
I TOLD HIM WE COULD HANDLE IT...AND NOW EVERYTHING'S--
KRAK
KER-PAKK

CLK WHRR YOU ARE--

--THE FUTURE--

--FROM--WHR--FUTURE--STOP--CLK--VEDOMI--

Y-YES! WE ARE! CAN YOU--CAN YOU HELP US?

TAKE--CLKCLK--THIS. IT WILL STOP--THEM

WILL NOT--WHR--HURT--THEM

NO ONE--TAK--NEEDS TO HURT--EVER--

HE IS--GOOD--TK--HE NEEDS--WHRR--KINDNESSSSS--

--UNDERUNDERST-STANDING--

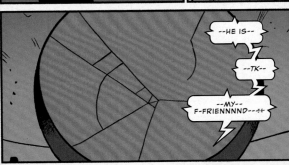

--HE IS--

--TK--

--MY--F-FRIENNNND---

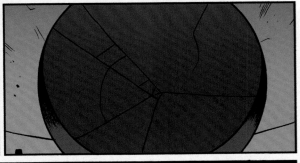

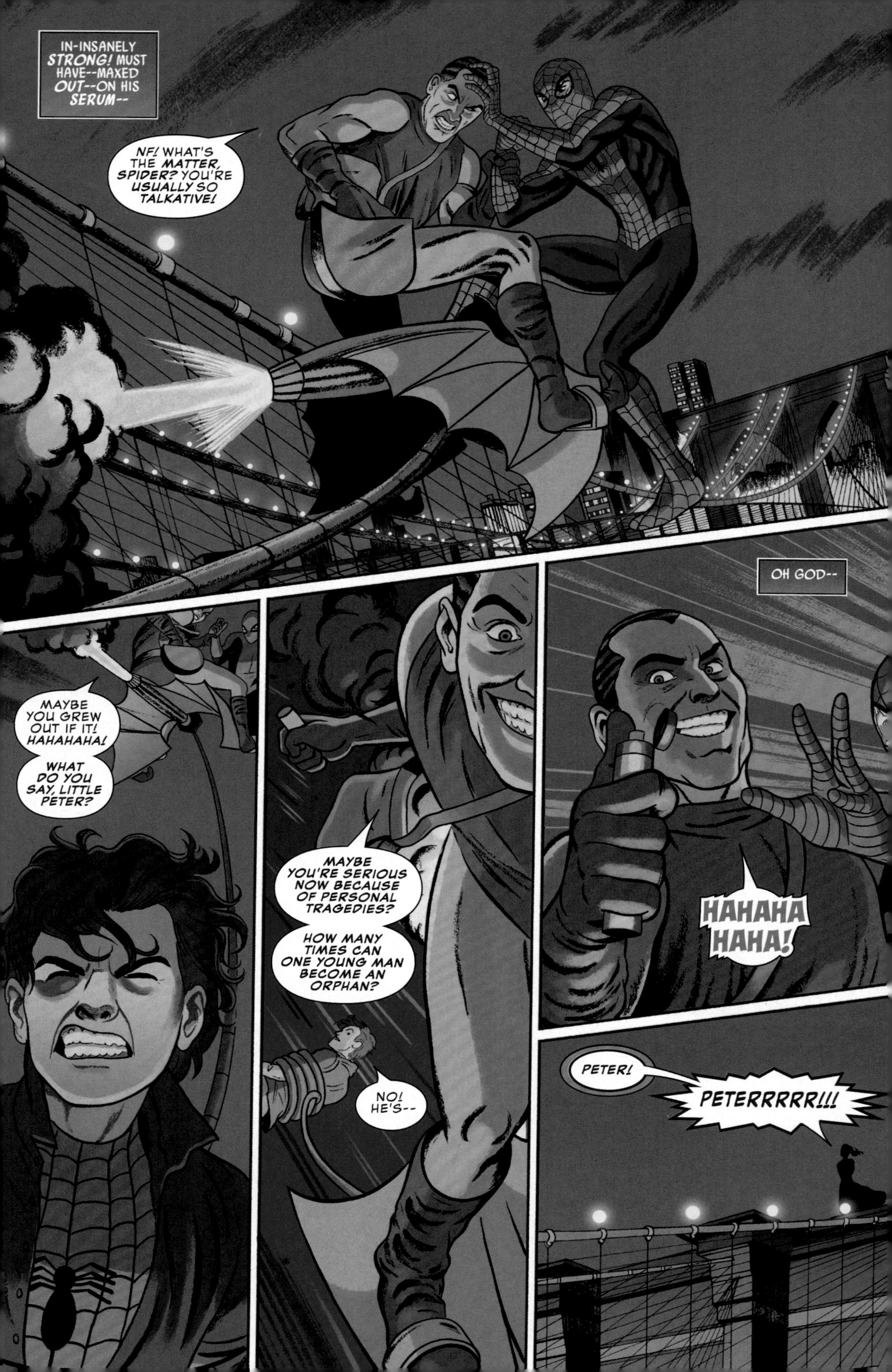
IN-INSANELY STRONG! MUST HAVE--MAXED OUT--ON HIS SERUM--
NF! WHAT'S THE MATTER, SPIDER? YOU'RE USUALLY SO TALKATIVE!
OH GOD--
MAYBE YOU GREW OUT IF IT! HAHAHAHA!
WHAT DO YOU SAY, LITTLE PETER?
MAYBE YOU'RE SERIOUS NOW BECAUSE OF PERSONAL TRAGEDIES?
HOW MANY TIMES CAN ONE YOUNG MAN BECOME AN ORPHAN?
NO! HE'S--
HAHAHA HAHA!
PETER!
PETERRRRR!!!

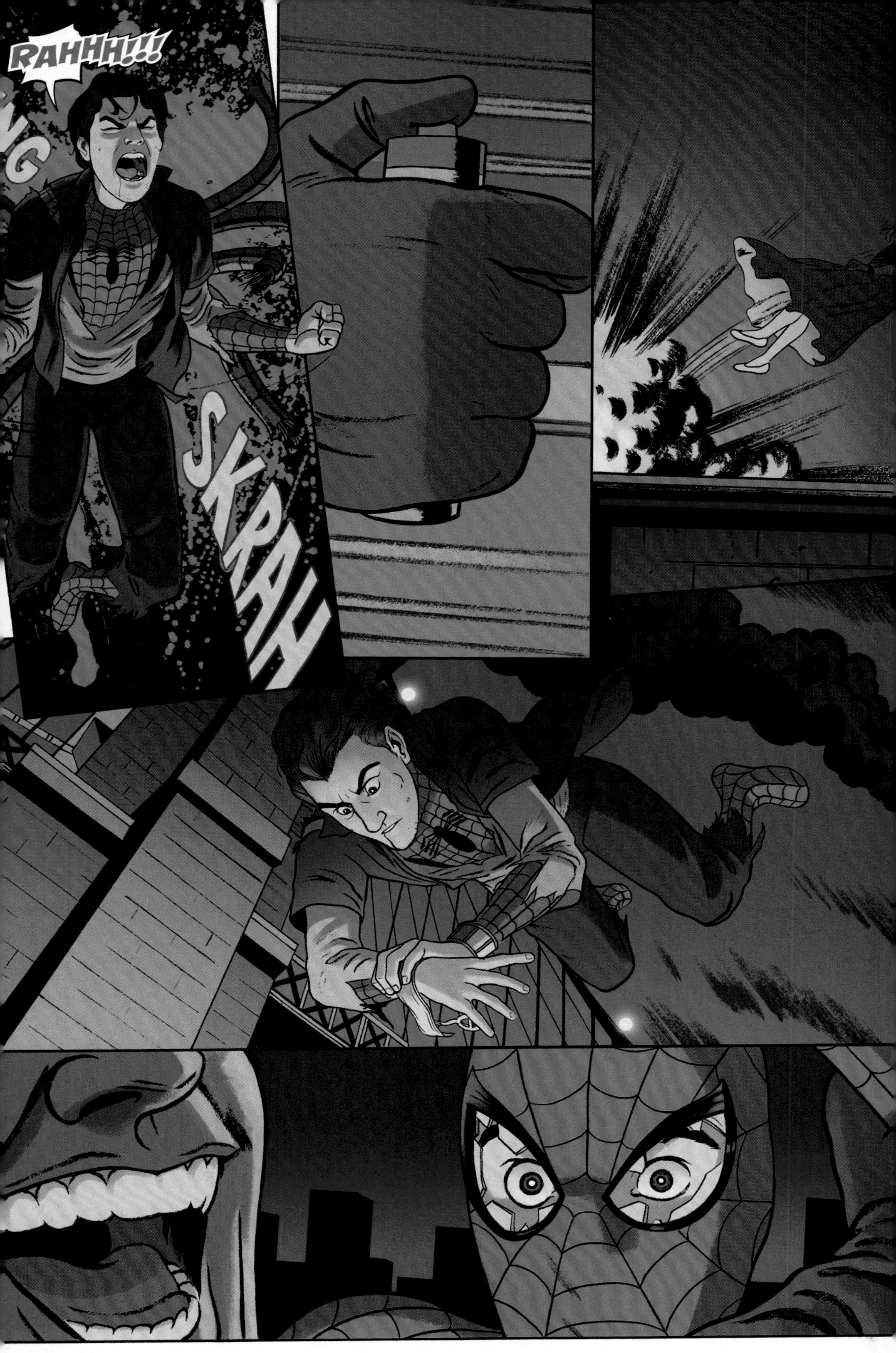
RAHHH!!!
SKRAH

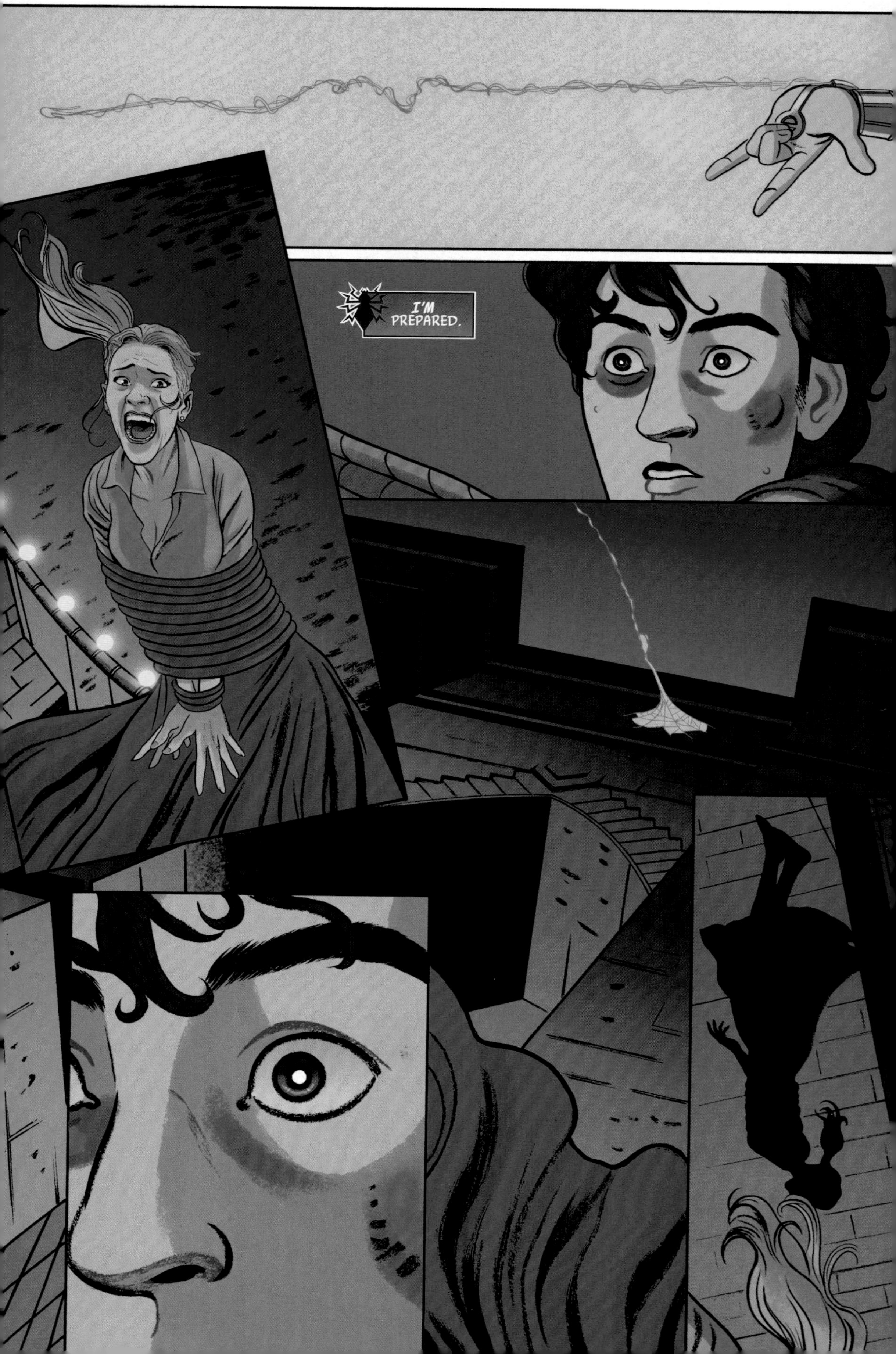
I'M PREPARED.

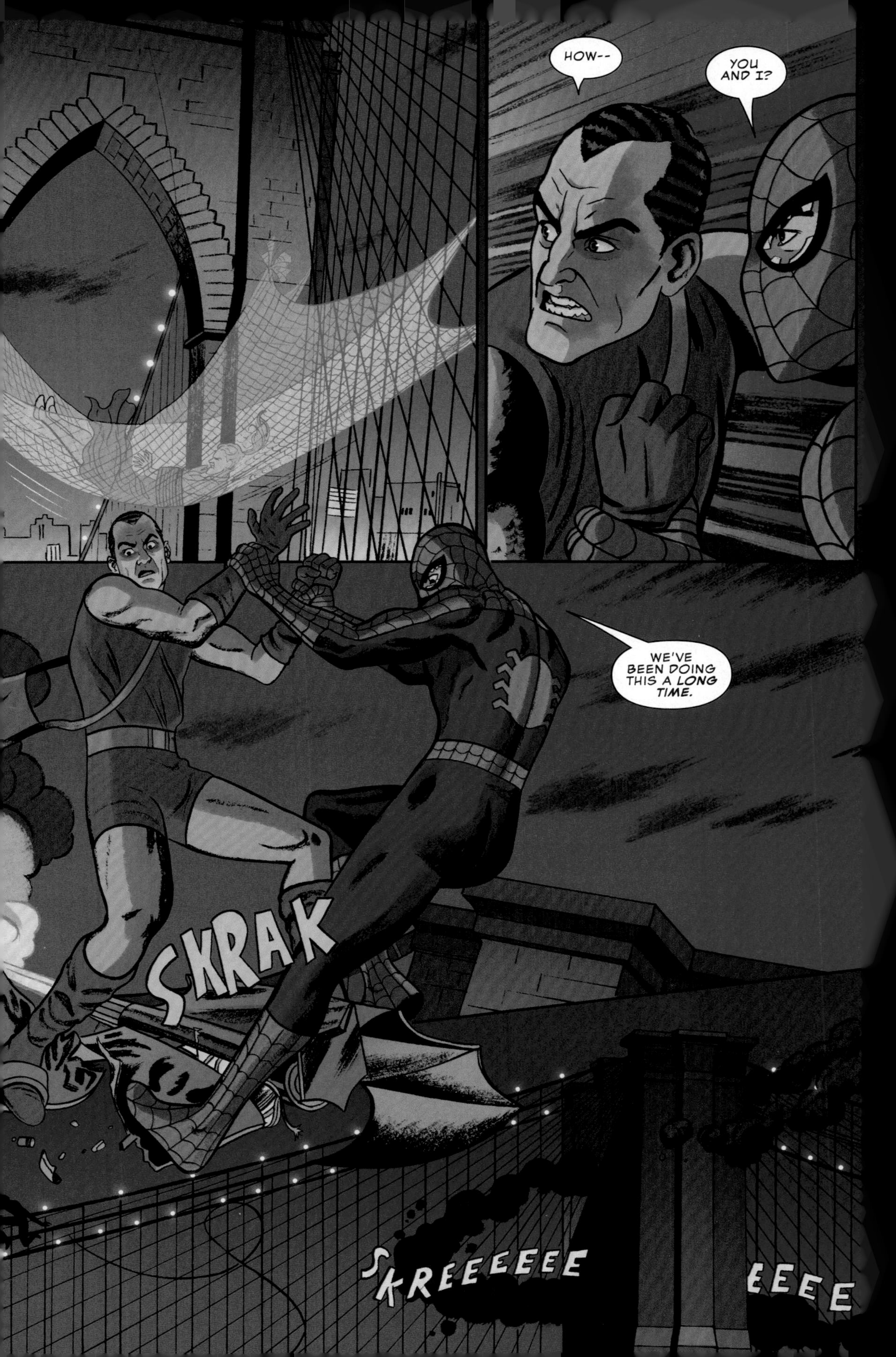
HOW--
YOU AND I?
WE'VE BEEN DOING THIS A *LONG TIME.*
SKRAK
SKREEEEEE
EEEE

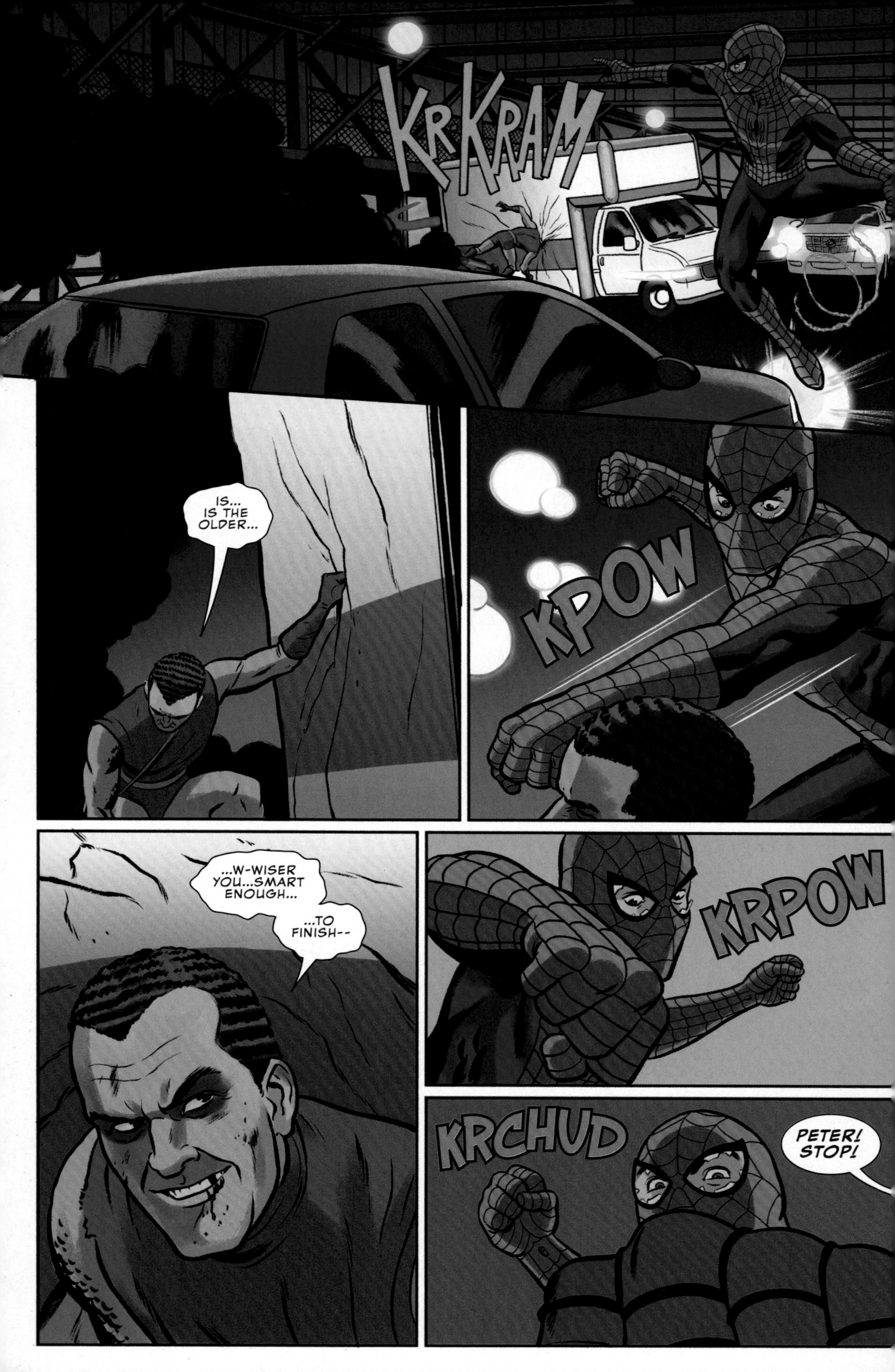
KRKRAM
IS... IS THE OLDER...
KPOW
...W-WISER YOU...SMART ENOUGH...
...TO FINISH--
KRPOW
KRCHUD
PETER! STOP!

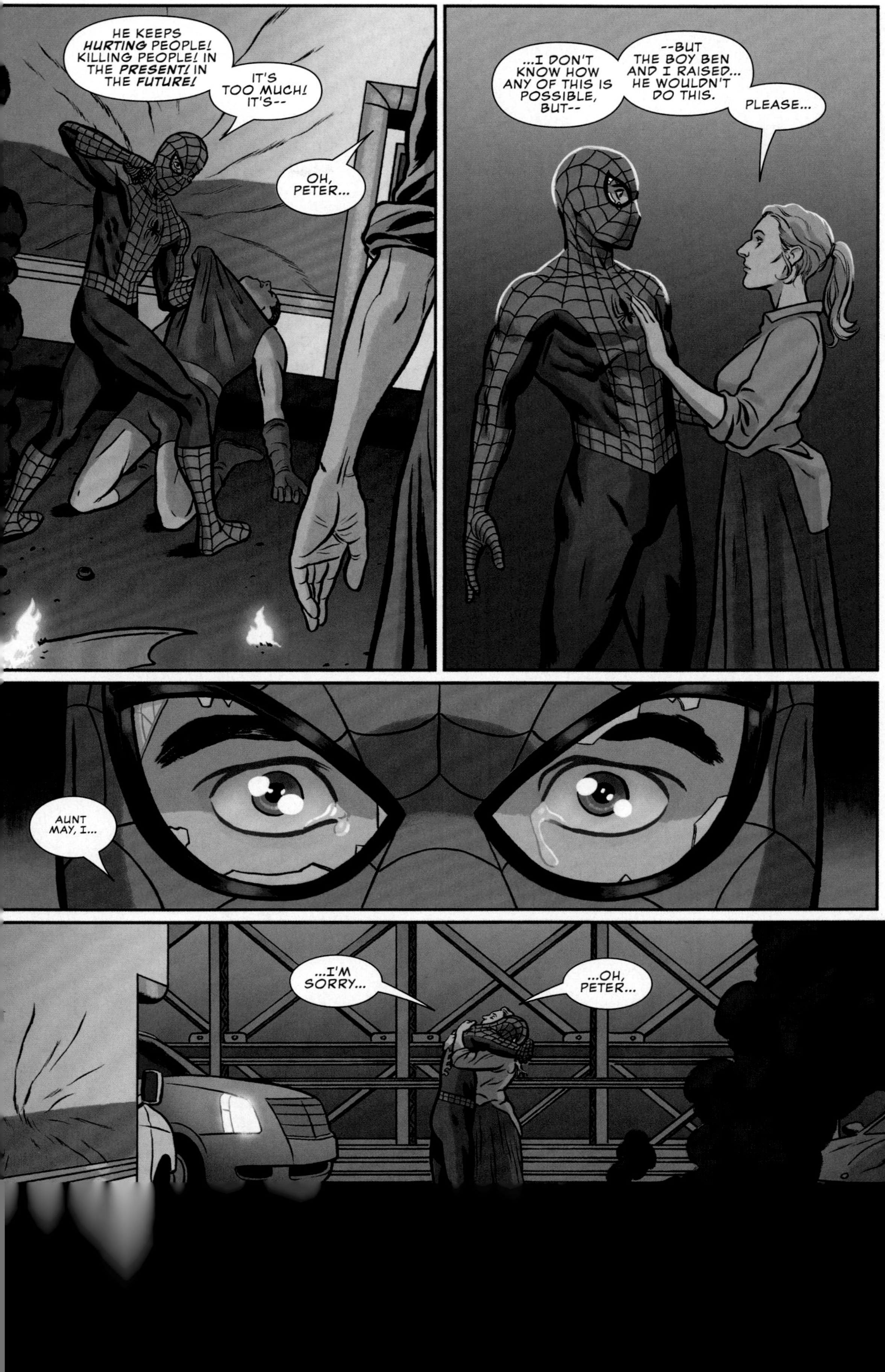
HE KEEPS *HURTING* PEOPLE! KILLING PEOPLE! IN THE *PRESENT!* IN THE *FUTURE!*
IT'S TOO MUCH! IT'S--
OH, PETER...
...I DON'T KNOW HOW ANY OF THIS IS POSSIBLE, BUT--
--BUT THE BOY BEN AND I RAISED... HE WOULDN'T DO THIS.
PLEASE...
AUNT MAY, I...
...I'M SORRY...
...OH, PETER...

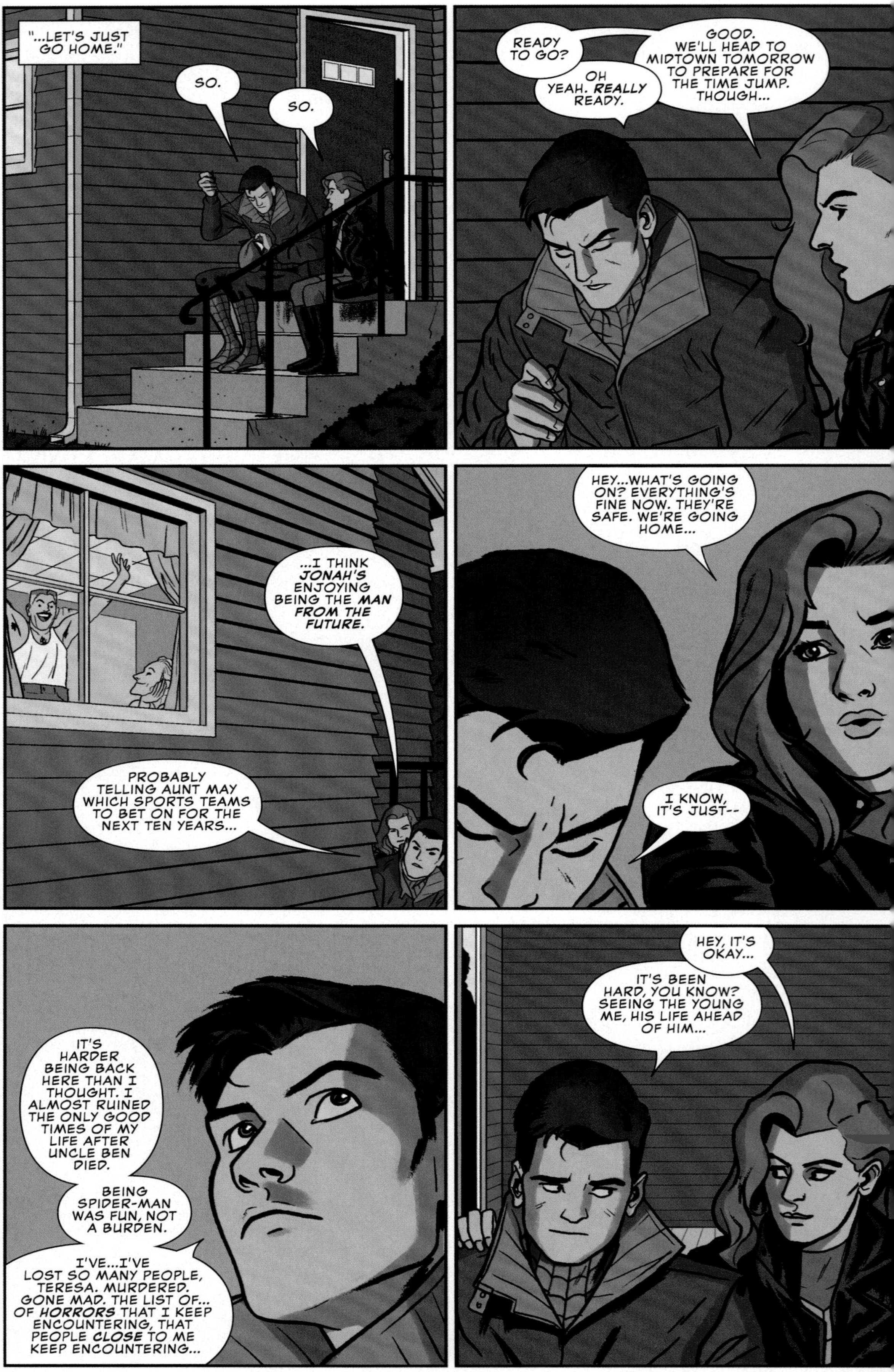
"...LET'S JUST GO HOME."
SO.
SO.
READY TO GO?
OH YEAH. REALLY READY.
GOOD. WE'LL HEAD TO MIDTOWN TOMORROW TO PREPARE FOR THE TIME JUMP. THOUGH...
...I THINK JONAH'S ENJOYING BEING THE MAN FROM THE FUTURE.
PROBABLY TELLING AUNT MAY WHICH SPORTS TEAMS TO BET ON FOR THE NEXT TEN YEARS...
HEY...WHAT'S GOING ON? EVERYTHING'S FINE NOW. THEY'RE SAFE. WE'RE GOING HOME...
I KNOW, IT'S JUST--
IT'S HARDER BEING BACK HERE THAN I THOUGHT. I ALMOST RUINED THE ONLY GOOD TIMES OF MY LIFE AFTER UNCLE BEN DIED.
BEING SPIDER-MAN WAS FUN, NOT A BURDEN.
I'VE...I'VE LOST SO MANY PEOPLE, TERESA. MURDERED. GONE MAD. THE LIST OF... OF HORRORS THAT I KEEP ENCOUNTERING, THAT PEOPLE CLOSE TO ME KEEP ENCOUNTERING...
HEY, IT'S OKAY...
IT'S BEEN HARD, YOU KNOW? SEEING THE YOUNG ME, HIS LIFE AHEAD OF HIM...

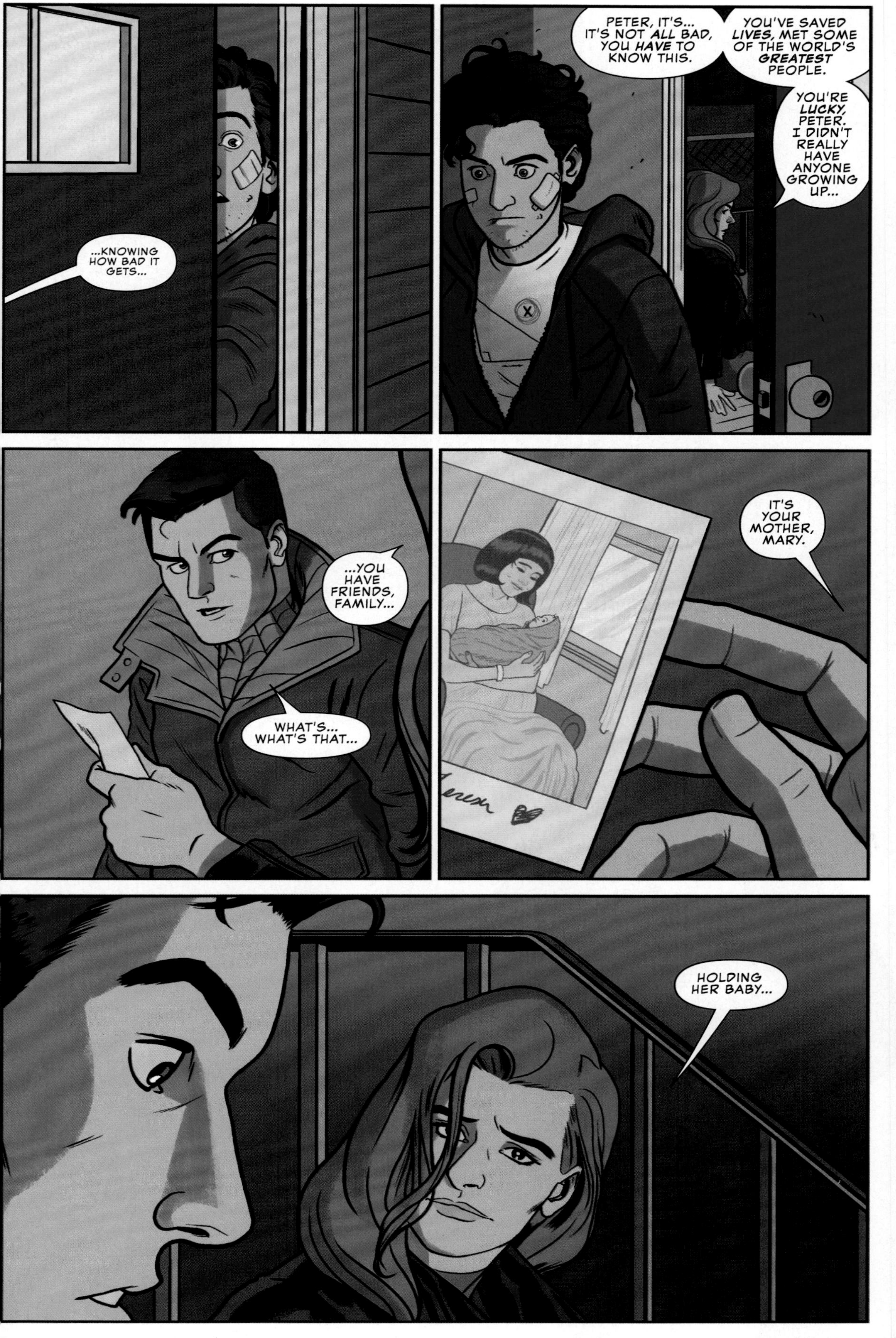
...KNOWING HOW BAD IT GETS...
PETER, IT'S... IT'S NOT ALL BAD, YOU HAVE TO KNOW THIS.
YOU'VE SAVED LIVES, MET SOME OF THE WORLD'S GREATEST PEOPLE.
YOU'RE LUCKY, PETER. I DIDN'T REALLY HAVE ANYONE GROWING UP...
...YOU HAVE FRIENDS, FAMILY...
WHAT'S... WHAT'S THAT...
IT'S YOUR MOTHER, MARY.
HOLDING HER BABY...

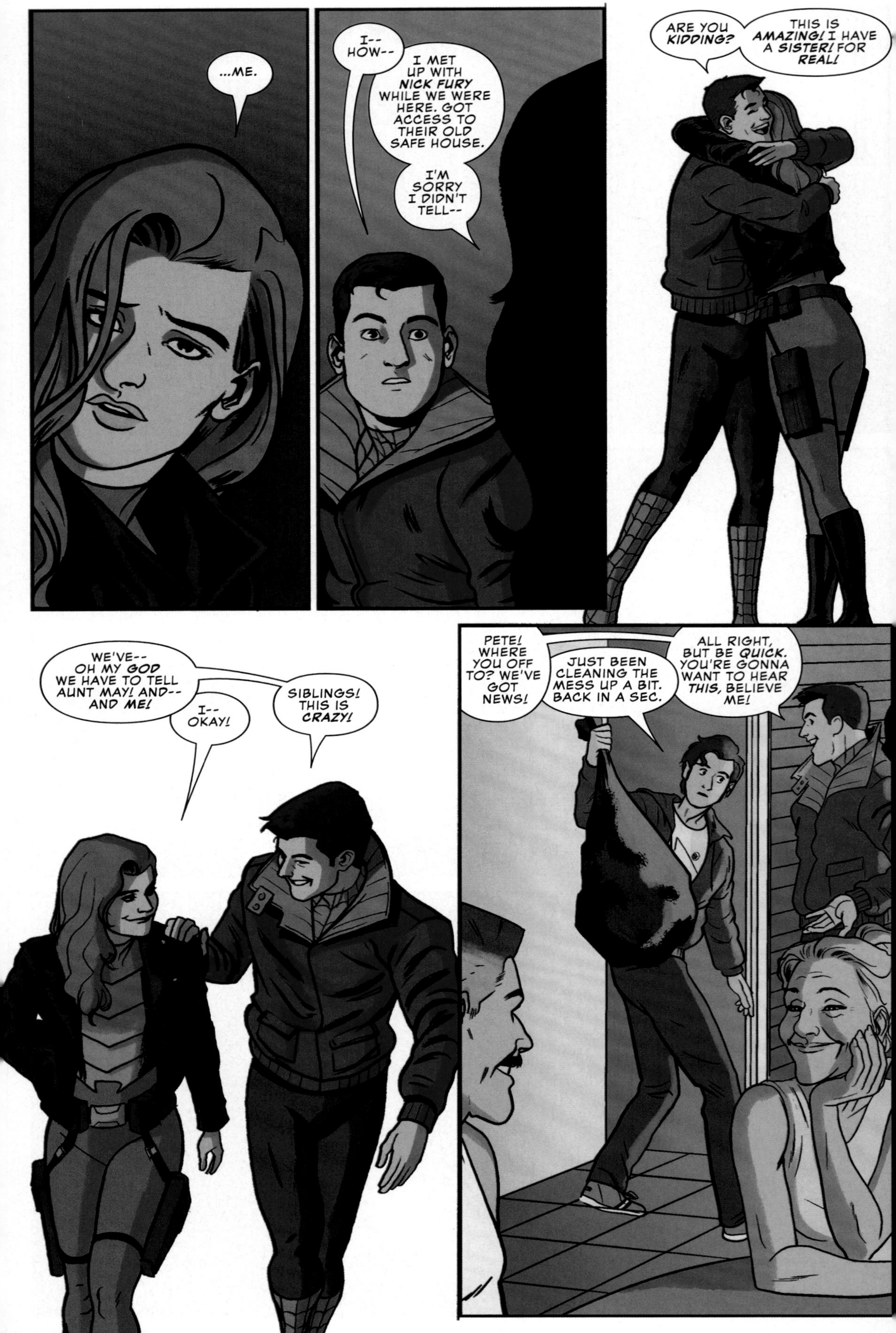
...ME.
I-- HOW--
I MET UP WITH NICK FURY WHILE WE WERE HERE. GOT ACCESS TO THEIR OLD SAFE HOUSE.
I'M SORRY I DIDN'T TELL--
ARE YOU KIDDING?
THIS IS AMAZING! I HAVE A SISTER! FOR REAL!
WE'VE-- OH MY GOD WE HAVE TO TELL AUNT MAY! AND-- AND MJ!
I-- OKAY!
SIBLINGS! THIS IS CRAZY!
PETE! WHERE YOU OFF TO? WE'VE GOT NEWS!
JUST BEEN CLEANING THE MESS UP A BIT. BACK IN A SEC.
ALL RIGHT, BUT BE QUICK. YOU'RE GONNA WANT TO HEAR THIS, BELIEVE ME!

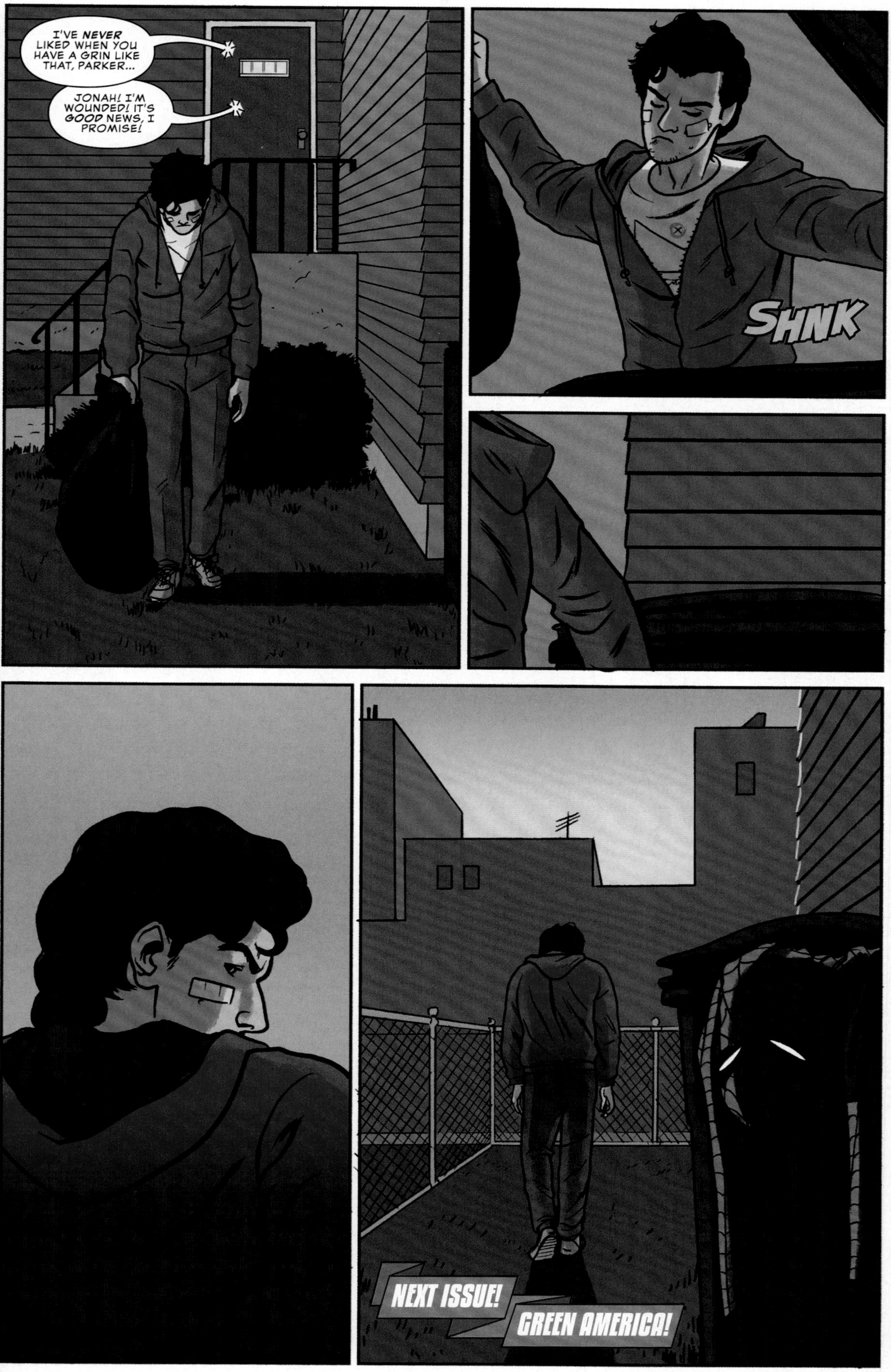
I'VE NEVER LIKED WHEN YOU HAVE A GRIN LIKE THAT, PARKER...
JONAH! I'M WOUNDED! IT'S GOOD NEWS, I PROMISE!
SHNK
NEXT ISSUE!
GREEN AMERICA!

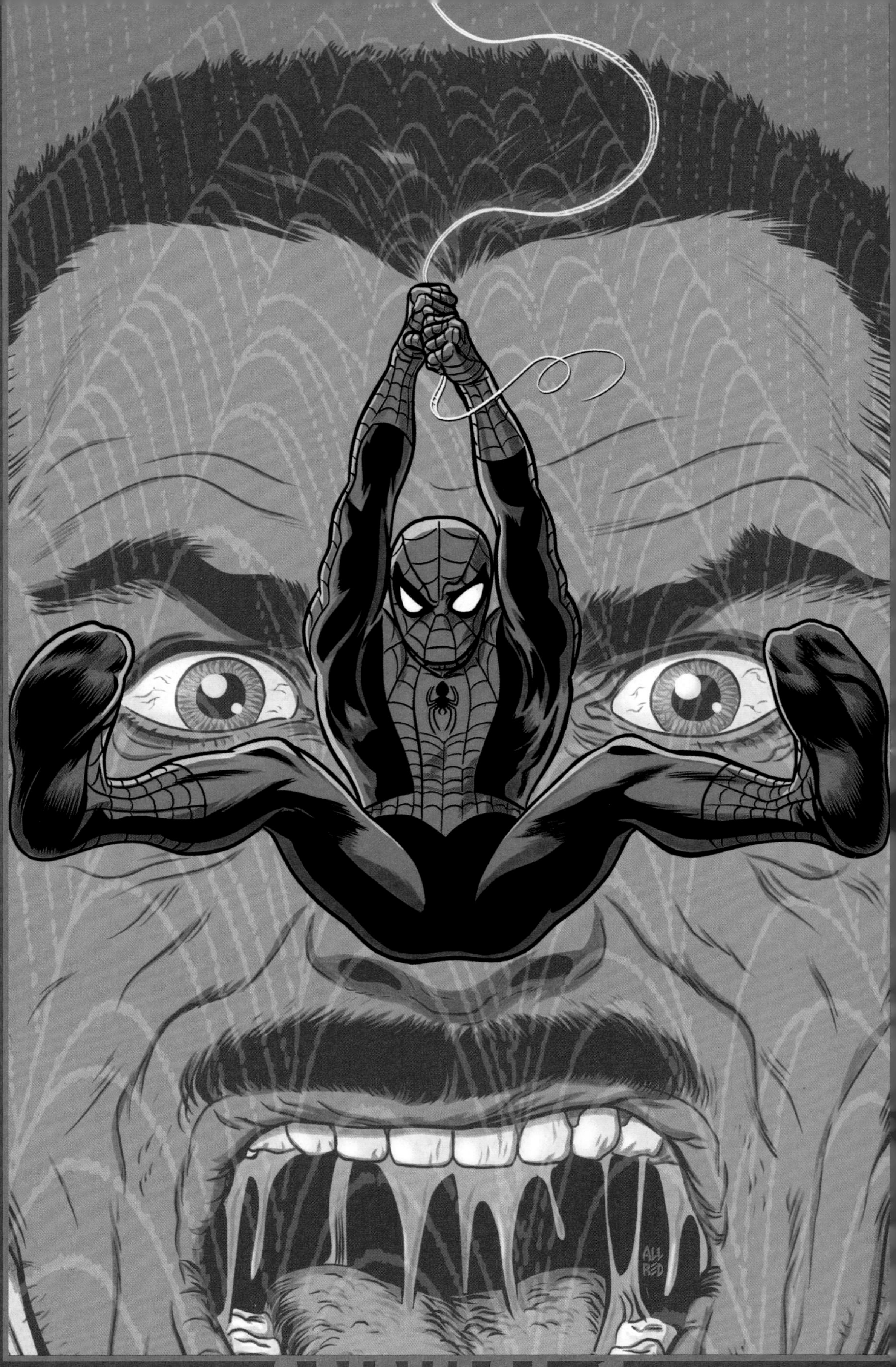
ALL
RED

ANNUAL 1

ALL RIGHT. FILL ME IN. WHAT'S GOING ON IN THIS SO-CALLED "ANNUAL"?

HMM… EVER HEARD OF J. JONAH JAMESON?

COOL—JUST SUPER-BASIC STUFF THIS TIME. 'COURSE I KNOW JAMESON!
FORMERLY PETER PARKER'S BOSS AT THE *DAILY BUGLE*,
ETERNALLY DISTINCTIVE 'STACHE, SHORT-TEMPERED, HATES SPIDER-MAN—

HOLD UP A MINUTE--THAT PART'S DIFFERENT. SEE, SPIDER-MAN FINALLY
ADMITTED HE AND PETER PARKER WERE THE SAME GUY, AND J.J.J.'S BEEN TRYING
TO "HELP" HIM/MAKE UP FOR YEARS OF SPIDER-PERSECUTION EVER SINCE.

ACROSS TWO COMICS TITLES AND WITH MIXED RESULTS, I IMAGINE?

TO SAY THE LEAST, MY PERSPICACIOUS FRIEND.

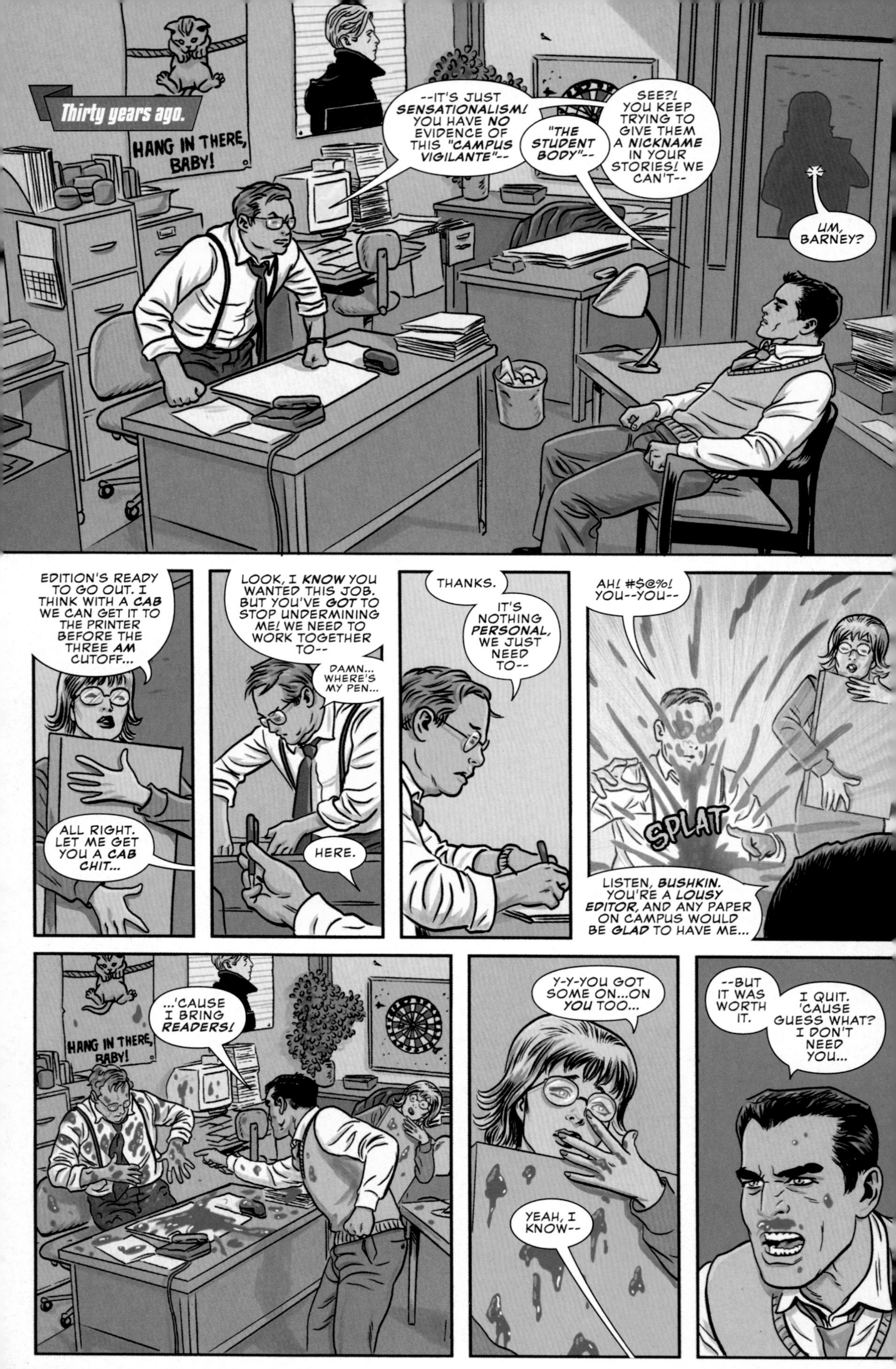
Thirty years ago.
HANG IN THERE, BABY!
--IT'S JUST SENSATIONALISM! YOU HAVE NO EVIDENCE OF THIS "CAMPUS VIGILANTE"--
SEE?! YOU KEEP TRYING TO GIVE THEM A NICKNAME IN YOUR STORIES! WE CAN'T--
"THE STUDENT BODY"--
UM, BARNEY?
EDITION'S READY TO GO OUT. I THINK WITH A CAB WE CAN GET IT TO THE PRINTER BEFORE THE THREE AM CUTOFF...
ALL RIGHT. LET ME GET YOU A CAB CHIT...
LOOK, I KNOW YOU WANTED THIS JOB. BUT YOU'VE GOT TO STOP UNDERMINING ME! WE NEED TO WORK TOGETHER TO--
DAMN... WHERE'S MY PEN...
HERE.
THANKS.
IT'S NOTHING PERSONAL, WE JUST NEED TO--
AH! #$@%! YOU--YOU--
SPLAT
LISTEN, BUSHKIN. YOU'RE A LOUSY EDITOR, AND ANY PAPER ON CAMPUS WOULD BE GLAD TO HAVE ME...
HANG IN THERE, BABY!
...'CAUSE I BRING READERS!
Y-Y-YOU GOT SOME ON...ON YOU TOO...
YEAH, I KNOW--
--BUT IT WAS WORTH IT.
I QUIT. 'CAUSE GUESS WHAT? I DON'T NEED YOU...

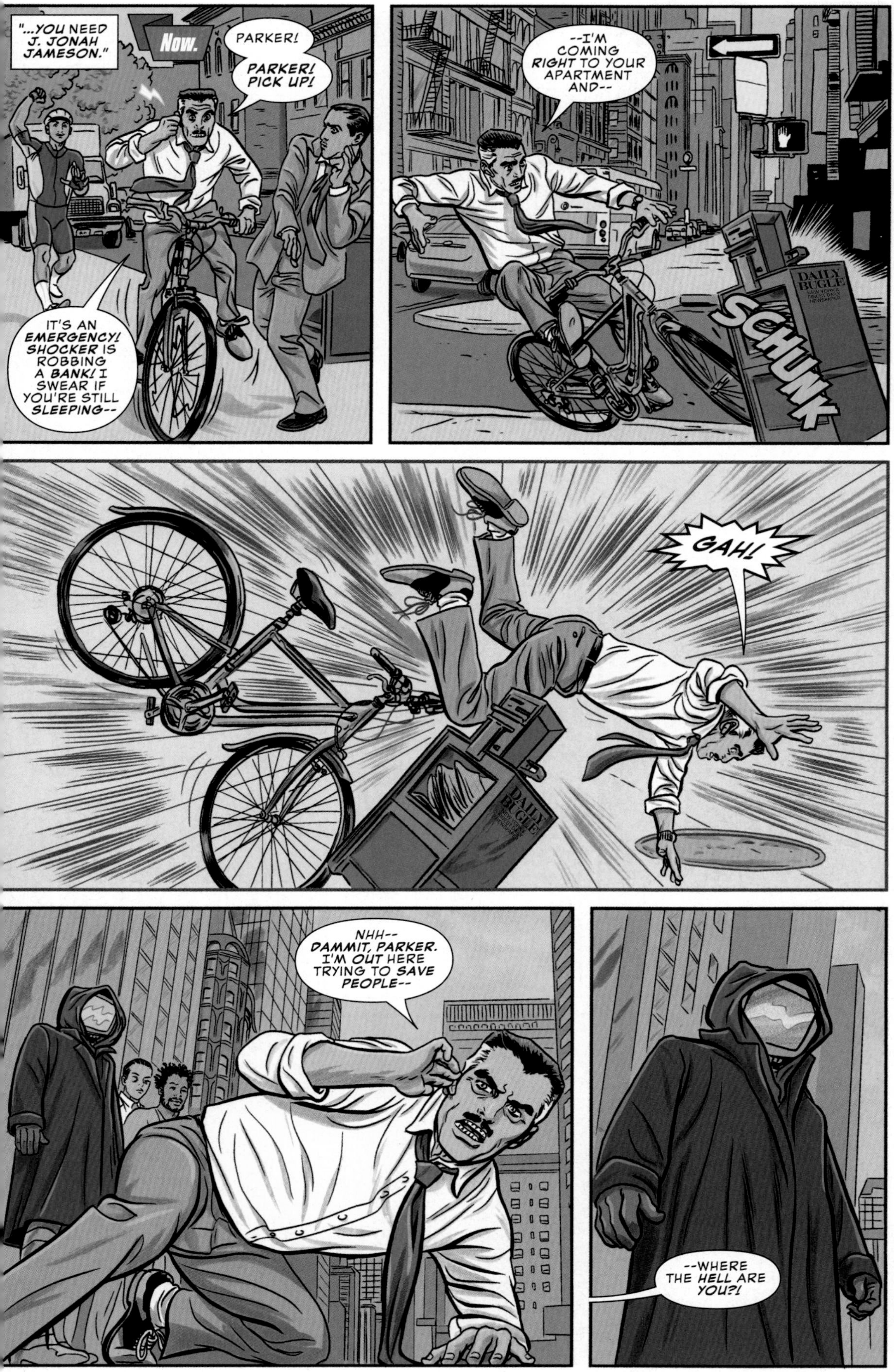
"...YOU NEED J. JONAH JAMESON."
Now.
PARKER!
PARKER! PICK UP!
IT'S AN EMERGENCY! SHOCKER IS ROBBING A BANK! I SWEAR IF YOU'RE STILL SLEEPING--
--I'M COMING RIGHT TO YOUR APARTMENT AND--
DAILY BUGLE
SCHUNK
GAH!
DAILY BUGLE
NHH-- DAMMIT, PARKER. I'M OUT HERE TRYING TO SAVE PEOPLE--
--WHERE THE HELL ARE YOU?!

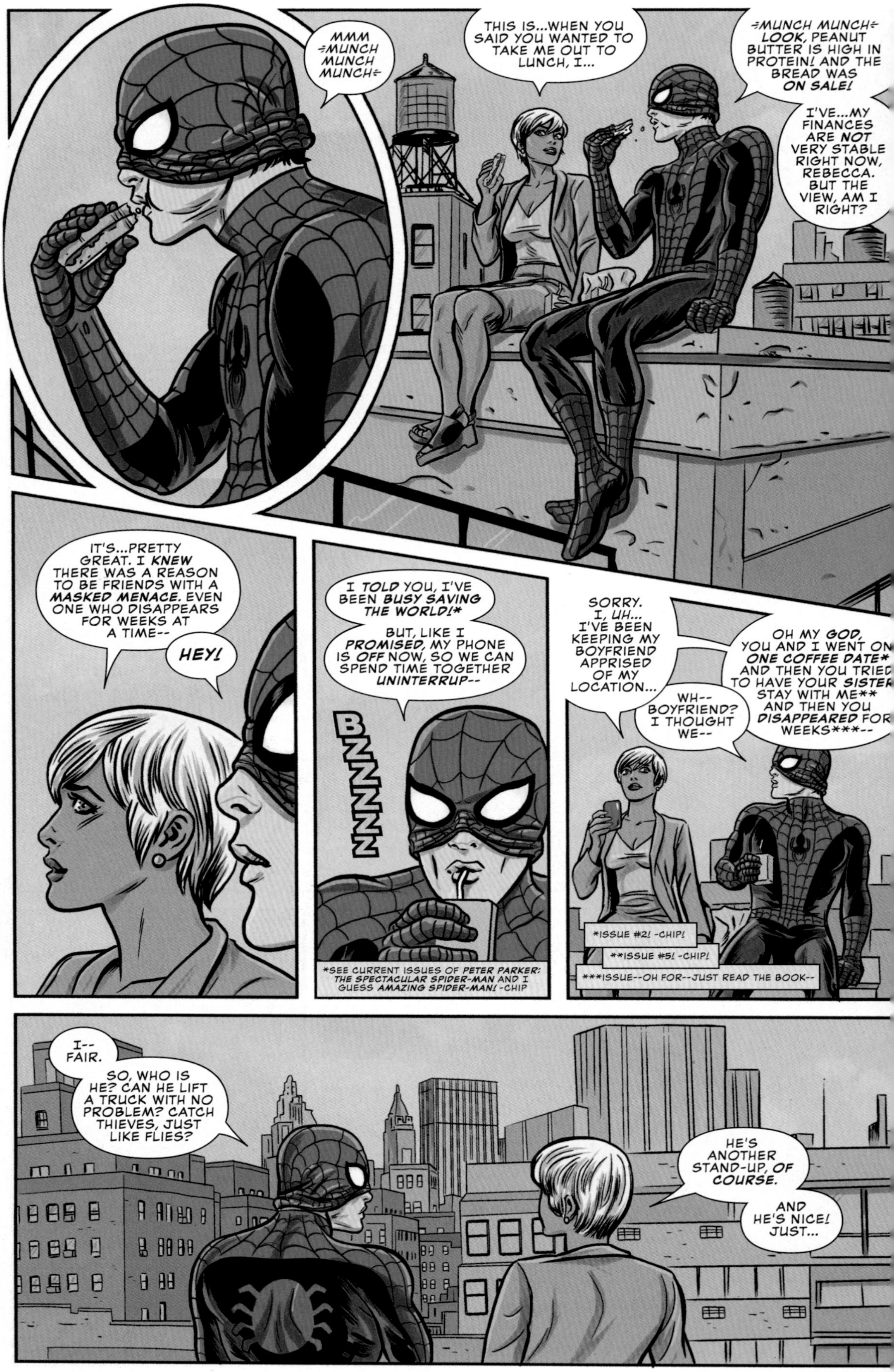

=MMM =MUNCH MUNCH MUNCH=
THIS IS...WHEN YOU SAID YOU WANTED TO TAKE ME OUT TO LUNCH, I...
=MUNCH MUNCH= LOOK, PEANUT BUTTER IS HIGH IN PROTEIN! AND THE BREAD WAS ON SALE!
I'VE...MY FINANCES ARE NOT VERY STABLE RIGHT NOW, REBECCA. BUT THE VIEW, AM I RIGHT?
IT'S...PRETTY GREAT. I KNEW THERE WAS A REASON TO BE FRIENDS WITH A MASKED MENACE. EVEN ONE WHO DISAPPEARS FOR WEEKS AT A TIME--
HEY!
I TOLD YOU, I'VE BEEN BUSY SAVING THE WORLD!*
BUT, LIKE I PROMISED, MY PHONE IS OFF NOW, SO WE CAN SPEND TIME TOGETHER UNINTERRUP--
BZZZZZ
*SEE CURRENT ISSUES OF PETER PARKER: THE SPECTACULAR SPIDER-MAN AND I GUESS AMAZING SPIDER-MAN! -CHIP
SORRY. I, UH... I'VE BEEN KEEPING MY BOYFRIEND APPRISED OF MY LOCATION...
WH-- BOYFRIEND? I THOUGHT WE--
OH MY GOD, YOU AND I WENT ON ONE COFFEE DATE* AND THEN YOU TRIED TO HAVE YOUR SISTER STAY WITH ME** AND THEN YOU DISAPPEARED FOR WEEKS***--
*ISSUE #2! -CHIP!
**ISSUE #5! -CHIP!
***ISSUE--OH FOR--JUST READ THE BOOK--
I-- FAIR.
SO, WHO IS HE? CAN HE LIFT A TRUCK WITH NO PROBLEM? CATCH THIEVES, JUST LIKE FLIES?
HE'S ANOTHER STAND-UP, OF COURSE.
AND HE'S NICE! JUST...

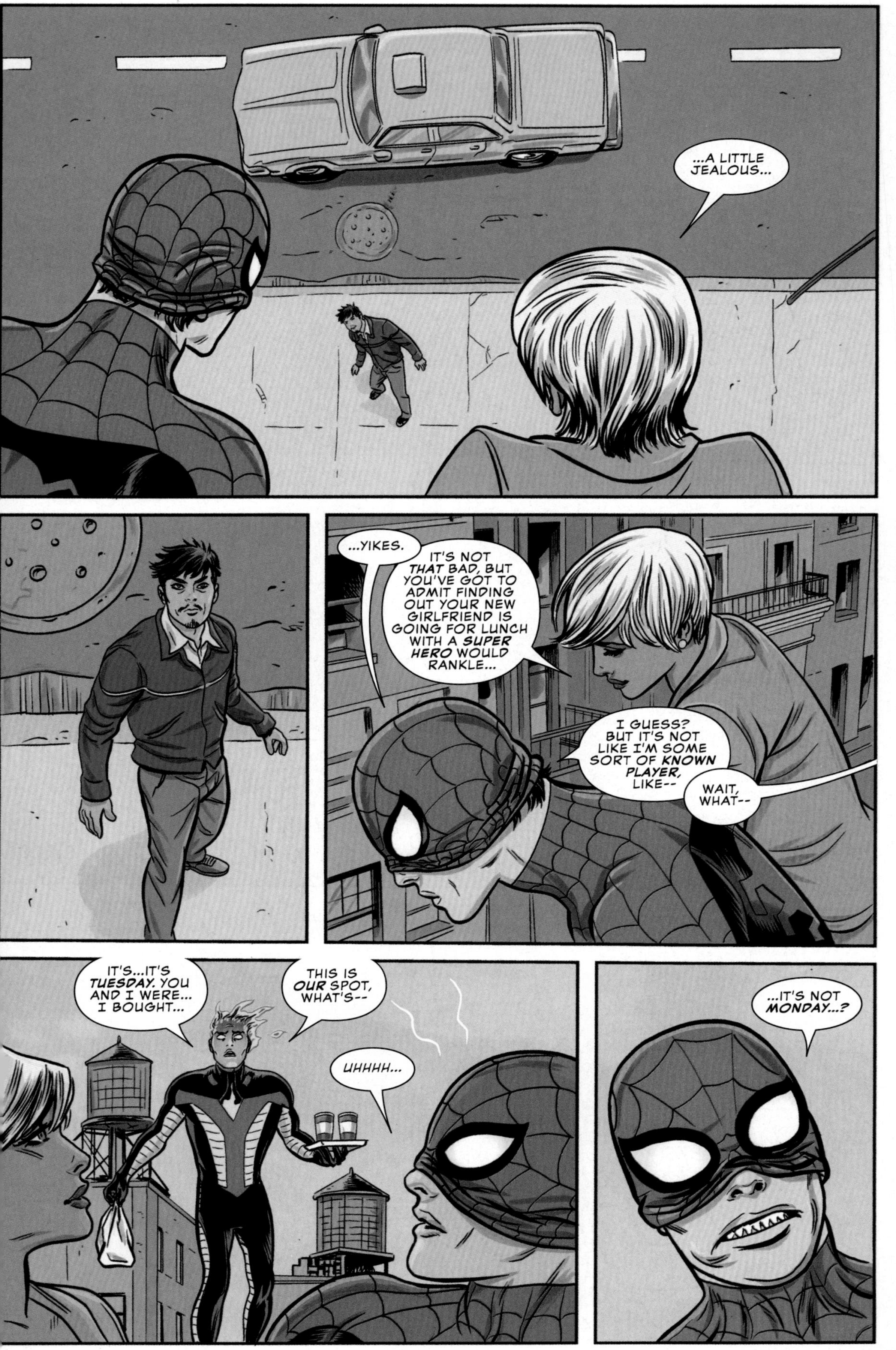
...A LITTLE JEALOUS...
...YIKES.
IT'S NOT *THAT* BAD, BUT YOU'VE GOT TO ADMIT FINDING OUT YOUR NEW GIRLFRIEND IS GOING FOR LUNCH WITH A *SUPER HERO* WOULD RANKLE...
I GUESS? BUT IT'S NOT LIKE I'M SOME SORT OF *KNOWN PLAYER,* LIKE--
WAIT, WHAT--
IT'S...IT'S *TUESDAY.* YOU AND I WERE... I BOUGHT...
THIS IS *OUR* SPOT, WHAT'S--
UHHHH...
...IT'S NOT *MONDAY...?*

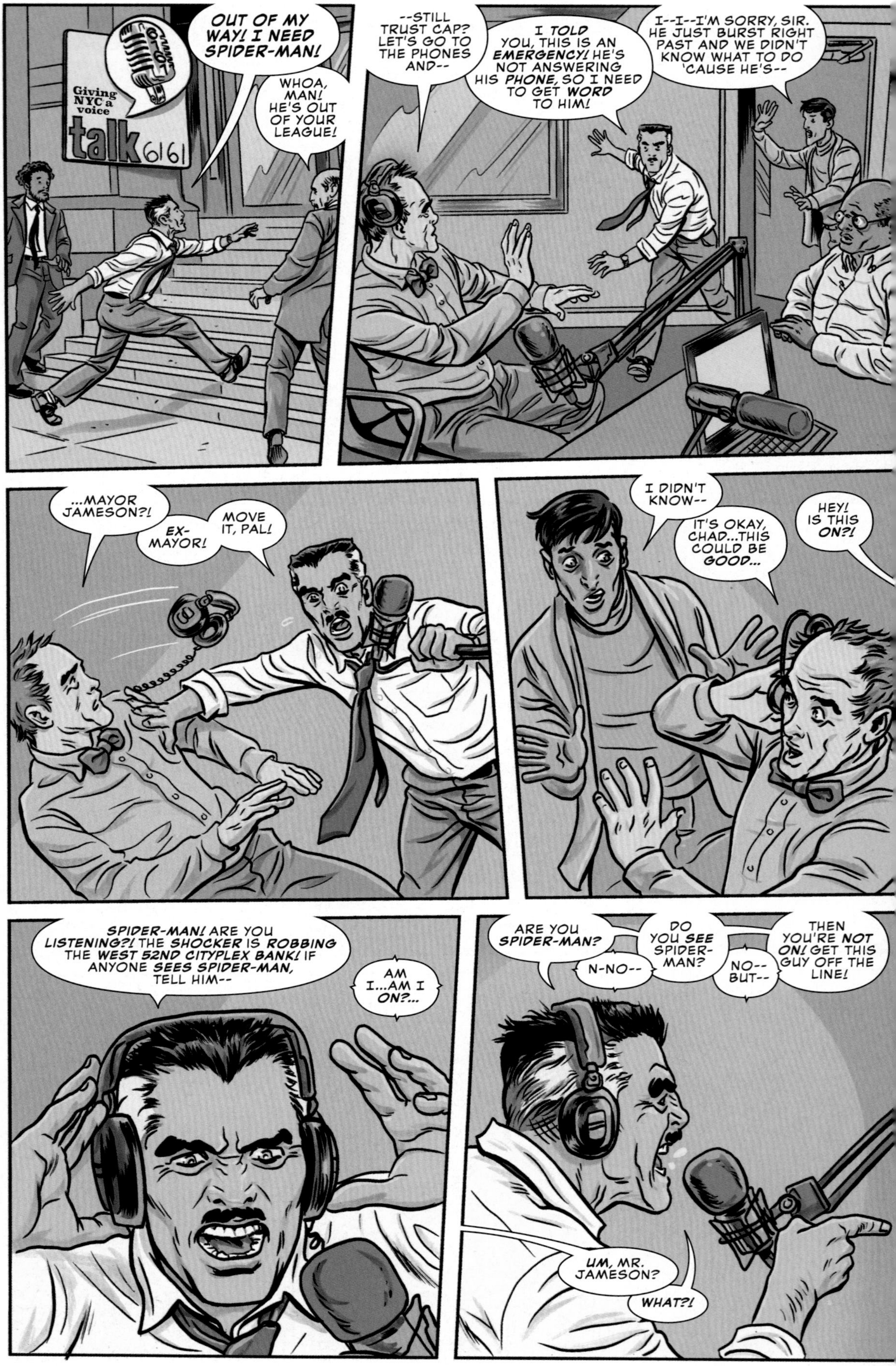
Giving NYC a voice
talk 61 61
OUT OF MY WAY! I NEED SPIDER-MAN!
WHOA, MAN! HE'S OUT OF YOUR LEAGUE!
--STILL TRUST CAP? LET'S GO TO THE PHONES AND--
I TOLD YOU, THIS IS AN EMERGENCY! HE'S NOT ANSWERING HIS PHONE, SO I NEED TO GET WORD TO HIM!
I--I--I'M SORRY, SIR. HE JUST BURST RIGHT PAST AND WE DIDN'T KNOW WHAT TO DO 'CAUSE HE'S--
...MAYOR JAMESON?!
EX-MAYOR!
MOVE IT, PAL!
I DIDN'T KNOW--
IT'S OKAY, CHAD...THIS COULD BE GOOD...
HEY! IS THIS ON?!
SPIDER-MAN! ARE YOU LISTENING?! THE SHOCKER IS ROBBING THE WEST 52ND CITYPLEX BANK! IF ANYONE SEES SPIDER-MAN, TELL HIM--
AM I...AM I ON?...
ARE YOU SPIDER-MAN?
N-NO--
DO YOU SEE SPIDER-MAN?
NO--BUT--
THEN YOU'RE NOT ON! GET THIS GUY OFF THE LINE!
UM, MR. JAMESON?
WHAT?!

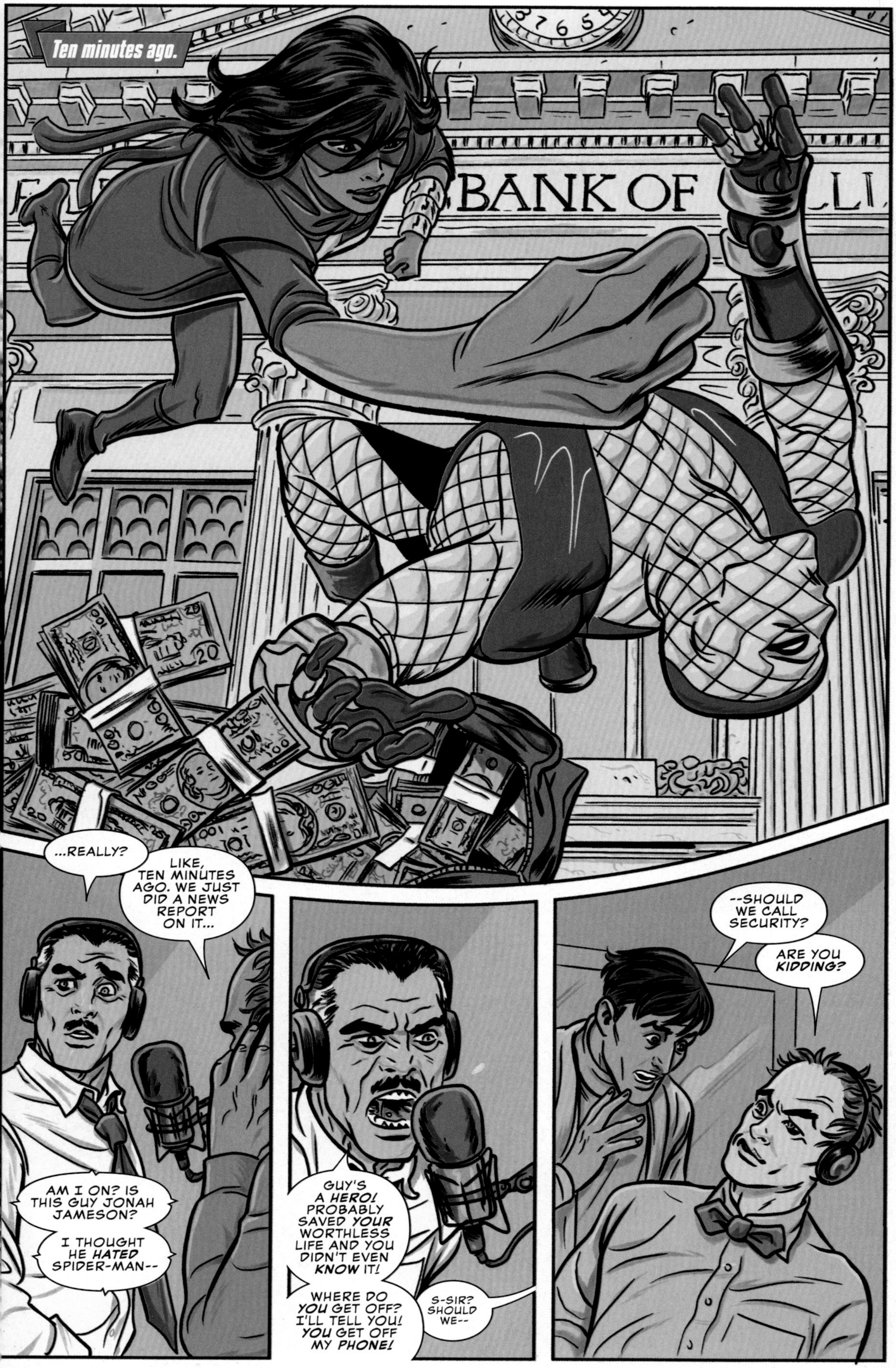
Ten minutes ago.
BANK OF
...REALLY?
LIKE, TEN MINUTES AGO. WE JUST DID A NEWS REPORT ON IT...
AM I ON? IS THIS GUY JONAH JAMESON?
I THOUGHT HE HATED SPIDER-MAN--
GUY'S A HERO! PROBABLY SAVED YOUR WORTHLESS LIFE AND YOU DIDN'T EVEN KNOW IT!
WHERE DO YOU GET OFF? I'LL TELL YOU! YOU GET OFF MY PHONE!
S-SIR? SHOULD WE--
--SHOULD WE CALL SECURITY?
ARE YOU KIDDING?

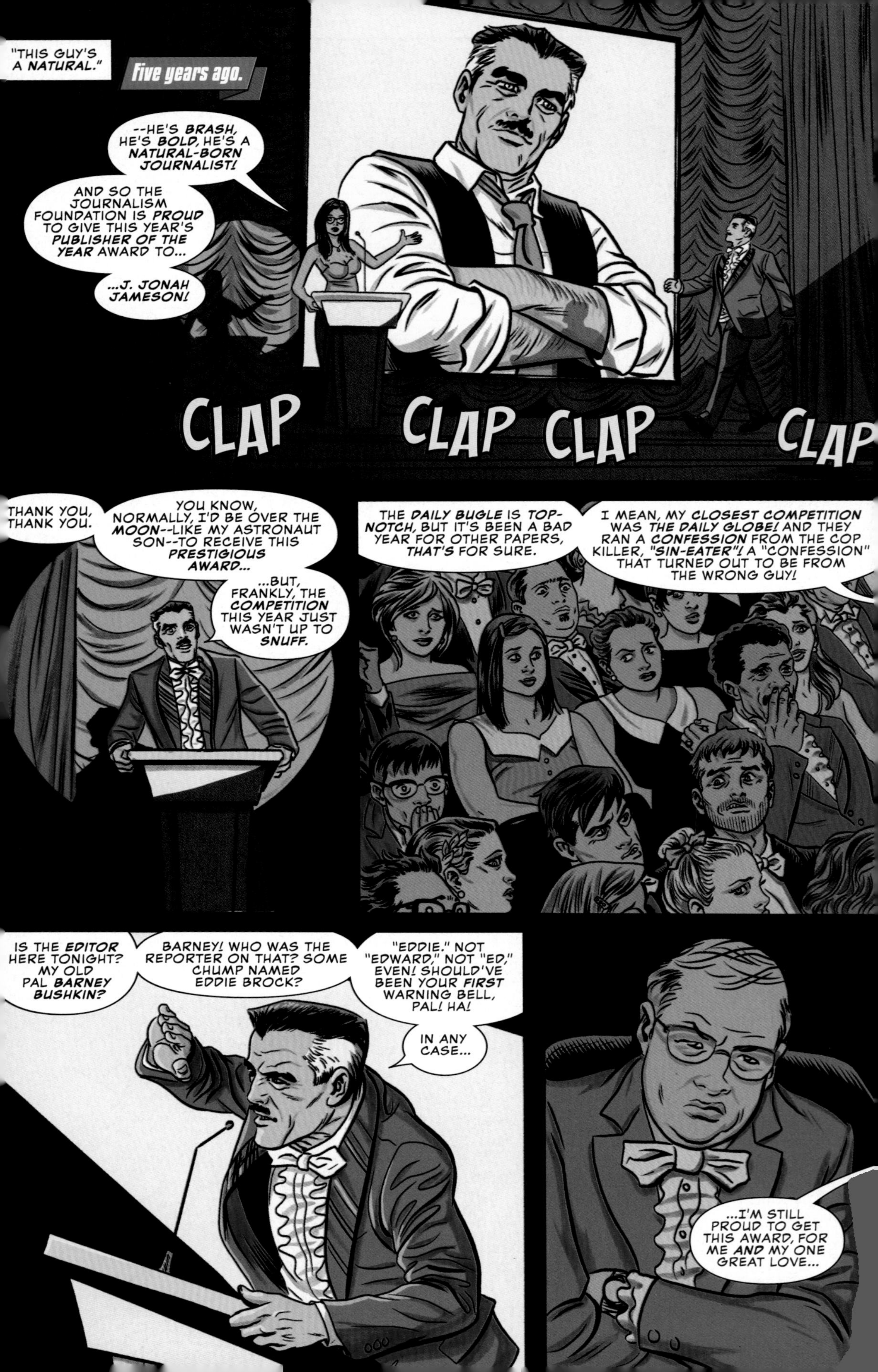
"THIS GUY'S A NATURAL."
Five years ago.
--HE'S BRASH, HE'S BOLD, HE'S A NATURAL-BORN JOURNALIST!
AND SO THE JOURNALISM FOUNDATION IS PROUD TO GIVE THIS YEAR'S PUBLISHER OF THE YEAR AWARD TO...
...J. JONAH JAMESON!
CLAP CLAP CLAP CLAP
THANK YOU, THANK YOU.
YOU KNOW, NORMALLY, I'D BE OVER THE MOON--LIKE MY ASTRONAUT SON--TO RECEIVE THIS PRESTIGIOUS AWARD...
...BUT, FRANKLY, THE COMPETITION THIS YEAR JUST WASN'T UP TO SNUFF.
THE DAILY BUGLE IS TOP-NOTCH, BUT IT'S BEEN A BAD YEAR FOR OTHER PAPERS, THAT'S FOR SURE.
I MEAN, MY CLOSEST COMPETITION WAS THE DAILY GLOBE! AND THEY RAN A CONFESSION FROM THE COP KILLER, "SIN-EATER"! A "CONFESSION" THAT TURNED OUT TO BE FROM THE WRONG GUY!
IS THE EDITOR HERE TONIGHT? MY OLD PAL BARNEY BUSHKIN?
BARNEY! WHO WAS THE REPORTER ON THAT? SOME CHUMP NAMED EDDIE BROCK?
"EDDIE." NOT "EDWARD," NOT "ED," EVEN! SHOULD'VE BEEN YOUR FIRST WARNING BELL, PAL! HA!
IN ANY CASE...
...I'M STILL PROUD TO GET THIS AWARD, FOR ME AND MY ONE GREAT LOVE...

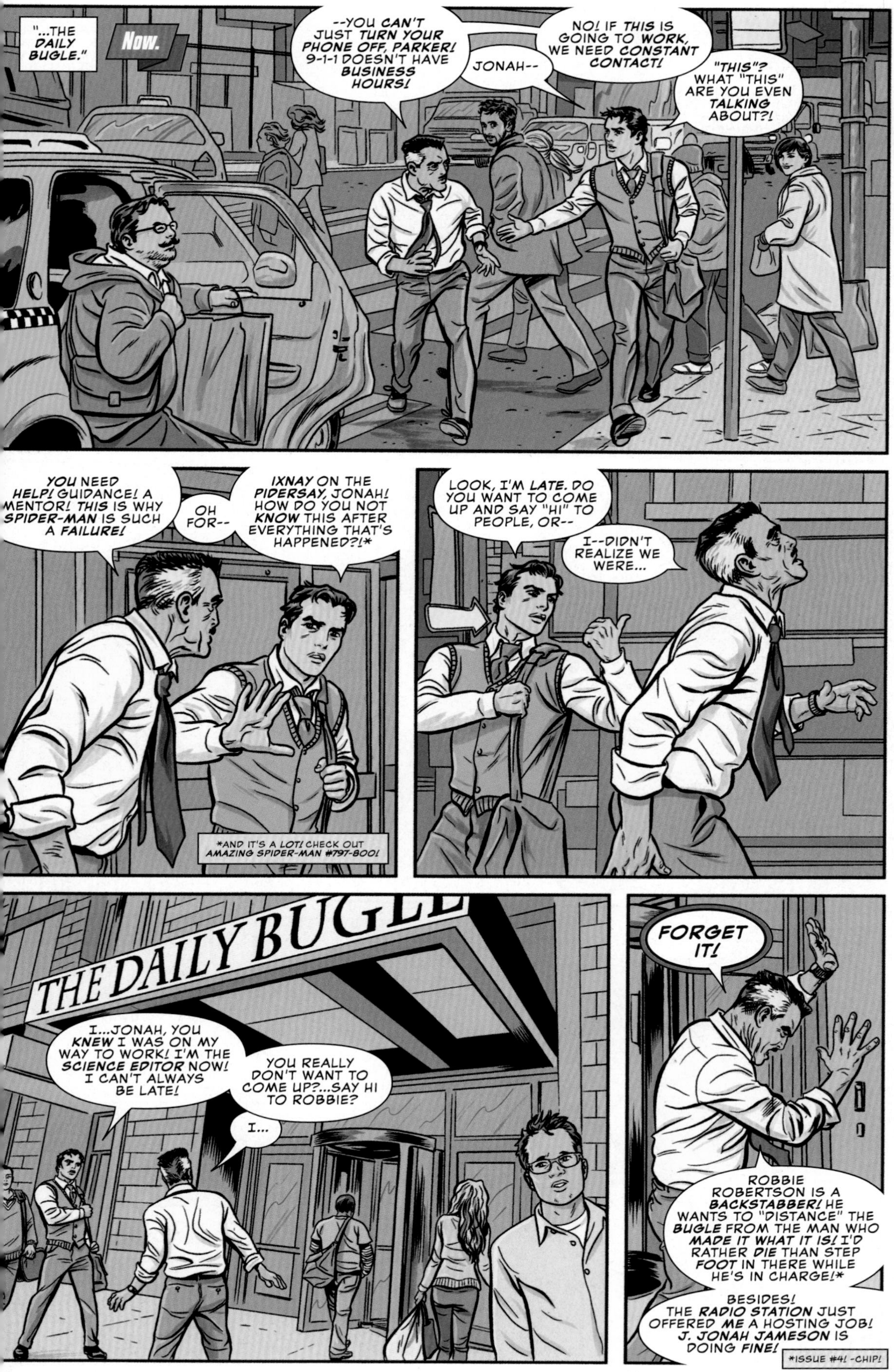
"...THE DAILY BUGLE."
Now.
--YOU CAN'T JUST TURN YOUR PHONE OFF, PARKER! 9-1-1 DOESN'T HAVE BUSINESS HOURS!
JONAH--
NO! IF THIS IS GOING TO WORK, WE NEED CONSTANT CONTACT!
"THIS"? WHAT "THIS" ARE YOU EVEN TALKING ABOUT?!
YOU NEED HELP! GUIDANCE! A MENTOR! THIS IS WHY SPIDER-MAN IS SUCH A FAILURE!
OH FOR--
IXNAY ON THE PIDERSAY, JONAH! HOW DO YOU NOT KNOW THIS AFTER EVERYTHING THAT'S HAPPENED?!*
*AND IT'S A LOT! CHECK OUT AMAZING SPIDER-MAN #797-800!
LOOK, I'M LATE. DO YOU WANT TO COME UP AND SAY "HI" TO PEOPLE, OR--
I--DIDN'T REALIZE WE WERE...
THE DAILY BUGLE
I...JONAH, YOU KNEW I WAS ON MY WAY TO WORK! I'M THE SCIENCE EDITOR NOW! I CAN'T ALWAYS BE LATE!
YOU REALLY DON'T WANT TO COME UP?...SAY HI TO ROBBIE?
I...
FORGET IT!
ROBBIE ROBERTSON IS A BACKSTABBER! HE WANTS TO "DISTANCE" THE BUGLE FROM THE MAN WHO MADE IT WHAT IT IS! I'D RATHER DIE THAN STEP FOOT IN THERE WHILE HE'S IN CHARGE!*
BESIDES! THE RADIO STATION JUST OFFERED ME A HOSTING JOB! J. JONAH JAMESON IS DOING FINE!
*ISSUE #4! -CHIP!

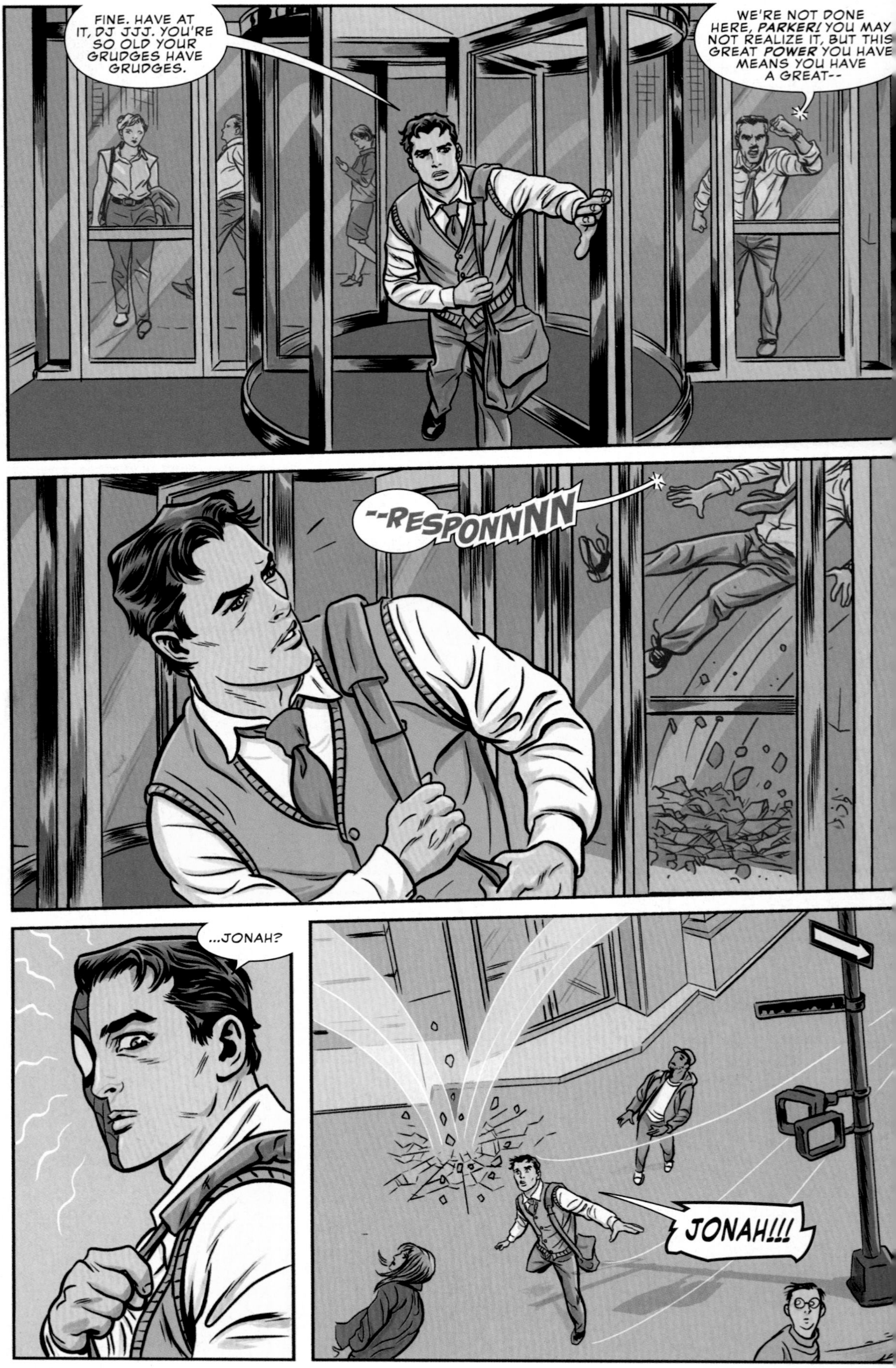
FINE. HAVE AT IT, DJ JJJ. YOU'RE SO OLD YOUR GRUDGES HAVE GRUDGES.
WE'RE NOT DONE HERE, PARKER! YOU MAY NOT REALIZE IT, BUT THIS GREAT POWER YOU HAVE MEANS YOU HAVE A GREAT--
--RESPONNNN
...JONAH?
JONAH!!!

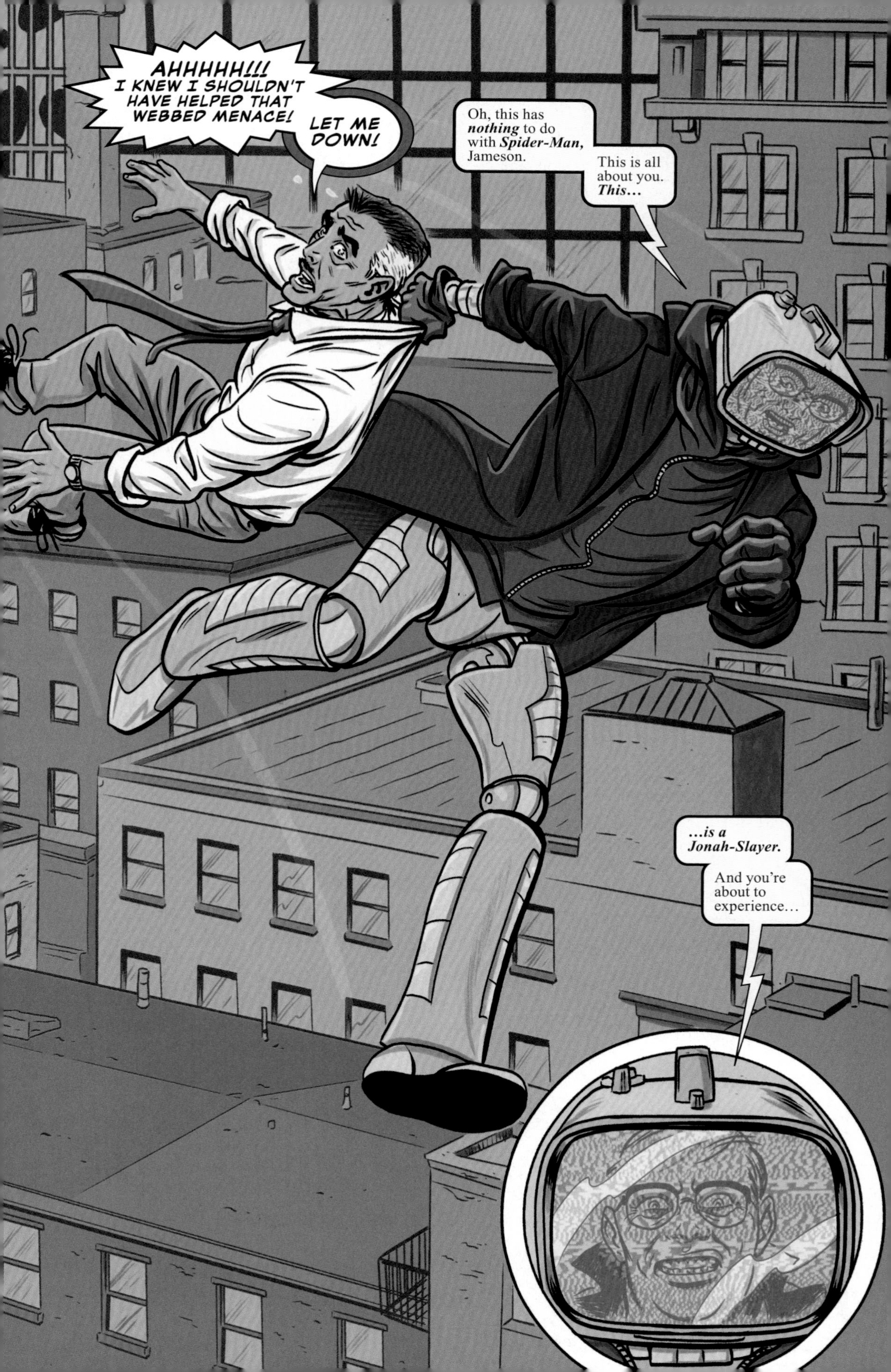
AHHHHH!!! I KNEW I SHOULDN'T HAVE HELPED THAT WEBBED MENACE!
LET ME DOWN!
Oh, this has *nothing* to do with *Spider-Man,* Jameson.
This is all about you. *This…*
…is a Jonah-Slayer.
And you're about to experience…

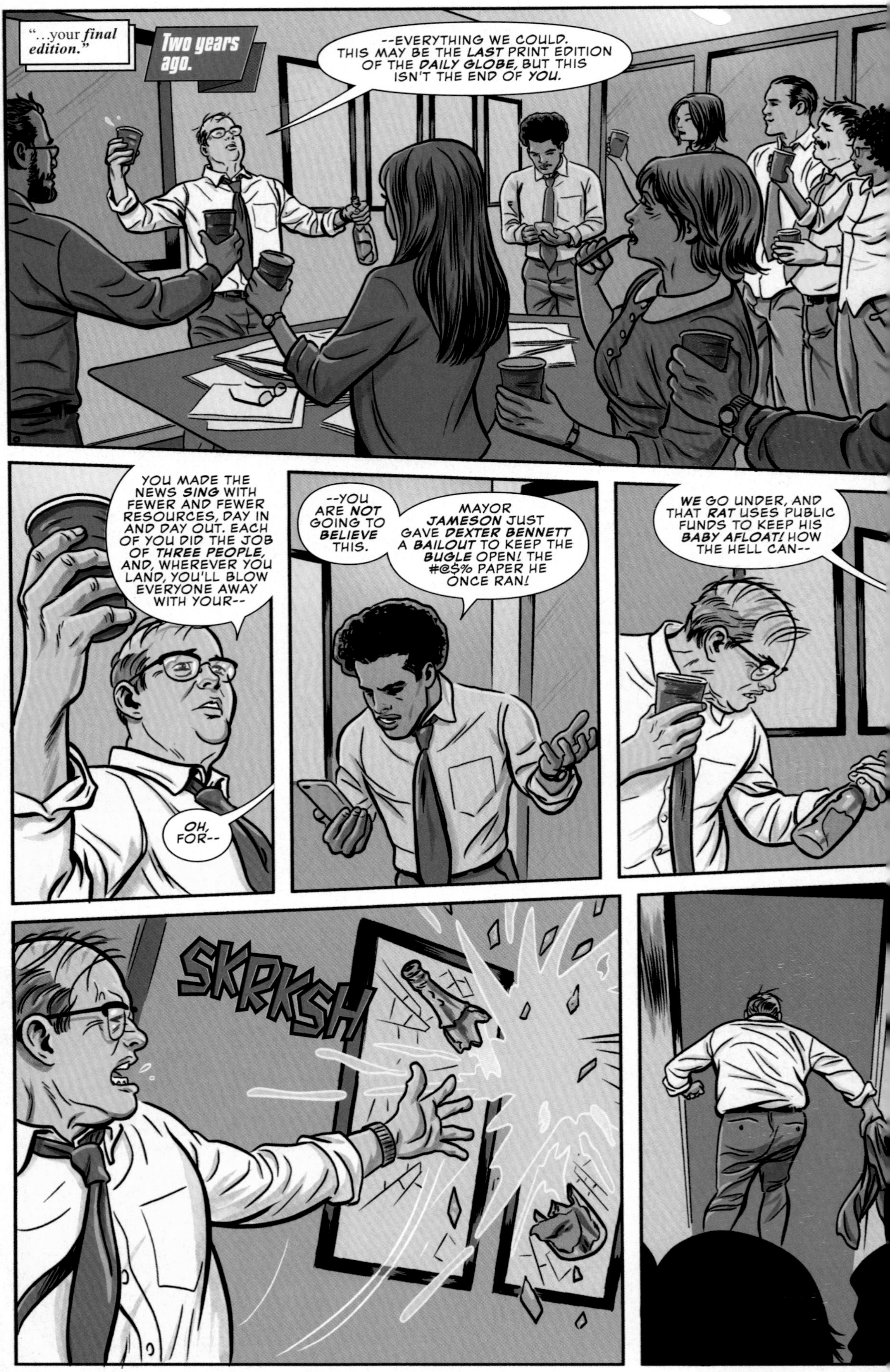
"...your *final* edition."
Two years ago.
--EVERYTHING WE COULD. THIS MAY BE THE *LAST* PRINT EDITION OF THE *DAILY GLOBE*, BUT THIS ISN'T THE END OF *YOU.*
YOU MADE THE NEWS *SING* WITH FEWER AND FEWER RESOURCES, DAY IN AND DAY OUT. EACH OF YOU DID THE JOB OF *THREE PEOPLE*, AND, WHEREVER YOU LAND, YOU'LL BLOW EVERYONE AWAY WITH YOUR--
OH, FOR--
--YOU ARE *NOT* GOING TO *BELIEVE* THIS.
MAYOR *JAMESON* JUST GAVE *DEXTER BENNETT* A *BAILOUT* TO KEEP THE *BUGLE* OPEN! THE #@$% PAPER HE ONCE RAN!
WE GO UNDER, AND THAT *RAT* USES PUBLIC FUNDS TO KEEP HIS *BABY AFLOAT!* HOW THE HELL CAN--
SKRKSH

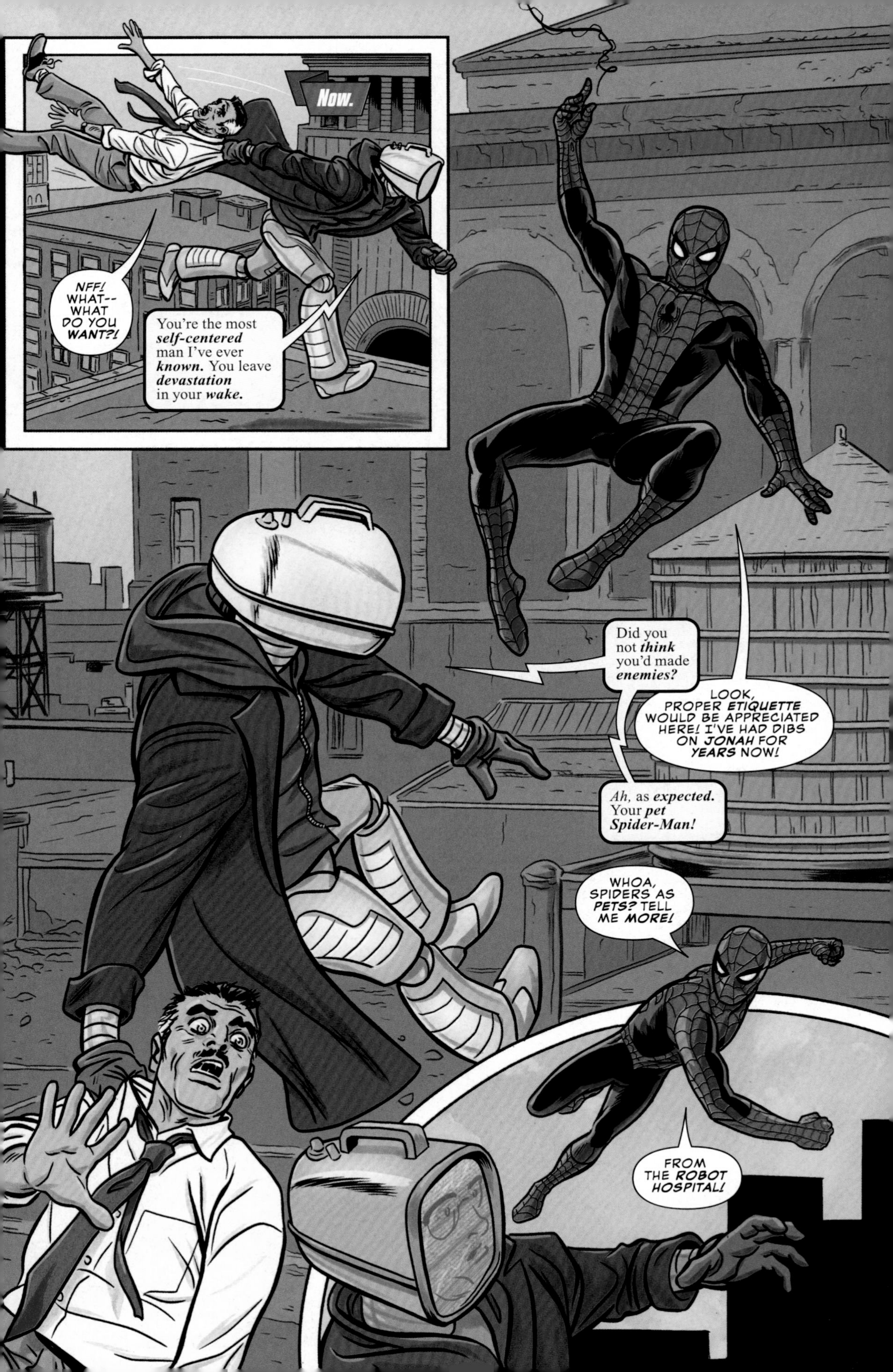

Now.
NFF! WHAT-- WHAT DO YOU WANT?!
You're the most self-centered man I've ever known. You leave devastation in your wake.
Did you not think you'd made enemies?
LOOK, PROPER ETIQUETTE WOULD BE APPRECIATED HERE! I'VE HAD DIBS ON JONAH FOR YEARS NOW!
Ah, as expected. Your pet Spider-Man!
WHOA, SPIDERS AS PETS? TELL ME MORE!
FROM THE ROBOT HOSPITAL!

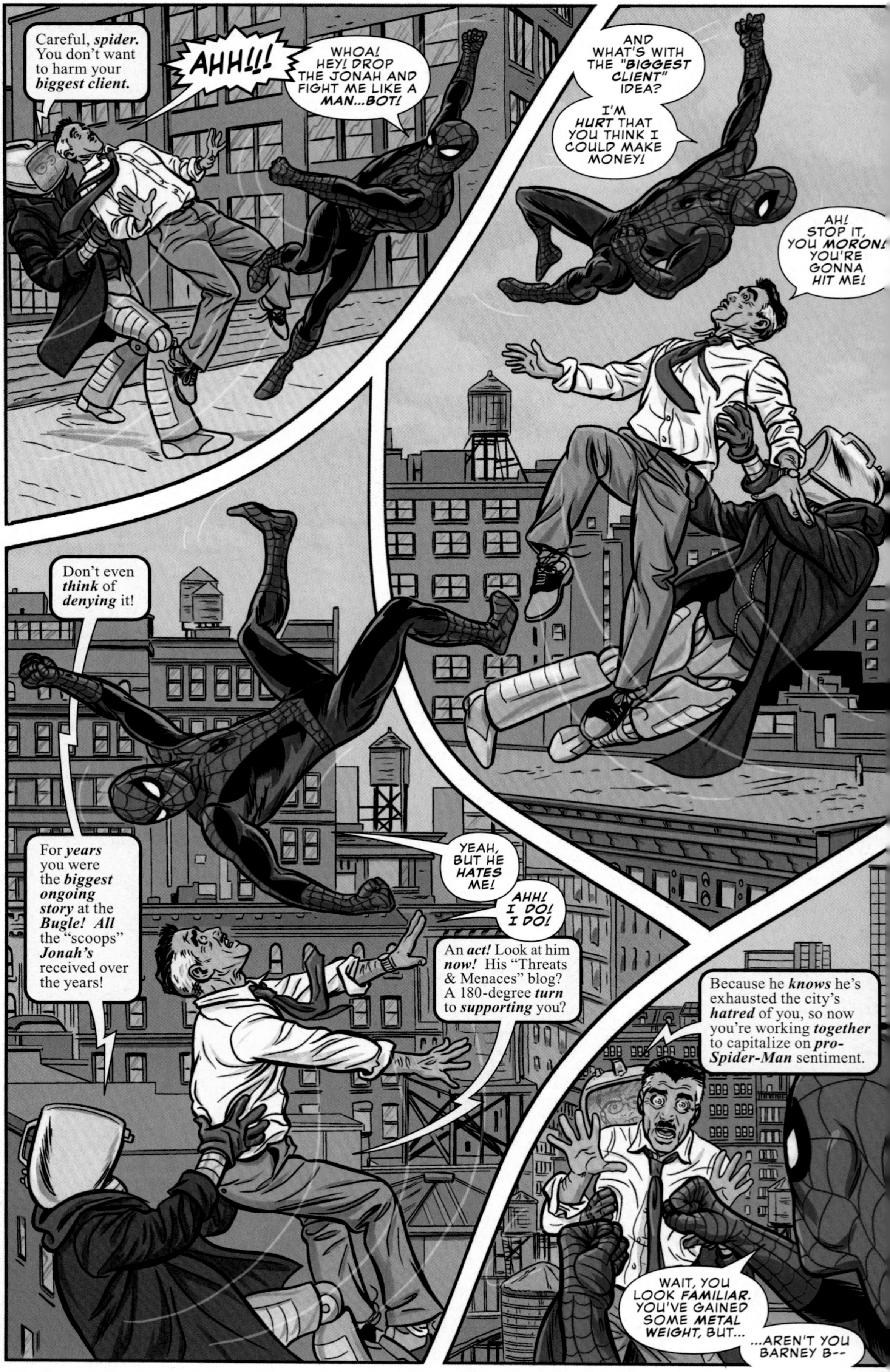
Careful, ***spider.*** You don't want to harm your ***biggest client.***
AHH!!!
WHOA! HEY! DROP THE JONAH AND FIGHT ME LIKE A ***MAN...BOT!***
AND WHAT'S WITH THE ***"BIGGEST CLIENT"*** IDEA?
I'M ***HURT*** THAT YOU THINK I COULD MAKE MONEY!
AH! STOP IT, YOU ***MORON!*** YOU'RE GONNA ***HIT ME!***
Don't even ***think*** of ***denying*** it!
For ***years*** you were the ***biggest ongoing story*** at the ***Bugle! All*** the "scoops" ***Jonah's*** received over the years!
YEAH, BUT HE ***HATES*** ME!
AHH! I DO! I DO!
An ***act!*** Look at him ***now!*** His "Threats & Menaces" blog? A 180-degree ***turn*** to ***supporting*** you?
Because he ***knows*** he's exhausted the city's ***hatred*** of you, so now you're working ***together*** to capitalize on ***pro-Spider-Man*** sentiment.
WAIT, YOU LOOK ***FAMILIAR.*** YOU'VE GAINED SOME ***METAL WEIGHT,*** BUT...
...AREN'T YOU BARNEY B--

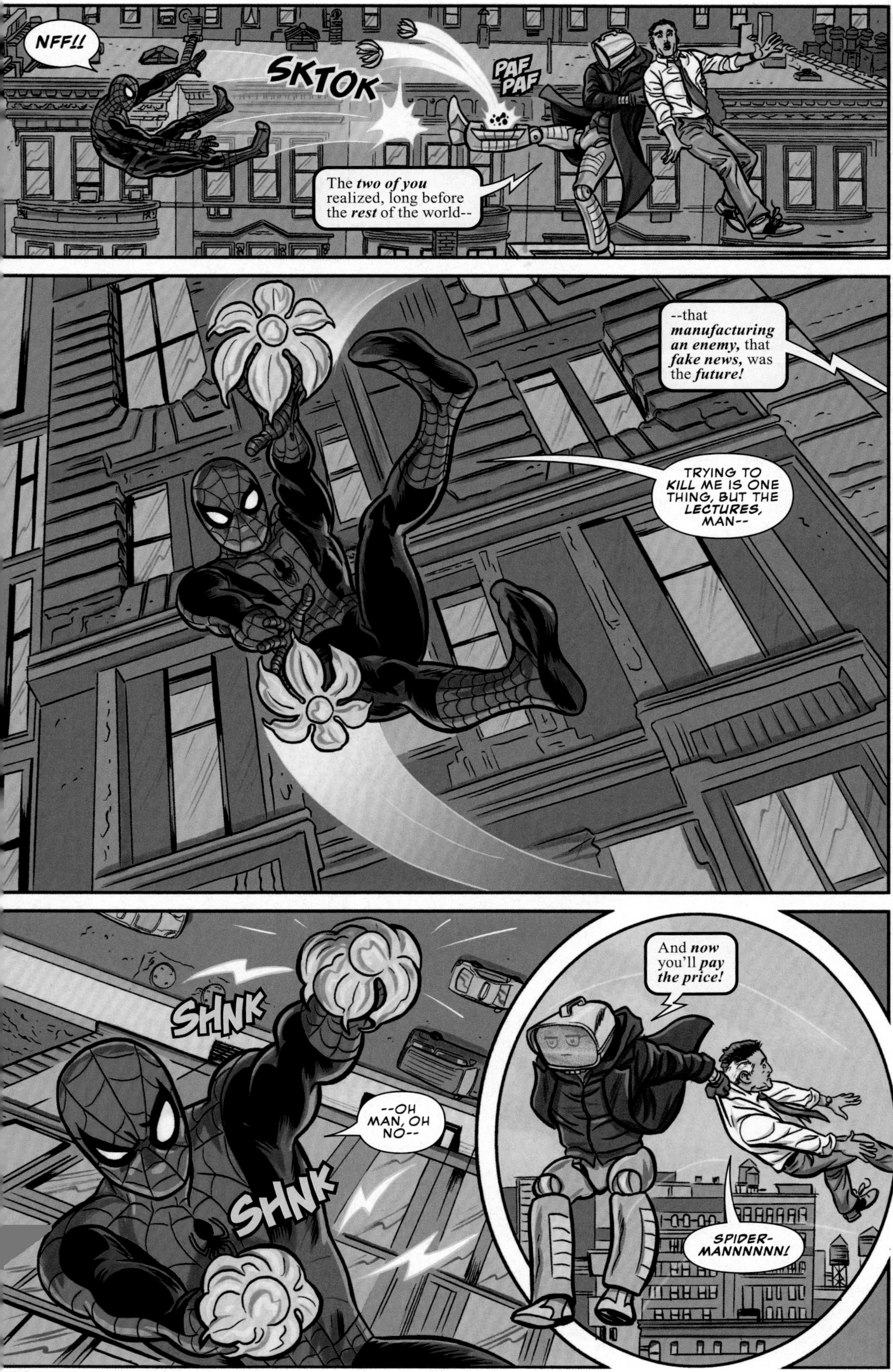
NFF!!
SKTOK
PAF PAF
The two of you realized, long before the rest of the world--
--that manufacturing an enemy, that fake news, was the future!
TRYING TO KILL ME IS ONE THING, BUT THE LECTURES, MAN--
SHNK
--OH MAN, OH NO--
SHNK
And now you'll pay the price!
SPIDER-MANNNNNN!

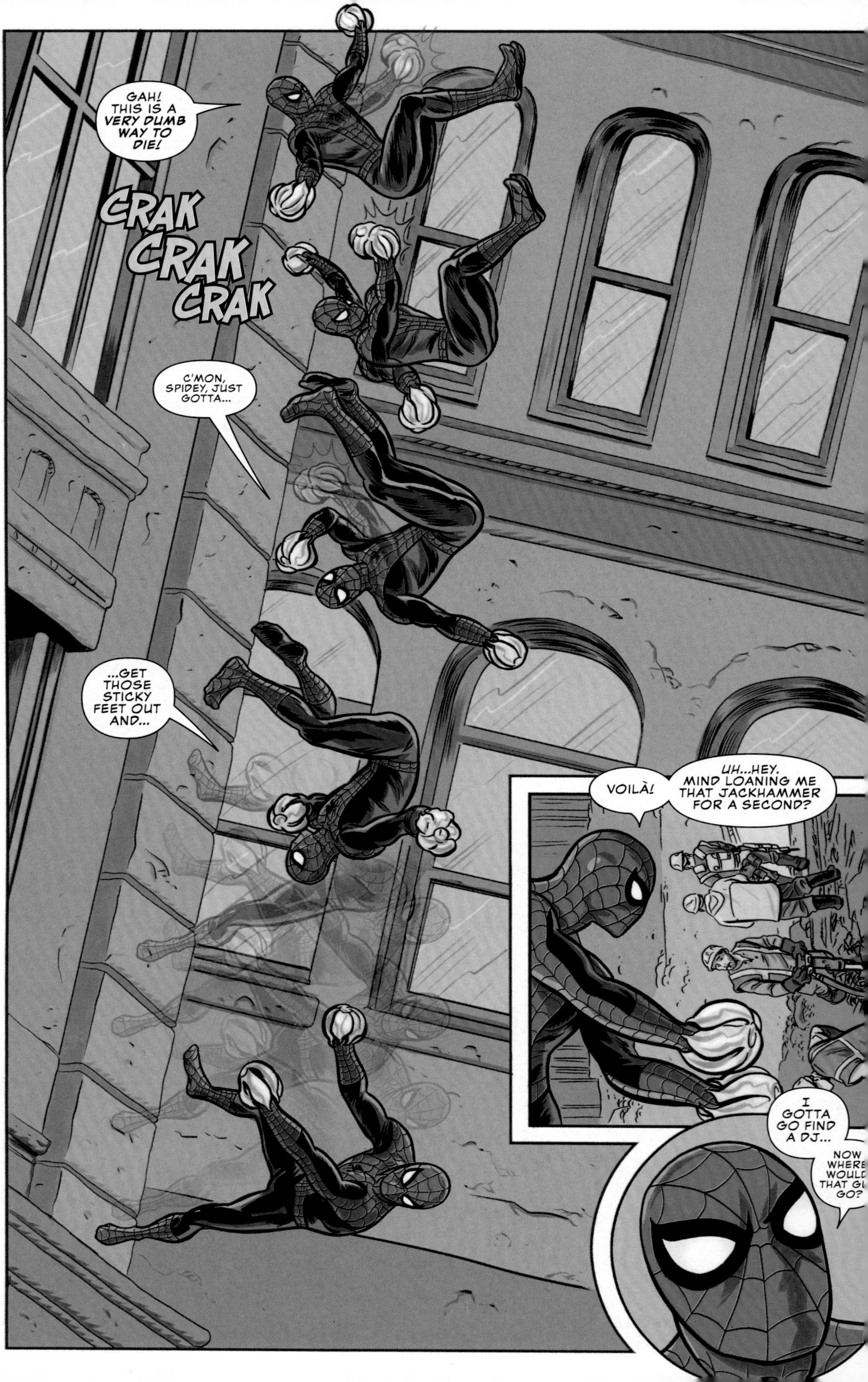
GAH! THIS IS A *VERY DUMB* WAY TO DIE!
CRAK CRAK CRAK
C'MON, SPIDEY, JUST GOTTA...
...GET THOSE STICKY FEET OUT AND...
VOILÀ!
UH...HEY. MIND LOANING ME THAT JACKHAMMER FOR A SECOND?
I GOTTA GO FIND A DJ...
NOW WHERE WOULD THAT GU GO?

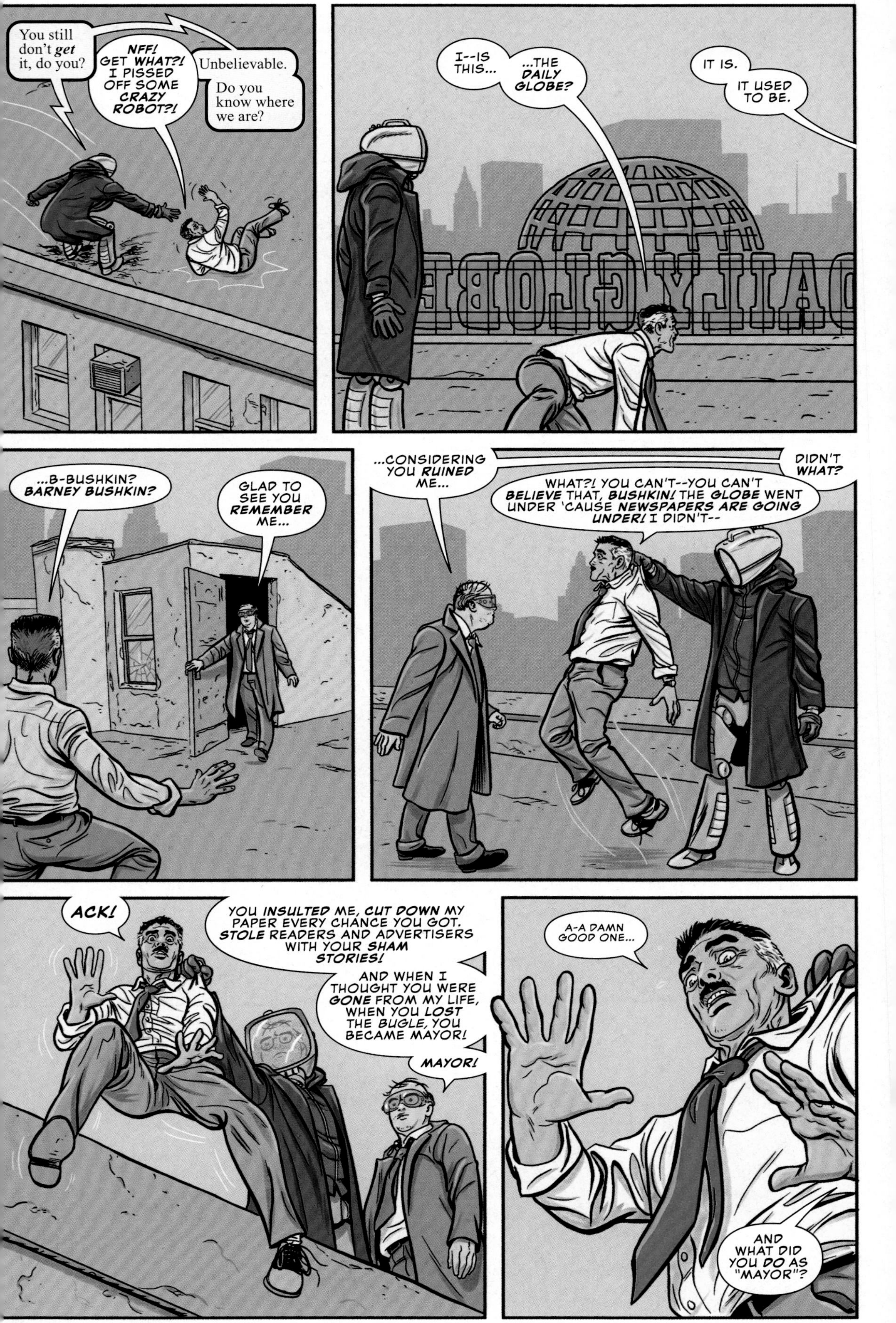

You still don't get it, do you?
NFF! GET WHAT?! I PISSED OFF SOME CRAZY ROBOT?!
Unbelievable.
Do you know where we are?
I--IS THIS...
...THE DAILY GLOBE?
IT IS.
IT USED TO BE.
DAILY GLOBE
...B-BUSHKIN? BARNEY BUSHKIN?
GLAD TO SEE YOU REMEMBER ME...
...CONSIDERING YOU RUINED ME...
WHAT?! YOU CAN'T--YOU CAN'T BELIEVE THAT, BUSHKIN! THE GLOBE WENT UNDER 'CAUSE NEWSPAPERS ARE GOING UNDER! I DIDN'T--
DIDN'T WHAT?
ACK!
YOU INSULTED ME, CUT DOWN MY PAPER EVERY CHANCE YOU GOT. STOLE READERS AND ADVERTISERS WITH YOUR SHAM STORIES!
AND WHEN I THOUGHT YOU WERE GONE FROM MY LIFE, WHEN YOU LOST THE BUGLE, YOU BECAME MAYOR!
MAYOR!
A-A DAMN GOOD ONE...
AND WHAT DID YOU DO AS "MAYOR"?

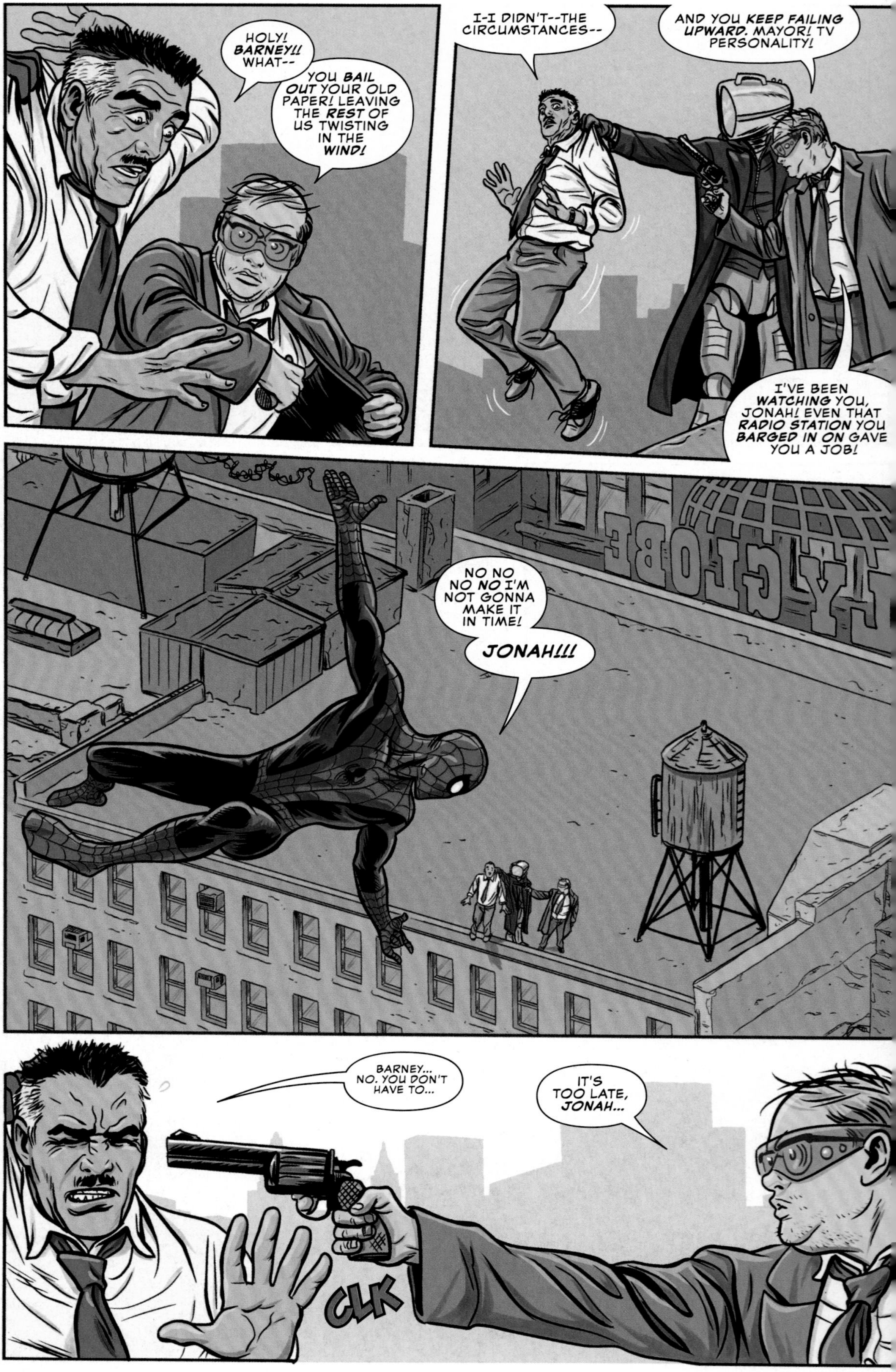
HOLY! BARNEY!! WHAT--
YOU BAIL OUT YOUR OLD PAPER! LEAVING THE REST OF US TWISTING IN THE WIND!
I-I DIDN'T--THE CIRCUMSTANCES--
AND YOU KEEP FAILING UPWARD. MAYOR! TV PERSONALITY!
I'VE BEEN WATCHING YOU, JONAH! EVEN THAT RADIO STATION YOU BARGED IN ON GAVE YOU A JOB!
NO NO NO NO I'M NOT GONNA MAKE IT IN TIME!
JONAH!!!
BARNEY... NO. YOU DON'T HAVE TO...
IT'S TOO LATE, JONAH...
CLK

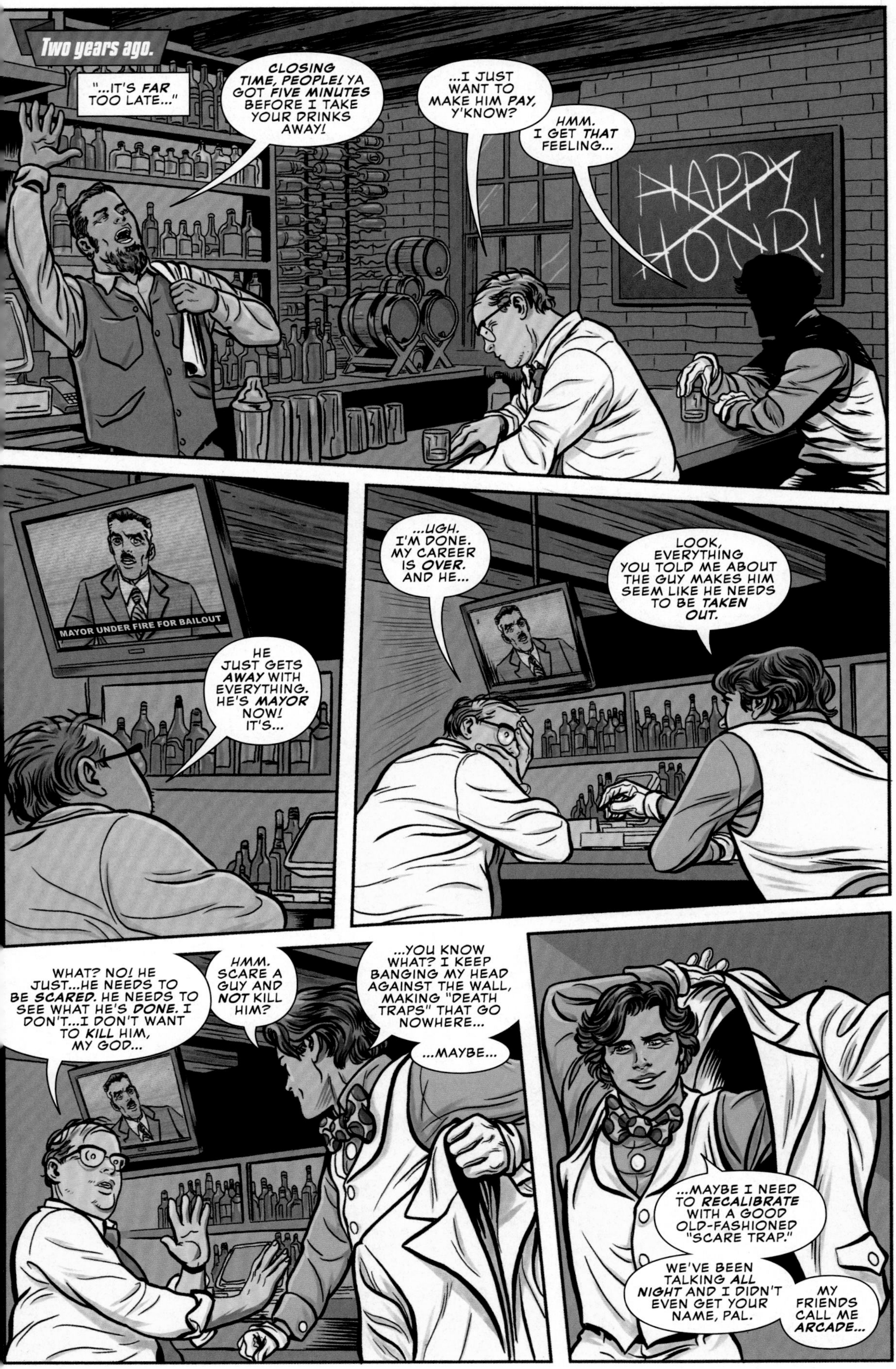
Two years ago.
"...IT'S FAR TOO LATE..."
CLOSING TIME, PEOPLE! YA GOT FIVE MINUTES BEFORE I TAKE YOUR DRINKS AWAY!
...I JUST WANT TO MAKE HIM PAY, Y'KNOW?
HMM. I GET THAT FEELING...
HAPPY HOUR!
MAYOR UNDER FIRE FOR BAILOUT
HE JUST GETS AWAY WITH EVERYTHING. HE'S MAYOR NOW! IT'S...
...UGH. I'M DONE. MY CAREER IS OVER. AND HE...
LOOK, EVERYTHING YOU TOLD ME ABOUT THE GUY MAKES HIM SEEM LIKE HE NEEDS TO BE TAKEN OUT.
WHAT? NO! HE JUST...HE NEEDS TO BE SCARED. HE NEEDS TO SEE WHAT HE'S DONE. I DON'T...I DON'T WANT TO KILL HIM, MY GOD...
HMM. SCARE A GUY AND NOT KILL HIM?
...YOU KNOW WHAT? I KEEP BANGING MY HEAD AGAINST THE WALL, MAKING "DEATH TRAPS" THAT GO NOWHERE...
...MAYBE...
...MAYBE I NEED TO RECALIBRATE WITH A GOOD OLD-FASHIONED "SCARE TRAP."
WE'VE BEEN TALKING ALL NIGHT AND I DIDN'T EVEN GET YOUR NAME, PAL.
MY FRIENDS CALL ME ARCADE...

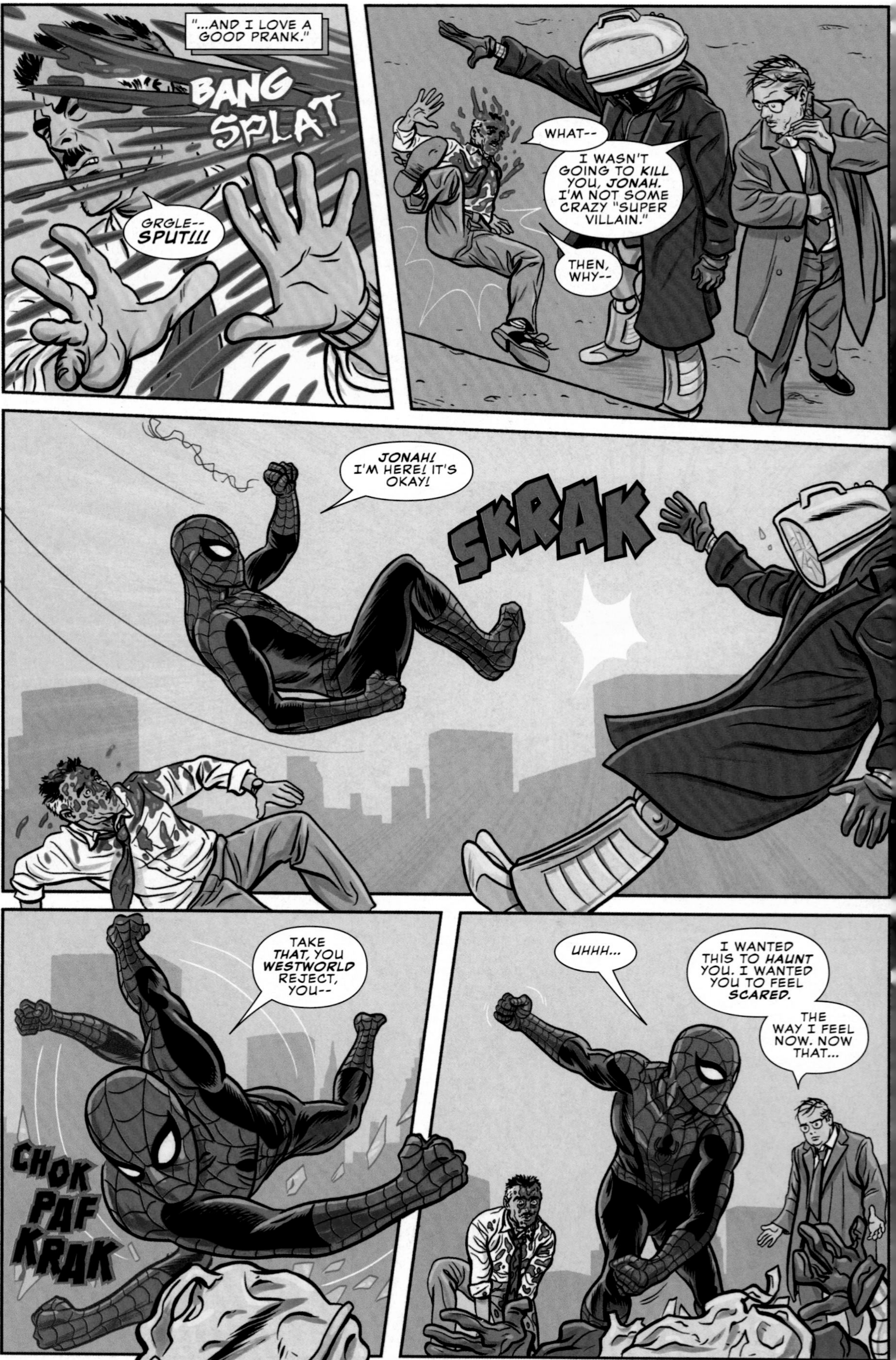
"...AND I LOVE A GOOD PRANK."
BANG
SPLAT
GRGLE-- SPUT!!!
WHAT--
I WASN'T GOING TO KILL YOU, JONAH. I'M NOT SOME CRAZY "SUPER VILLAIN."
THEN, WHY--
JONAH! I'M HERE! IT'S OKAY!
SKRAK
TAKE THAT, YOU WESTWORLD REJECT, YOU--
CHOK
PAF
KRAK
UHHH...
I WANTED THIS TO HAUNT YOU. I WANTED YOU TO FEEL SCARED.
THE WAY I FEEL NOW. NOW THAT...

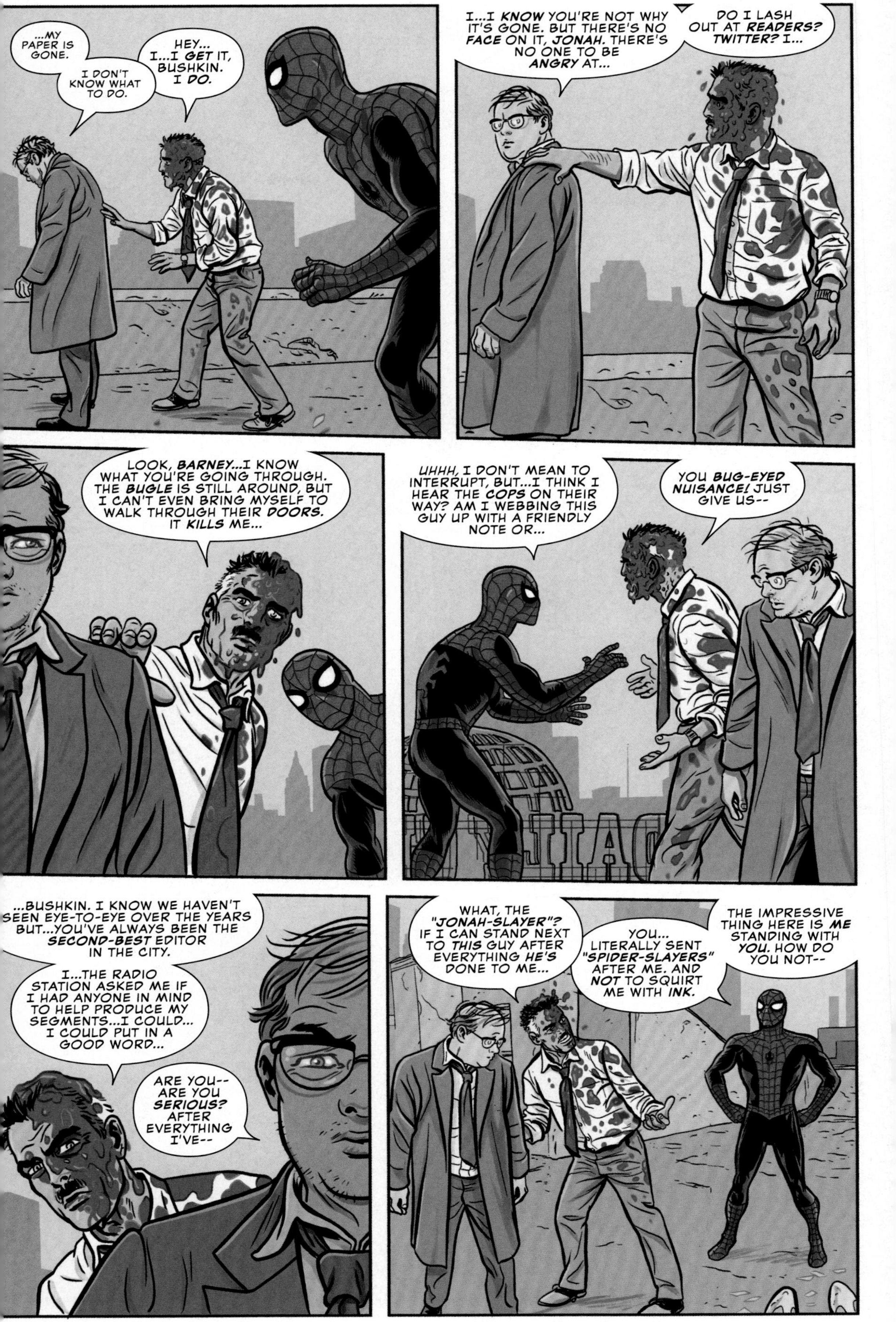
...MY PAPER IS GONE.
I DON'T KNOW WHAT TO DO.
HEY... I...I *GET* IT, BUSHKIN. I *DO.*
I...I *KNOW* YOU'RE NOT WHY IT'S GONE. BUT THERE'S NO *FACE* ON IT, *JONAH.* THERE'S NO ONE TO BE *ANGRY* AT...
DO I LASH OUT AT *READERS? TWITTER?* I...
LOOK, *BARNEY*...I KNOW WHAT YOU'RE GOING THROUGH. THE *BUGLE* IS STILL AROUND, BUT I CAN'T EVEN BRING MYSELF TO WALK THROUGH THEIR *DOORS.* IT *KILLS* ME...
UHHH, I DON'T MEAN TO INTERRUPT, BUT...I THINK I HEAR THE *COPS* ON THEIR WAY? AM I WEBBING THIS GUY UP WITH A FRIENDLY NOTE OR...
YOU *BUG-EYED NUISANCE!* JUST GIVE US--
...BUSHKIN. I KNOW WE HAVEN'T SEEN EYE-TO-EYE OVER THE YEARS BUT...YOU'VE ALWAYS BEEN THE *SECOND-BEST* EDITOR IN THE CITY.
I...THE RADIO STATION ASKED ME IF I HAD ANYONE IN MIND TO HELP PRODUCE MY SEGMENTS...I COULD... I COULD PUT IN A GOOD WORD...
ARE YOU-- ARE YOU *SERIOUS?* AFTER EVERYTHING I'VE--
WHAT, THE *"JONAH-SLAYER"*? IF I CAN STAND NEXT TO *THIS* GUY AFTER EVERYTHING *HE'S* DONE TO ME...
YOU... LITERALLY SENT *"SPIDER-SLAYERS"* AFTER ME. AND *NOT* TO SQUIRT ME WITH *INK.*
THE IMPRESSIVE THING HERE IS *ME* STANDING WITH *YOU.* HOW DO YOU NOT--

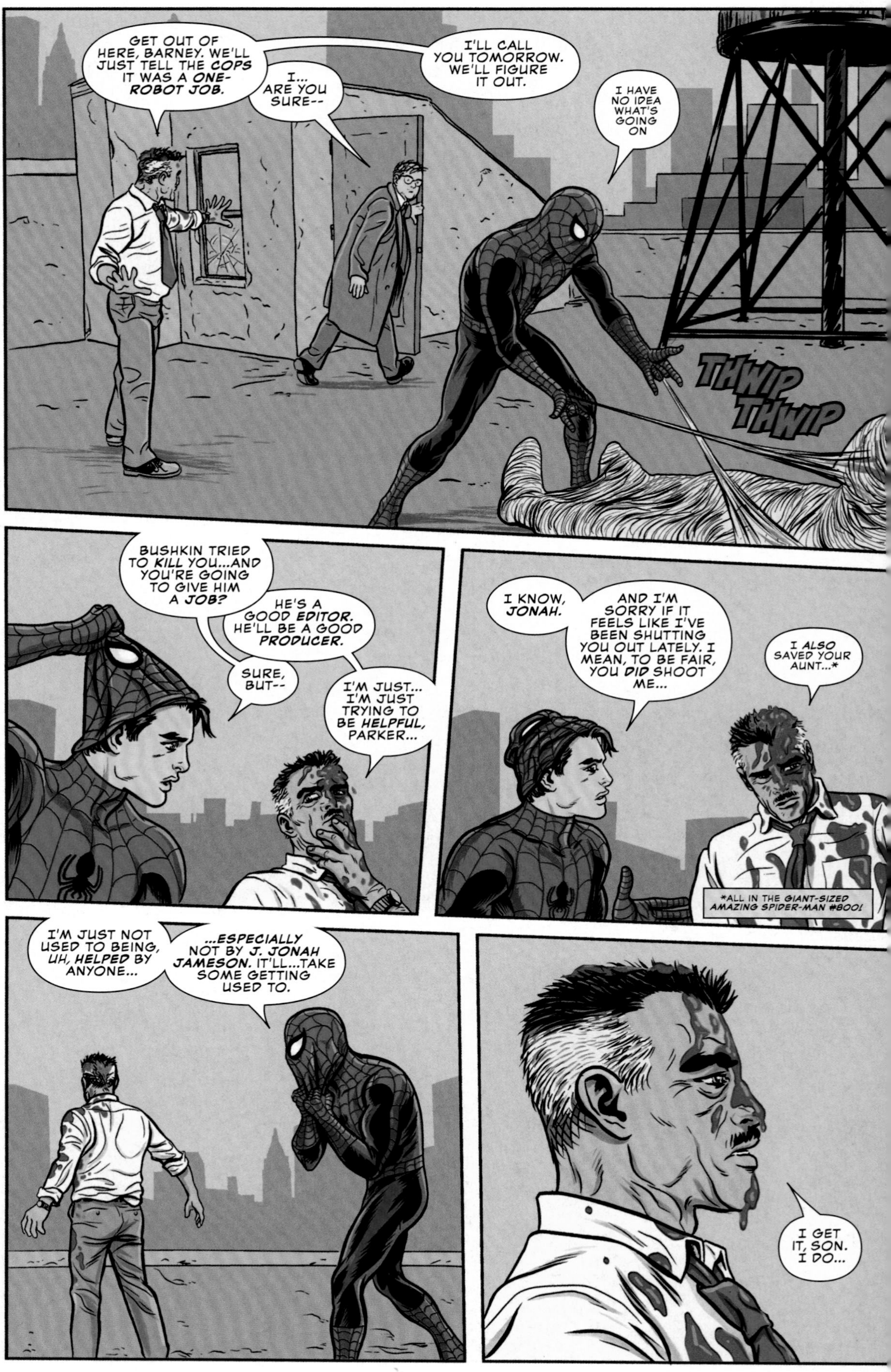
GET OUT OF HERE, BARNEY. WE'LL JUST TELL THE COPS IT WAS A ONE-ROBOT JOB.
I... ARE YOU SURE--
I'LL CALL YOU TOMORROW. WE'LL FIGURE IT OUT.
I HAVE NO IDEA WHAT'S GOING ON
THWIP THWIP
BUSHKIN TRIED TO KILL YOU...AND YOU'RE GOING TO GIVE HIM A JOB?
HE'S A GOOD EDITOR. HE'LL BE A GOOD PRODUCER.
SURE, BUT--
I'M JUST... I'M JUST TRYING TO BE HELPFUL, PARKER...
I KNOW, JONAH.
AND I'M SORRY IF IT FEELS LIKE I'VE BEEN SHUTTING YOU OUT LATELY. I MEAN, TO BE FAIR, YOU DID SHOOT ME...
I ALSO SAVED YOUR AUNT...*
*ALL IN THE GIANT-SIZED AMAZING SPIDER-MAN #800!
I'M JUST NOT USED TO BEING, UH, HELPED BY ANYONE...
...ESPECIALLY NOT BY J. JONAH JAMESON. IT'LL...TAKE SOME GETTING USED TO.
I GET IT, SON. I DO...

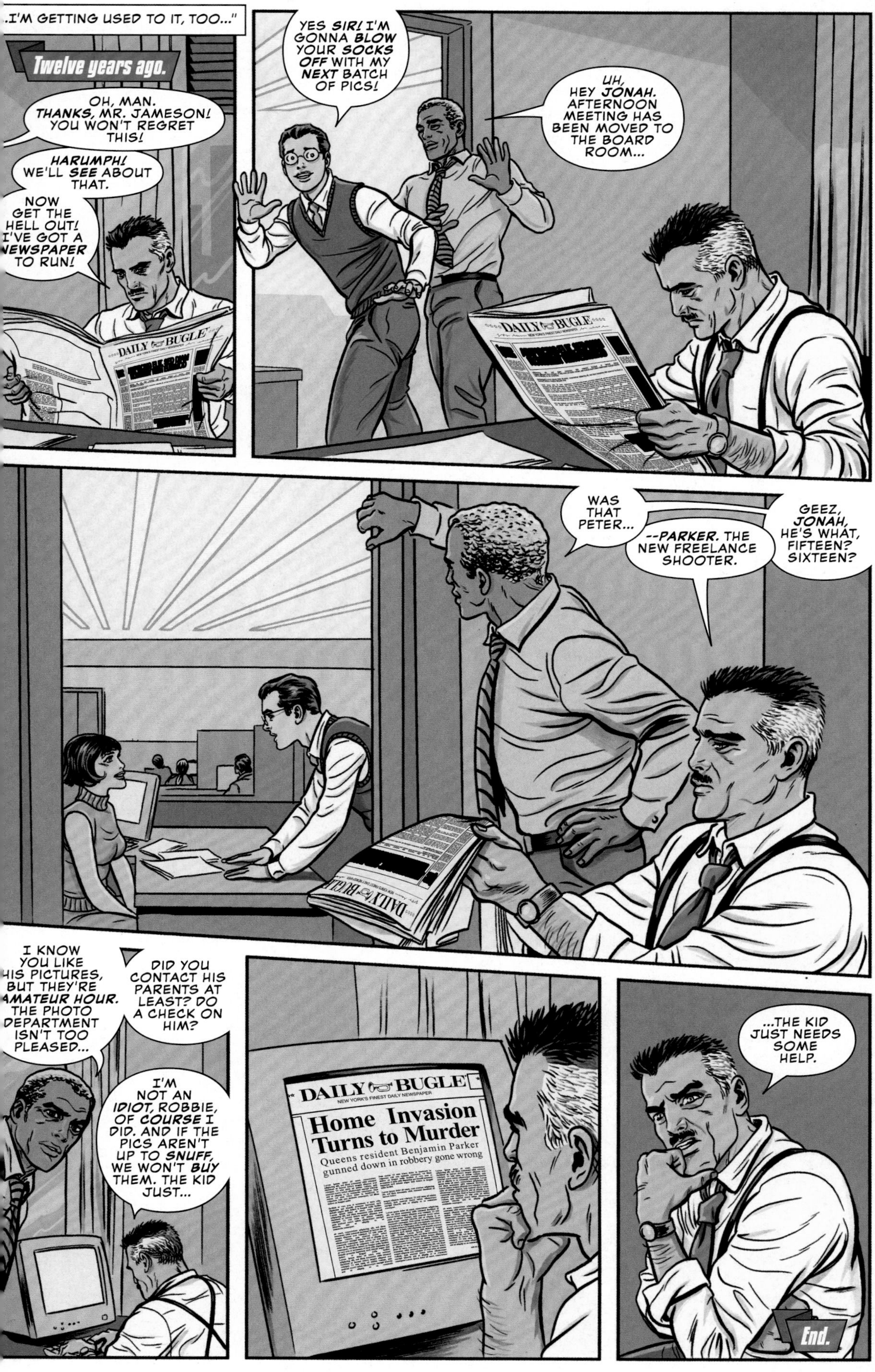
...I'M GETTING USED TO IT, TOO..."
Twelve years ago.
OH, MAN. THANKS, MR. JAMESON! YOU WON'T REGRET THIS!
HARUMPH! WE'LL SEE ABOUT THAT.
NOW GET THE HELL OUT! I'VE GOT A NEWSPAPER TO RUN!
YES SIR! I'M GONNA BLOW YOUR SOCKS OFF WITH MY NEXT BATCH OF PICS!
UH, HEY JONAH. AFTERNOON MEETING HAS BEEN MOVED TO THE BOARD ROOM...
DAILY BUGLE
WAS THAT PETER...
--PARKER. THE NEW FREELANCE SHOOTER.
GEEZ, JONAH, HE'S WHAT, FIFTEEN? SIXTEEN?
I KNOW YOU LIKE HIS PICTURES, BUT THEY'RE AMATEUR HOUR. THE PHOTO DEPARTMENT ISN'T TOO PLEASED...
DID YOU CONTACT HIS PARENTS AT LEAST? DO A CHECK ON HIM?
I'M NOT AN IDIOT, ROBBIE, OF COURSE I DID. AND IF THE PICS AREN'T UP TO SNUFF, WE WON'T BUY THEM. THE KID JUST...
DAILY BUGLE
NEW YORK'S FINEST DAILY NEWSPAPER
Home Invasion Turns to Murder
Queens resident Benjamin Parker gunned down in robbery gone wrong
...THE KID JUST NEEDS SOME HELP.
End.

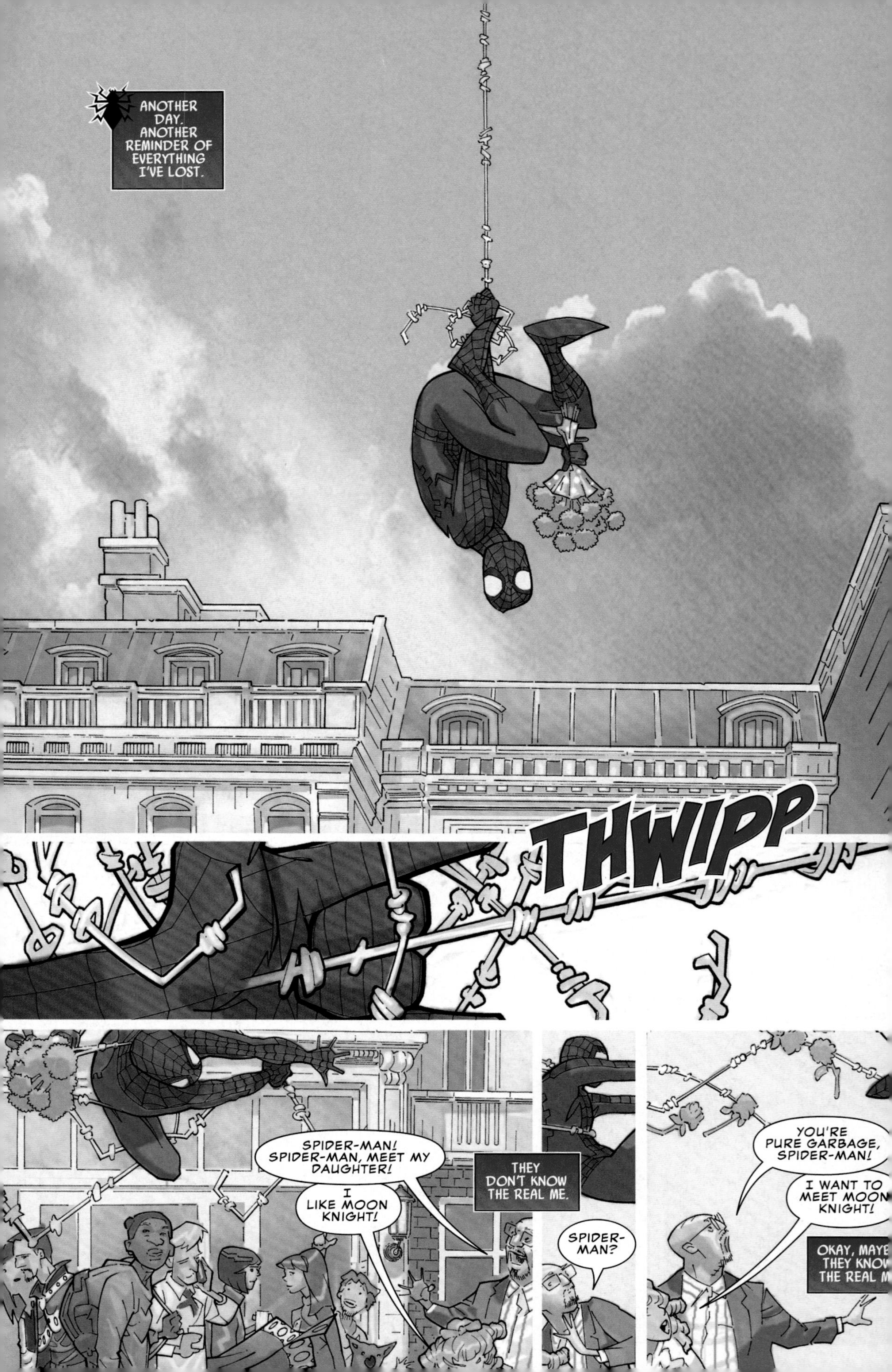
ANOTHER DAY. ANOTHER REMINDER OF EVERYTHING I'VE LOST.
THWIPP
SPIDER-MAN! SPIDER-MAN, MEET MY DAUGHTER!
I LIKE MOON KNIGHT!
THEY DON'T KNOW THE REAL ME.
SPIDER-MAN?
YOU'RE PURE GARBAGE, SPIDER-MAN!
I WANT TO MEET MOON KNIGHT!
OKAY, MAYBE THEY KNOW THE REAL M

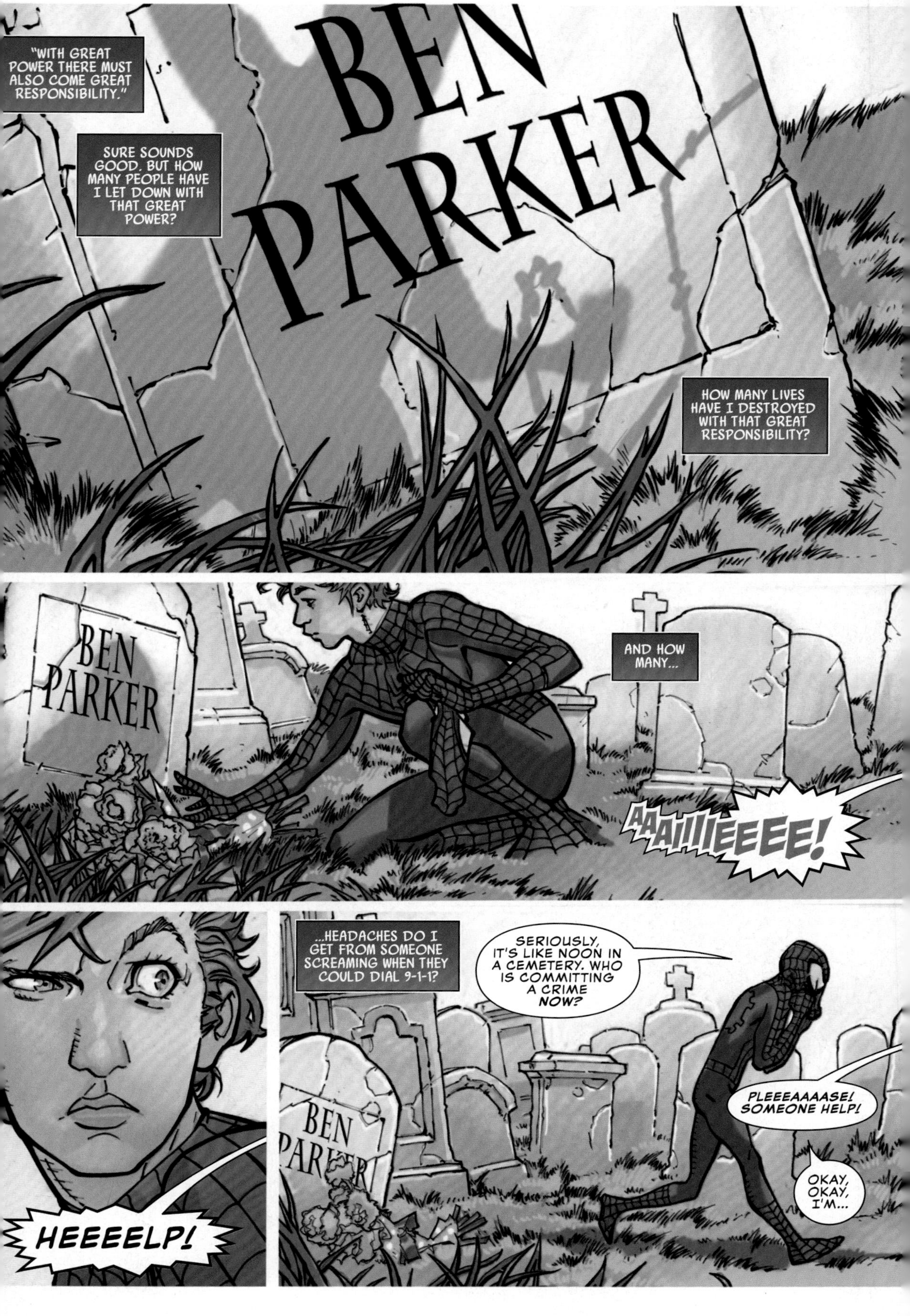
"WITH GREAT POWER THERE MUST ALSO COME GREAT RESPONSIBILITY."
BEN PARKER
SURE SOUNDS GOOD. BUT HOW MANY PEOPLE HAVE I LET DOWN WITH THAT GREAT POWER?
HOW MANY LIVES HAVE I DESTROYED WITH THAT GREAT RESPONSIBILITY?
BEN PARKER
AND HOW MANY...
AAAIIIIEEEE!
HEEEELP!
...HEADACHES DO I GET FROM SOMEONE SCREAMING WHEN THEY COULD DIAL 9-1-1?
SERIOUSLY, IT'S LIKE NOON IN A CEMETERY. WHO IS COMMITTING A CRIME NOW?
PLEEEAAAASE! SOMEONE HELP!
OKAY, OKAY, I'M...

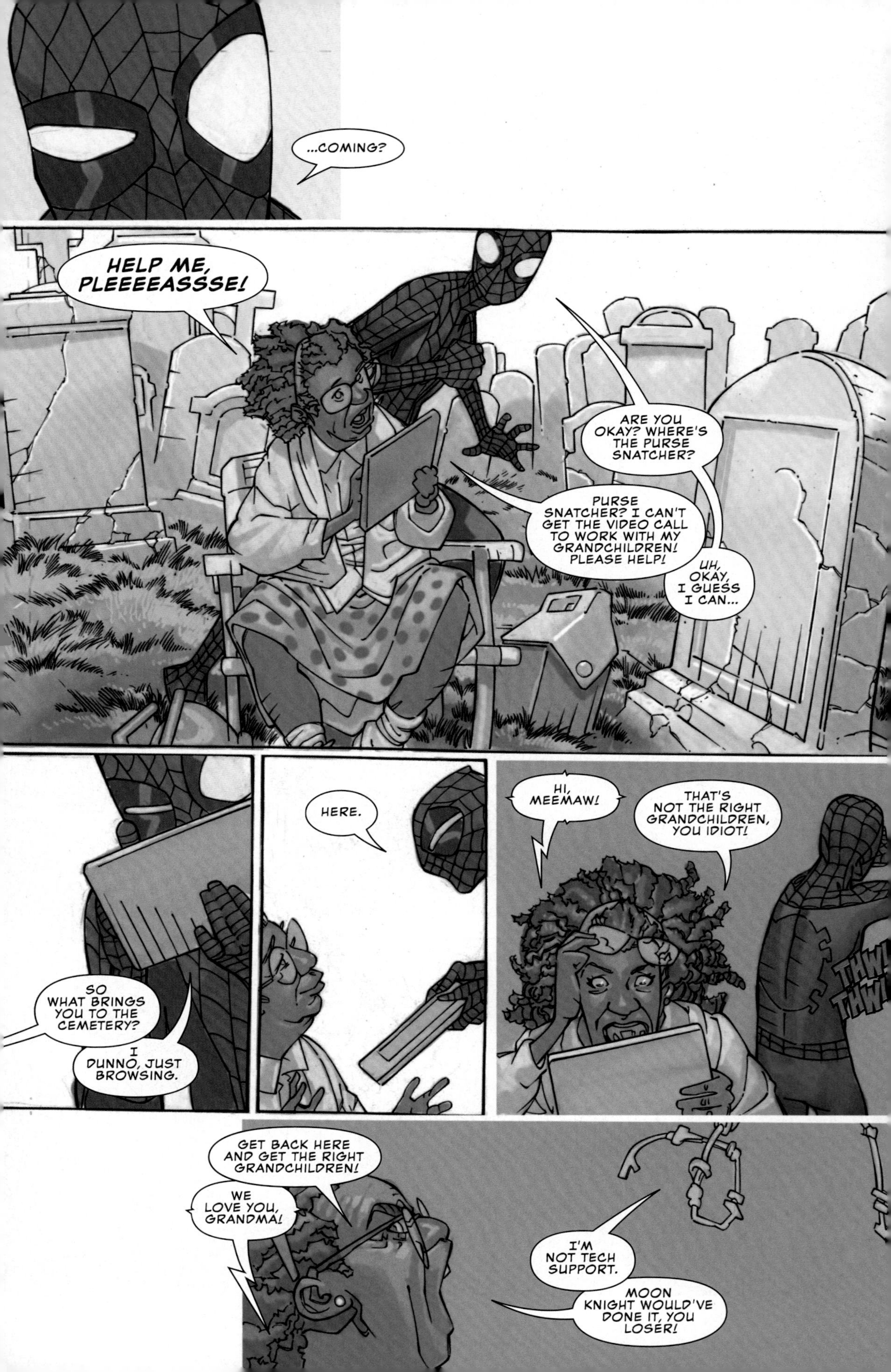
...COMING?
HELP ME, PLEEEEASSSE!
ARE YOU OKAY? WHERE'S THE PURSE SNATCHER?
PURSE SNATCHER? I CAN'T GET THE VIDEO CALL TO WORK WITH MY GRANDCHILDREN! PLEASE HELP!
UH, OKAY, I GUESS I CAN...
SO WHAT BRINGS YOU TO THE CEMETERY?
I DUNNO, JUST BROWSING.
HERE.
HI, MEEMAW!
THAT'S NOT THE RIGHT GRANDCHILDREN, YOU IDIOT!
GET BACK HERE AND GET THE RIGHT GRANDCHILDREN!
WE LOVE YOU, GRANDMA!
I'M NOT TECH SUPPORT.
MOON KNIGHT WOULD'VE DONE IT, YOU LOSER!

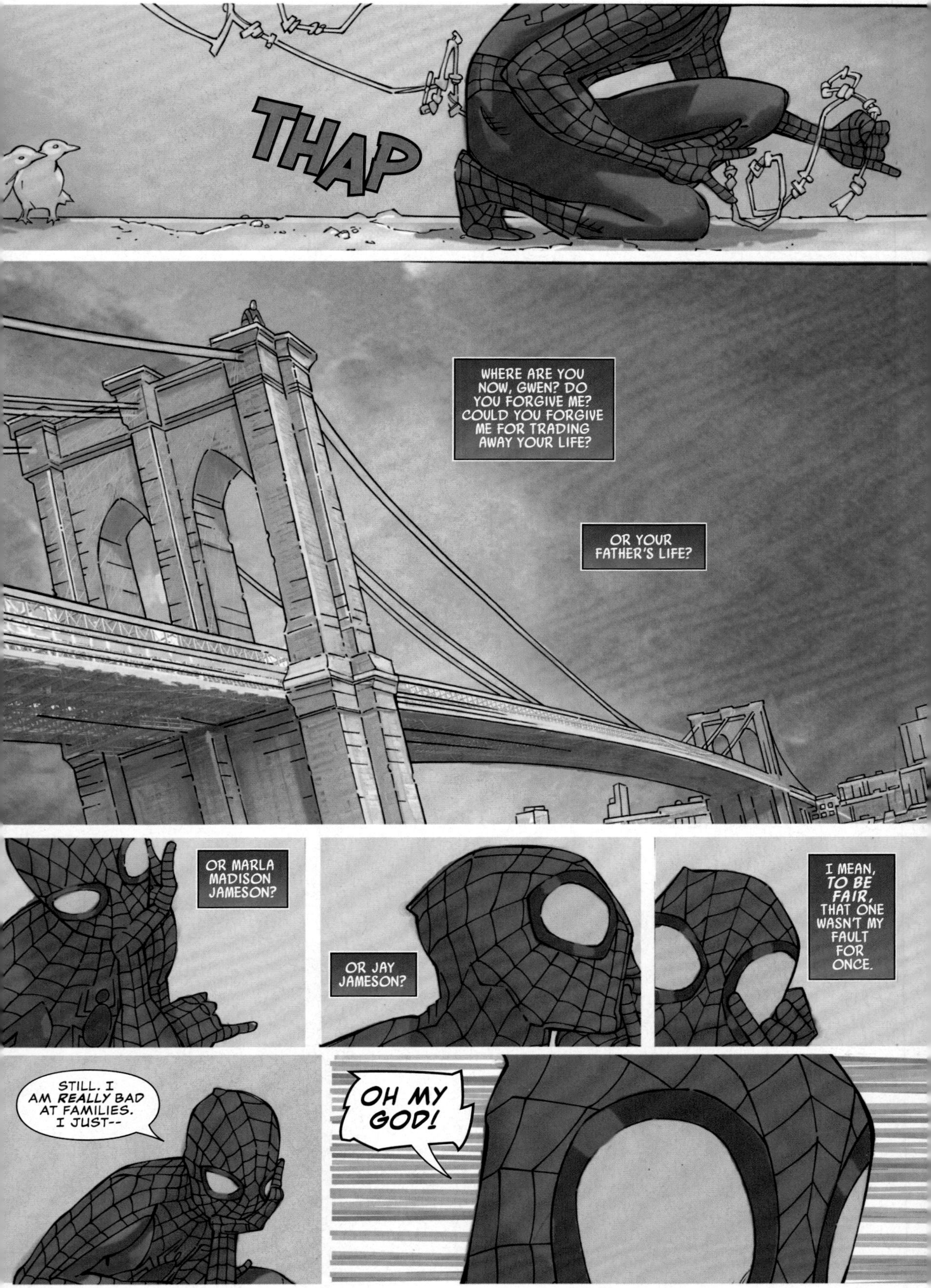
THAP
WHERE ARE YOU NOW, GWEN? DO YOU FORGIVE ME? COULD YOU FORGIVE ME FOR TRADING AWAY YOUR LIFE?
OR YOUR FATHER'S LIFE?
OR MARLA MADISON JAMESON?
OR JAY JAMESON?
I MEAN, *TO BE FAIR*, THAT ONE WASN'T MY FAULT FOR ONCE.
STILL. I AM *REALLY* BAD AT FAMILIES. I JUST--
OH MY GOD!

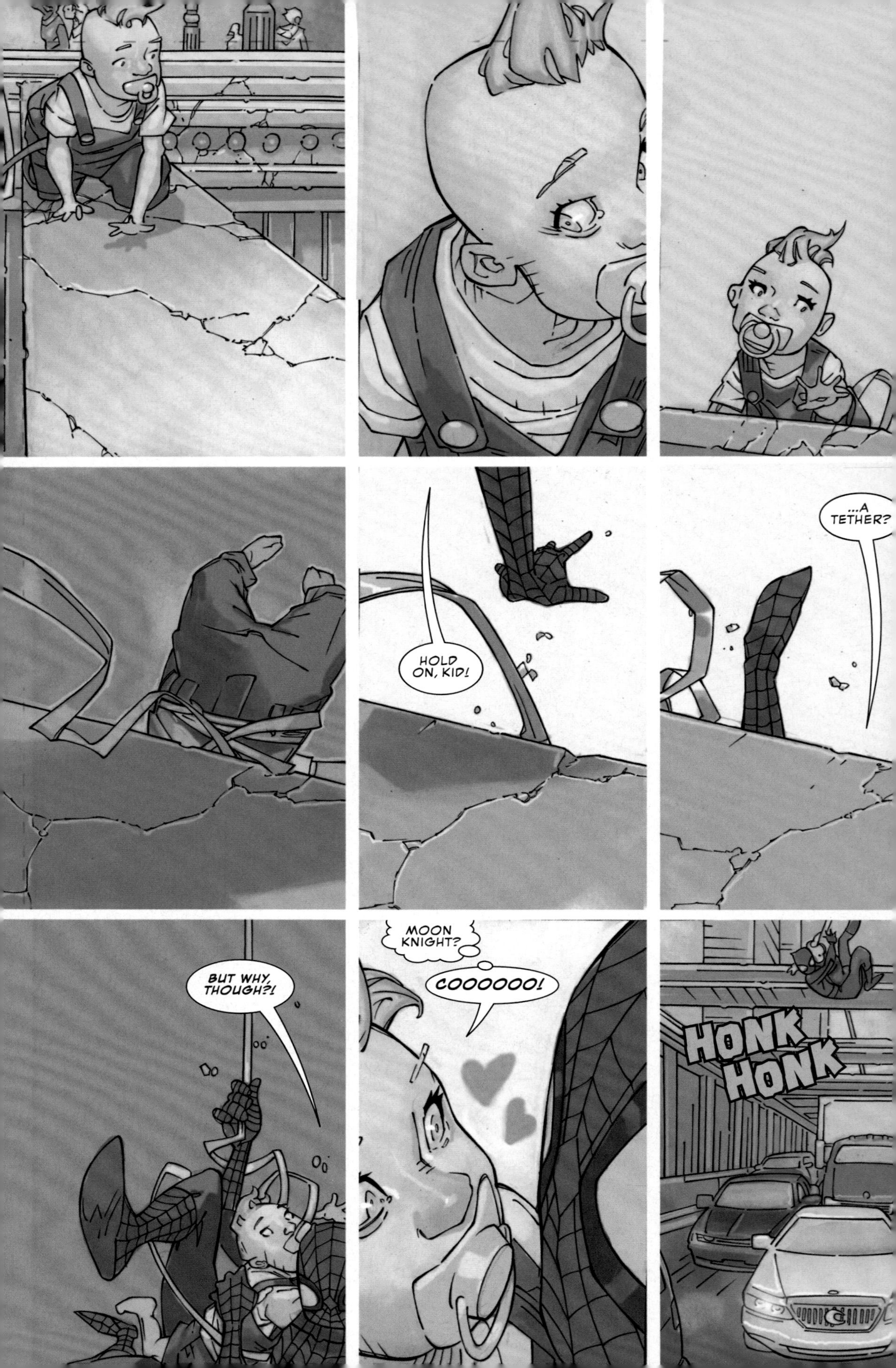
HOLD ON, KID!
...A TETHER?
BUT WHY, THOUGH?!
MOON KNIGHT?
COOOOOO!
HONK HONK

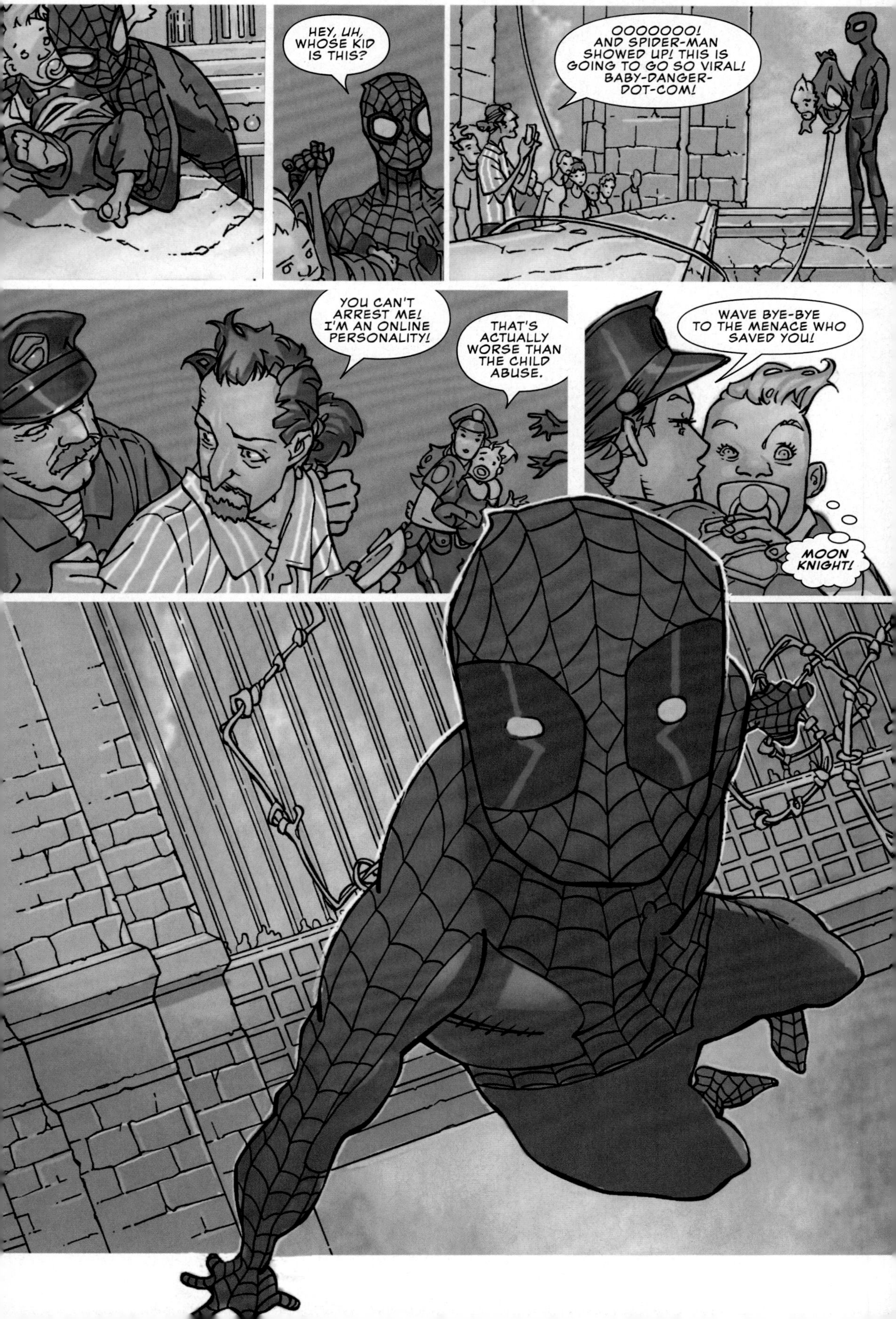
HEY, UH, WHOSE KID IS THIS?
OOOOOOO! AND SPIDER-MAN SHOWED UP! THIS IS GOING TO GO SO VIRAL! BABY-DANGER-DOT-COM!
YOU CAN'T ARREST ME! I'M AN ONLINE PERSONALITY!
THAT'S ACTUALLY WORSE THAN THE CHILD ABUSE.
WAVE BYE-BYE TO THE MENACE WHO SAVED YOU!
MOON KNIGHT!

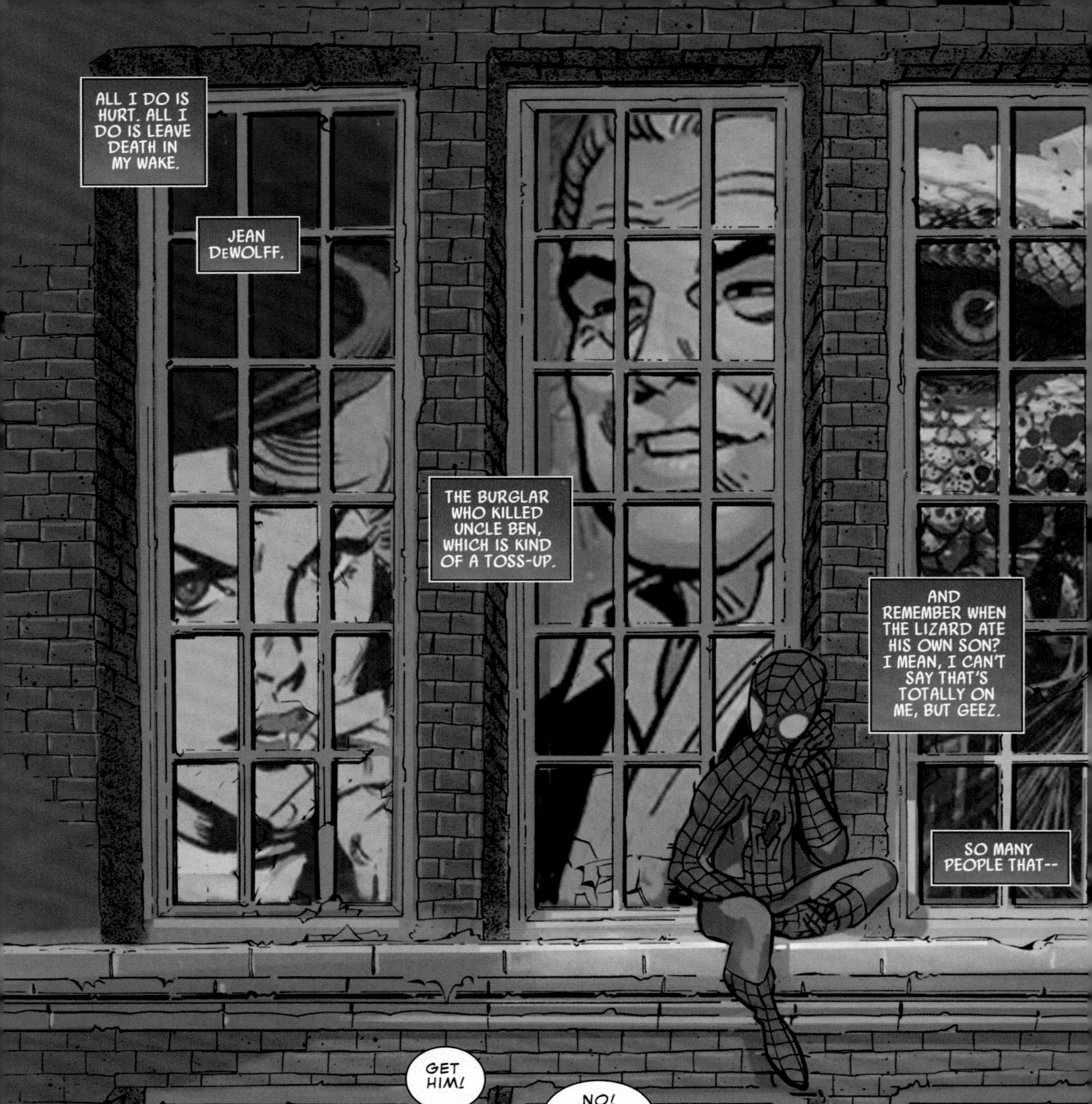
ALL I DO IS HURT. ALL I DO IS LEAVE DEATH IN MY WAKE.
JEAN DeWOLFF.
THE BURGLAR WHO KILLED UNCLE BEN, WHICH IS KIND OF A TOSS-UP.
AND REMEMBER WHEN THE LIZARD ATE HIS OWN SON? I MEAN, I CAN'T SAY THAT'S TOTALLY ON ME, BUT GEEZ.
SO MANY PEOPLE THAT--
GET HIM!
NO! PLEASE! PLEASE!
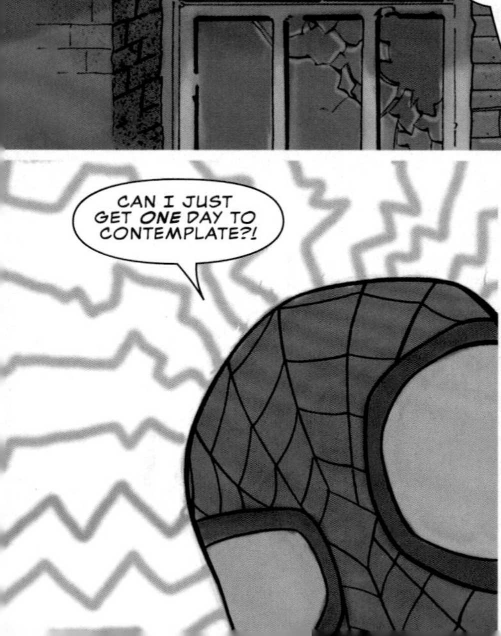
CAN I JUST GET ONE DAY TO CONTEMPLATE?!
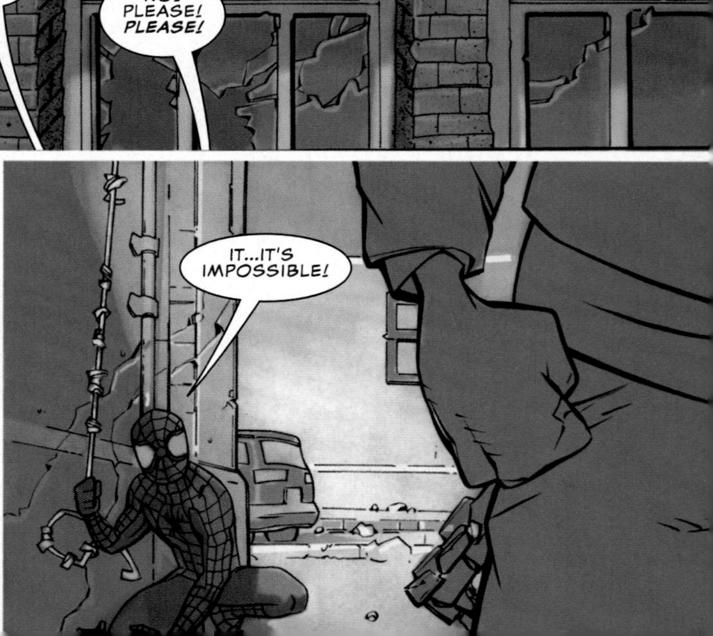
IT...IT'S IMPOSSIBLE!

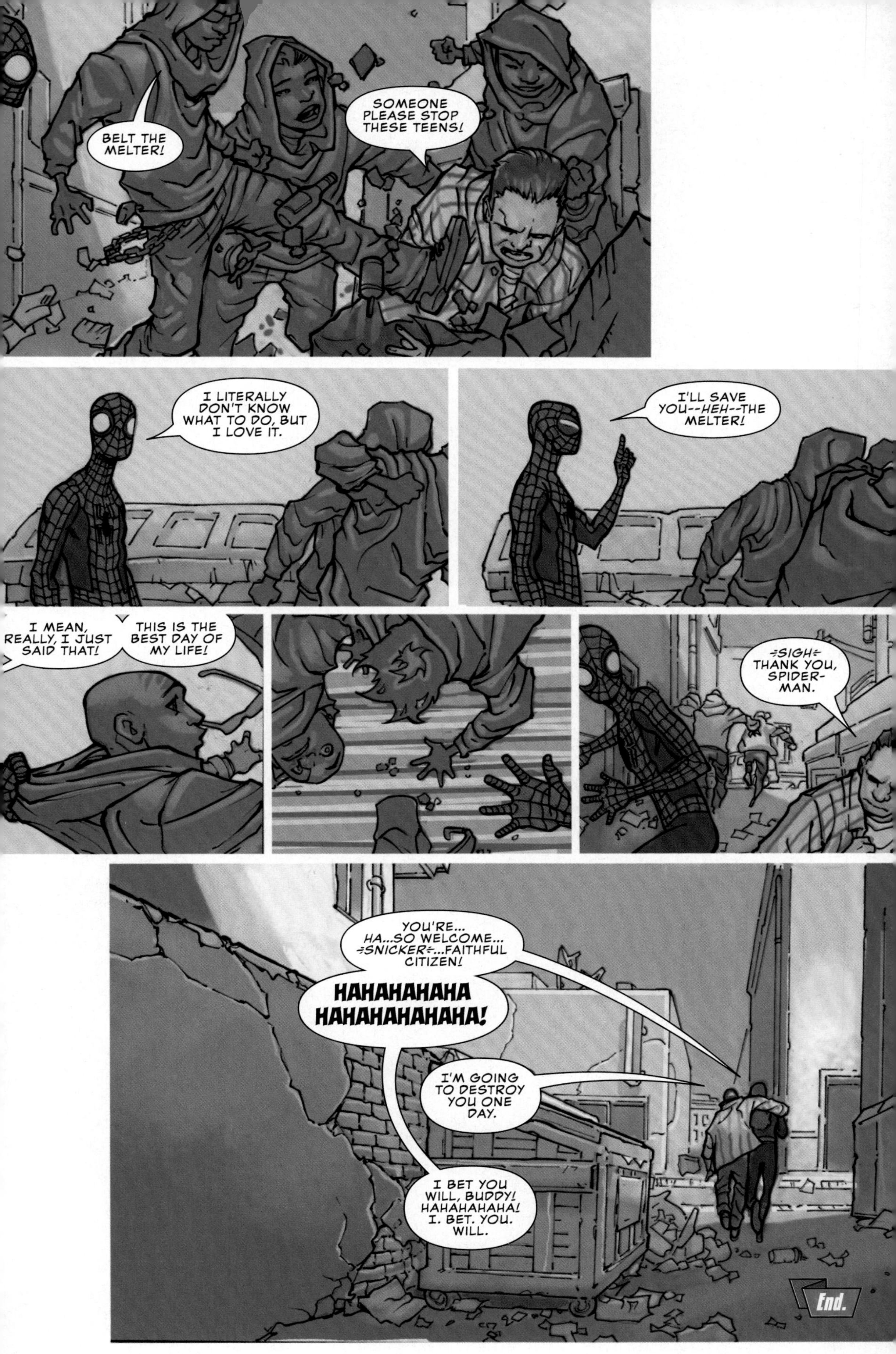
BELT THE MELTER!
SOMEONE PLEASE STOP THESE TEENS!
I LITERALLY DON'T KNOW WHAT TO DO, BUT I LOVE IT.
I'LL SAVE YOU--HEH--THE MELTER!
I MEAN, REALLY, I JUST SAID THAT!
THIS IS THE BEST DAY OF MY LIFE!
=SIGH= THANK YOU, SPIDER-MAN.
YOU'RE... HA...SO WELCOME... =SNICKER=...FAITHFUL CITIZEN!
HAHAHAHAHA HAHAHAHAHAHA!
I'M GOING TO DESTROY YOU ONE DAY.
I BET YOU WILL, BUDDY! HAHAHAHAHA! I. BET. YOU. WILL.
End.

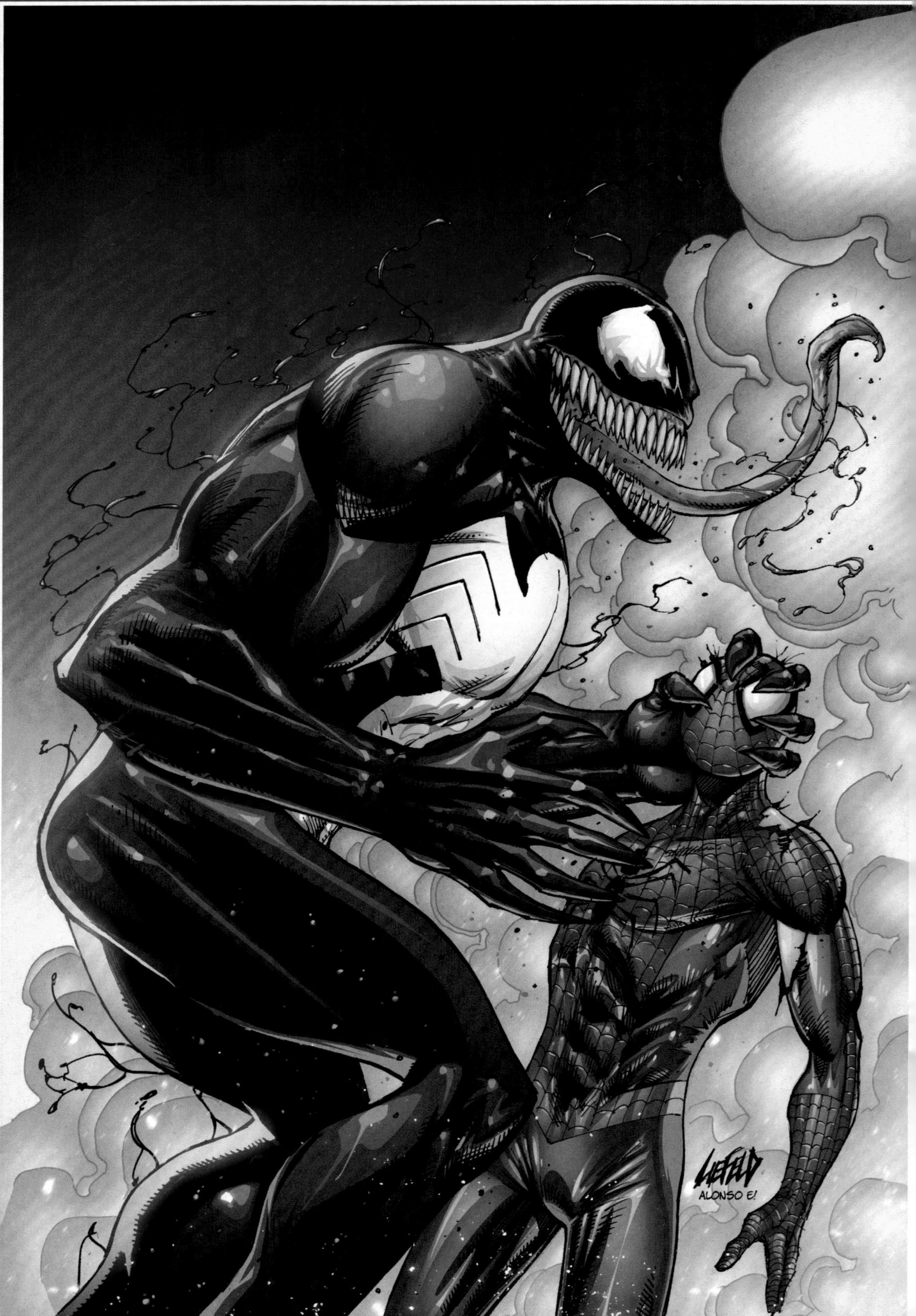
LIEFELD
ALONSO E!

#303 VENOM 30TH ANNIVERSARY VARIANT BY **ROB LIEFELD** & **ALONSO ESPINOZA**

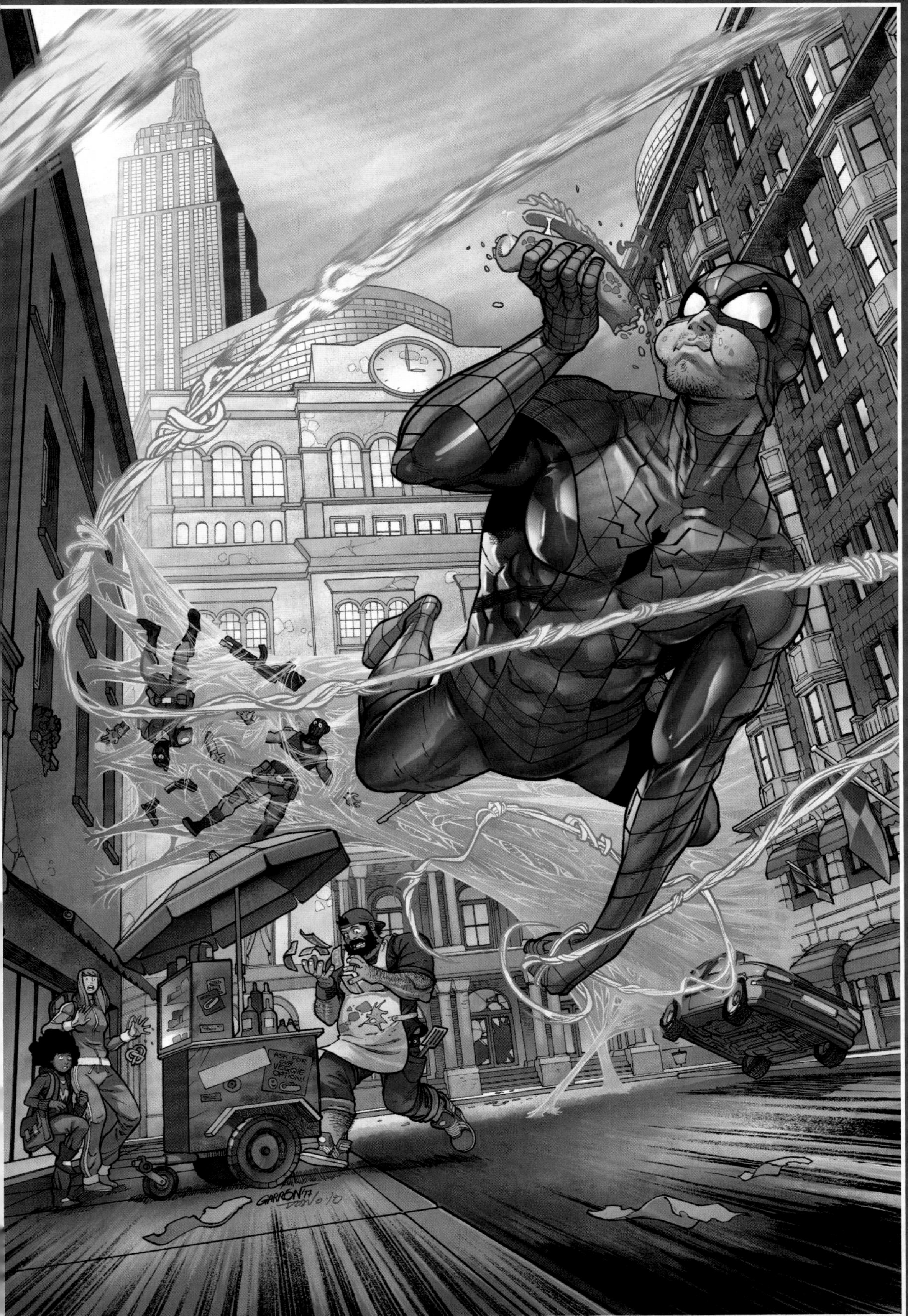
ASK FOR OUR VEGGIE OPTION!
GARRÓN '17

ANNUAL #1 VARIANT BY **JAVIER GARRÓN** & **DONO SÁNCHEZ-ALMARA**

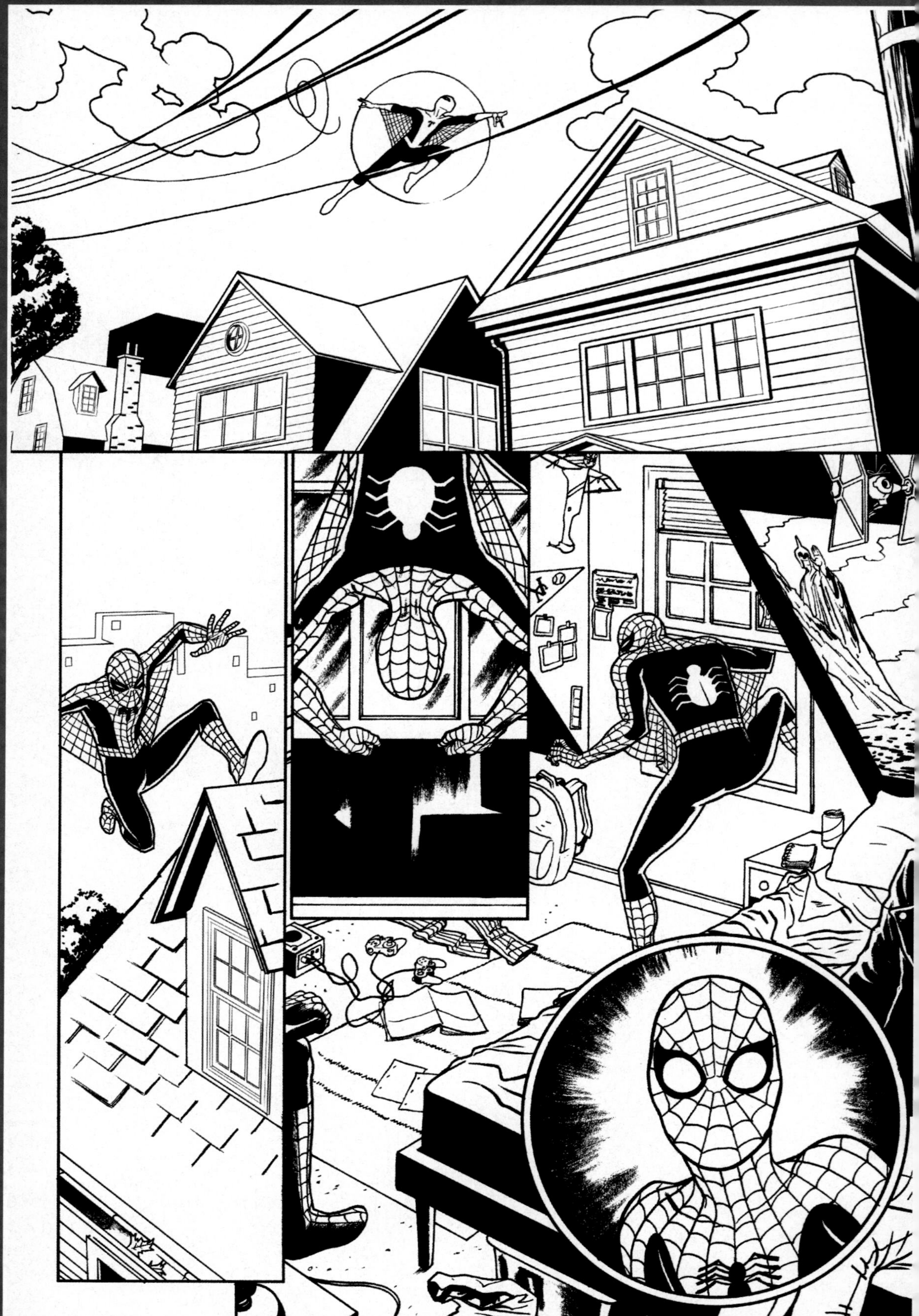

#301, PAGE 1 ART BY **JOE QUINONES** & **JOE RIVERA**

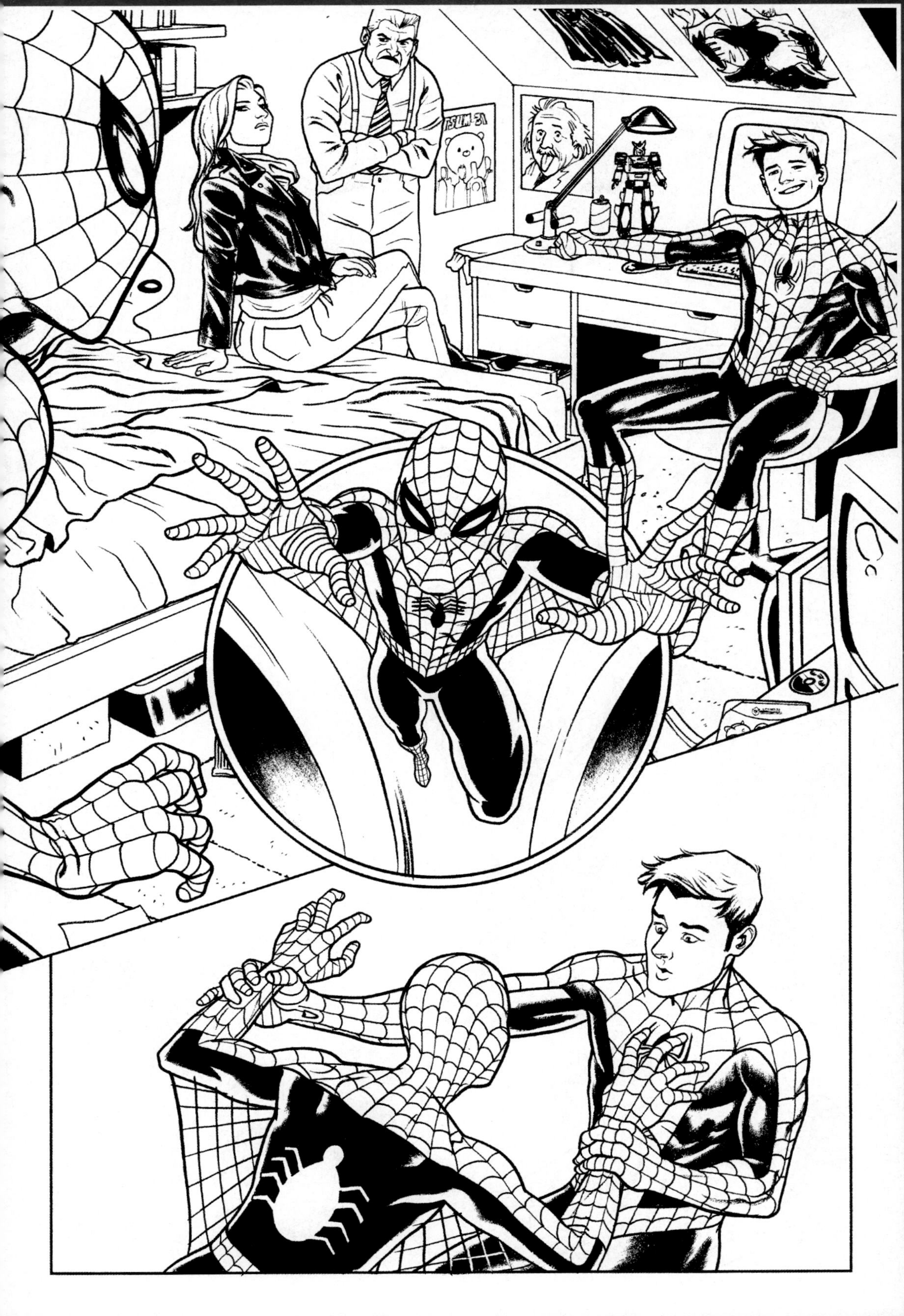

#301, PAGE 2 ART BY **JOE QUINONES** & **JOE RIVERA**

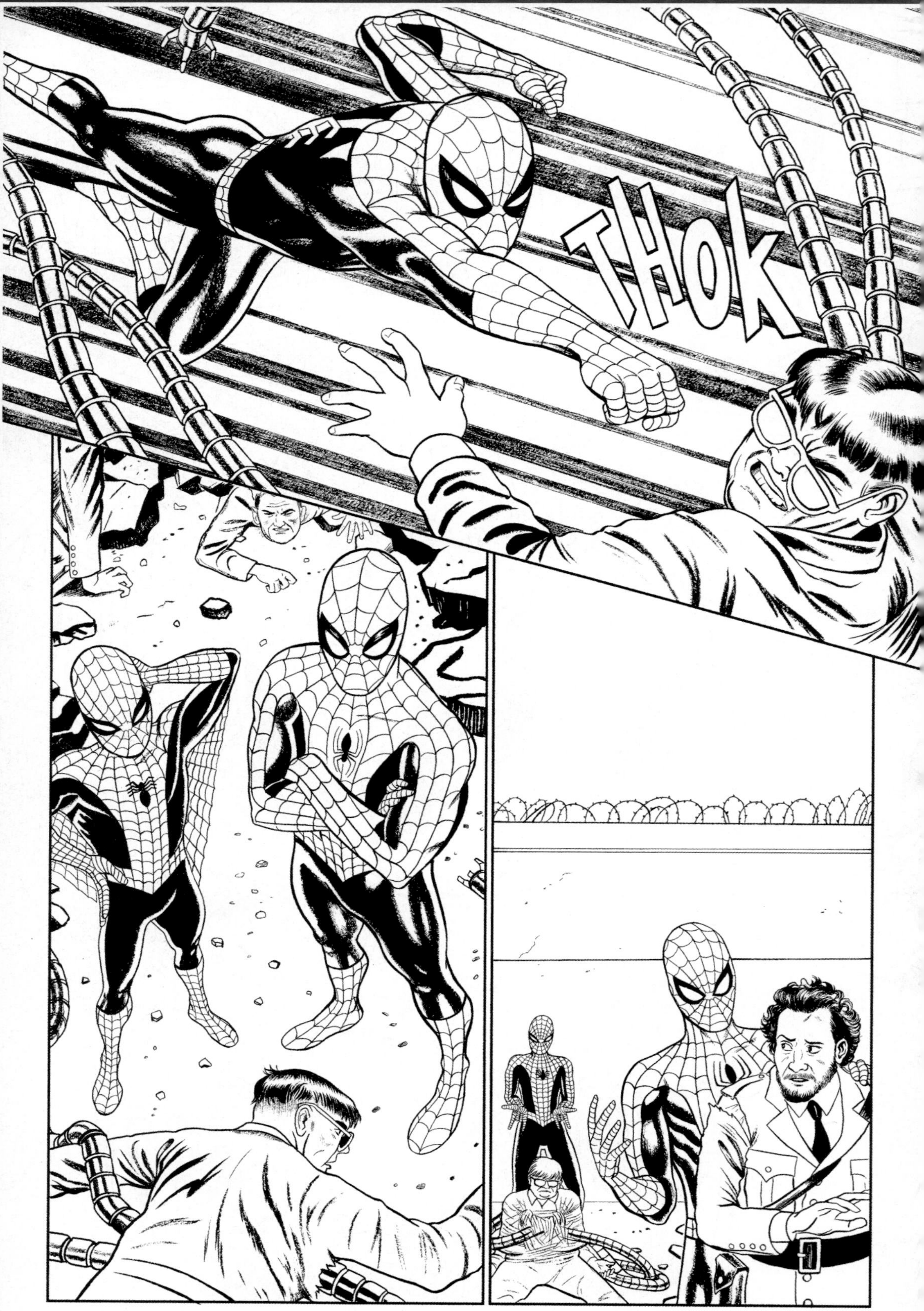
THOK

#301, PAGE 9 ART BY **JOE QUINONES** & **JOE RIVERA**

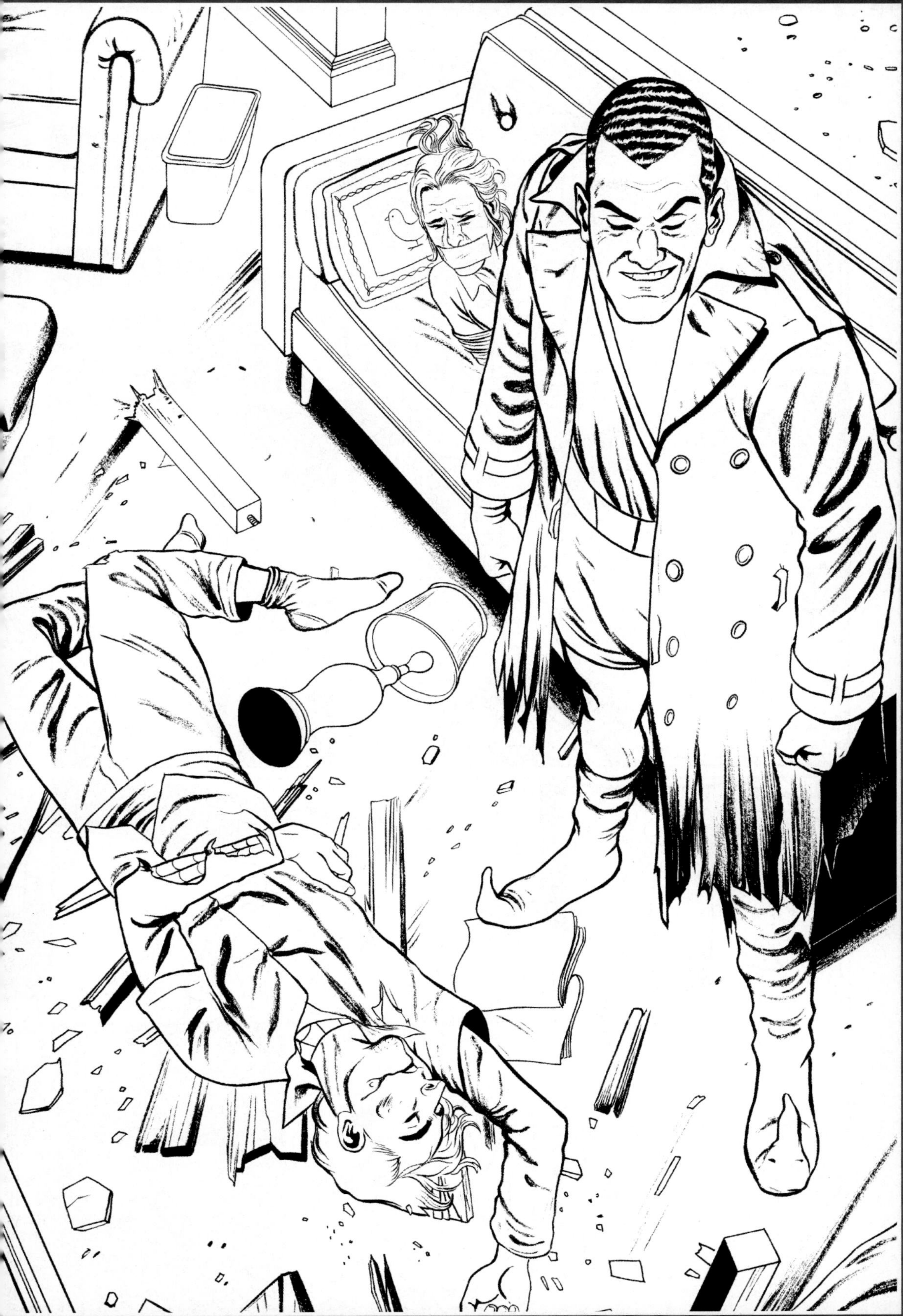

#302, PAGE 20 ART BY **JOE QUINONES** & **JOE RIVERA**

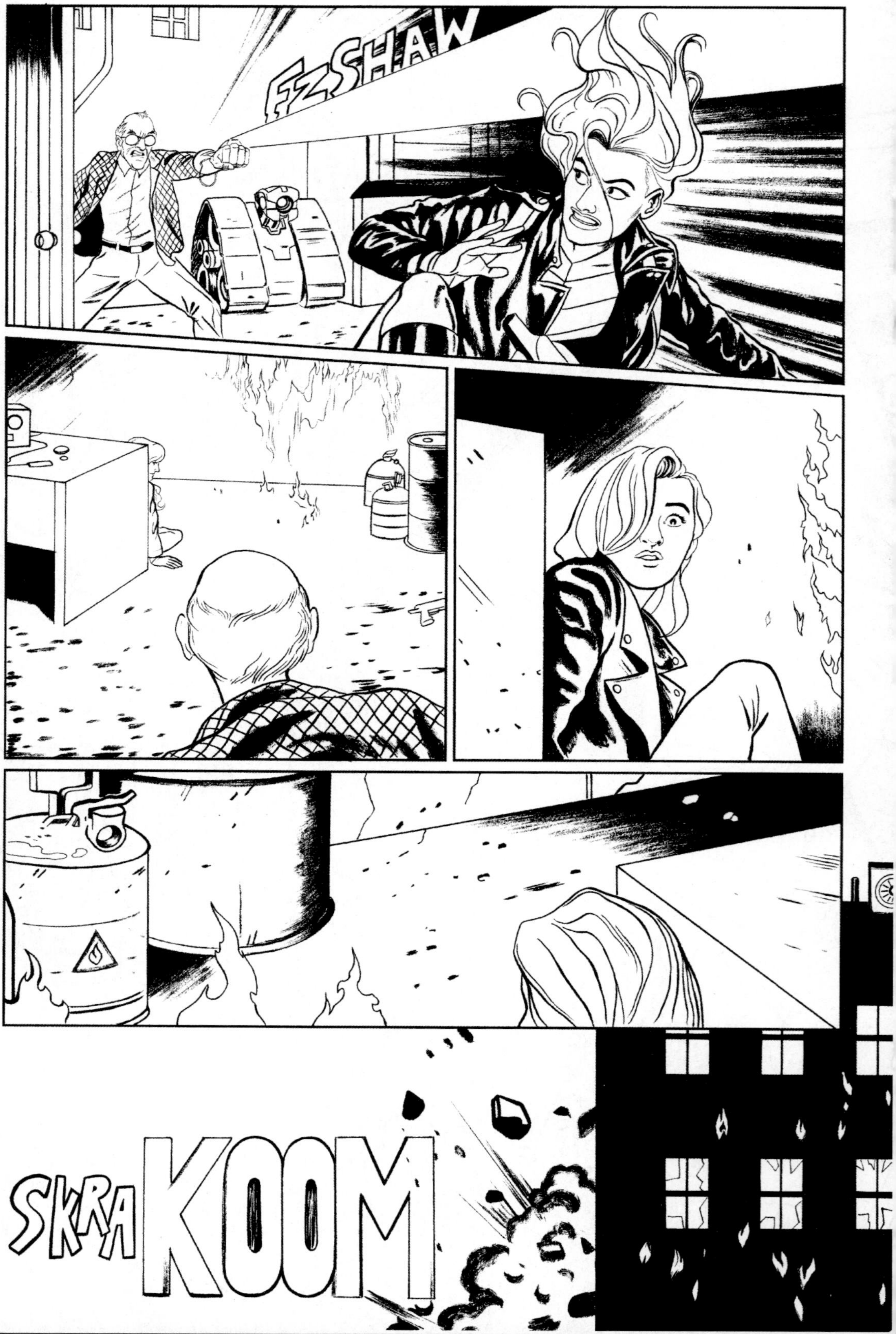
FZSHAW
SKRAKOOM

#303, PAGE 8 ART BY **JOE QUINONES, JOE RIVERA** & **PAOLO RIVERA**

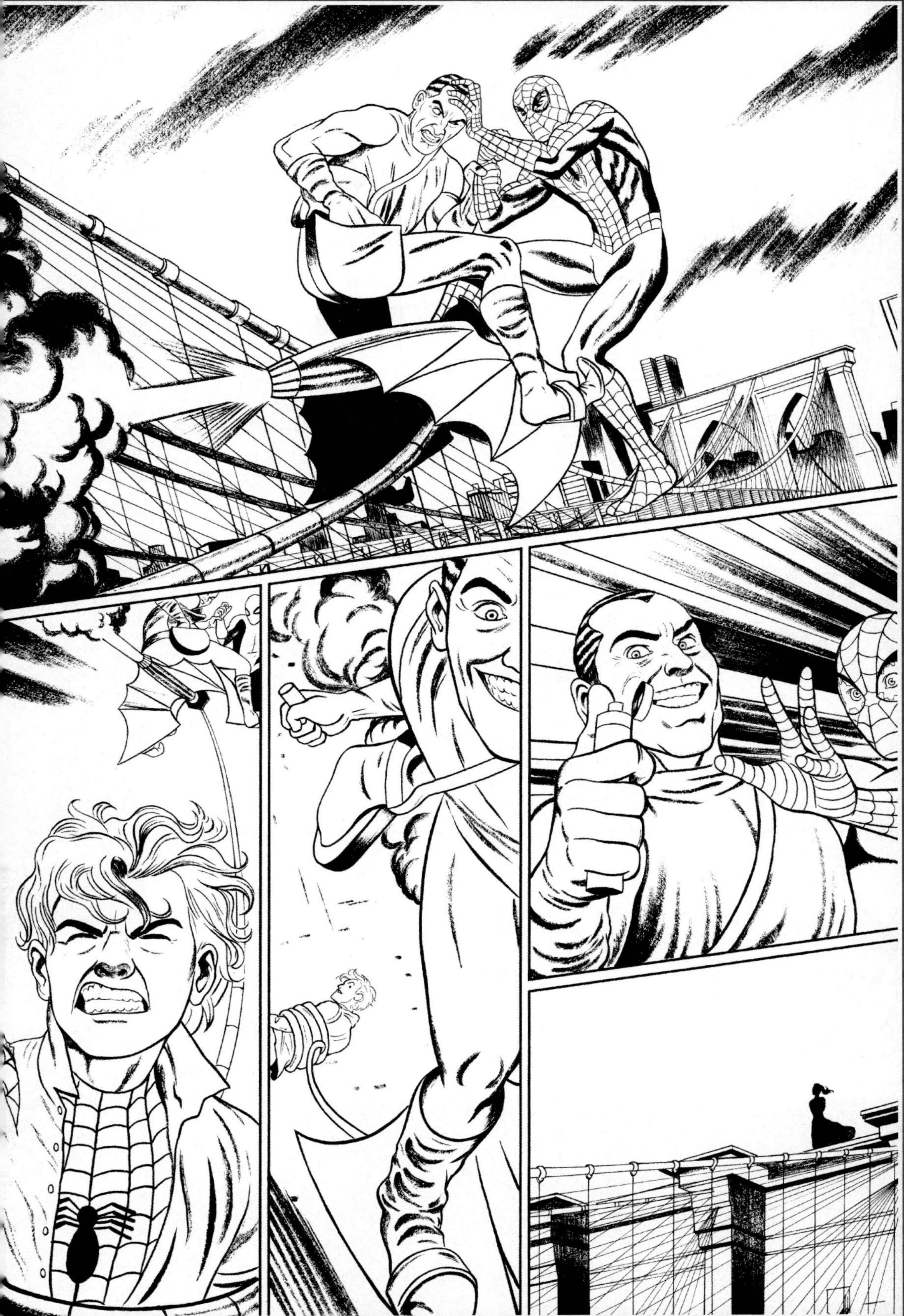

#303, PAGE 11 ART BY **JOE QUINONES, JOE RIVERA** & **PAOLO RIVERA**

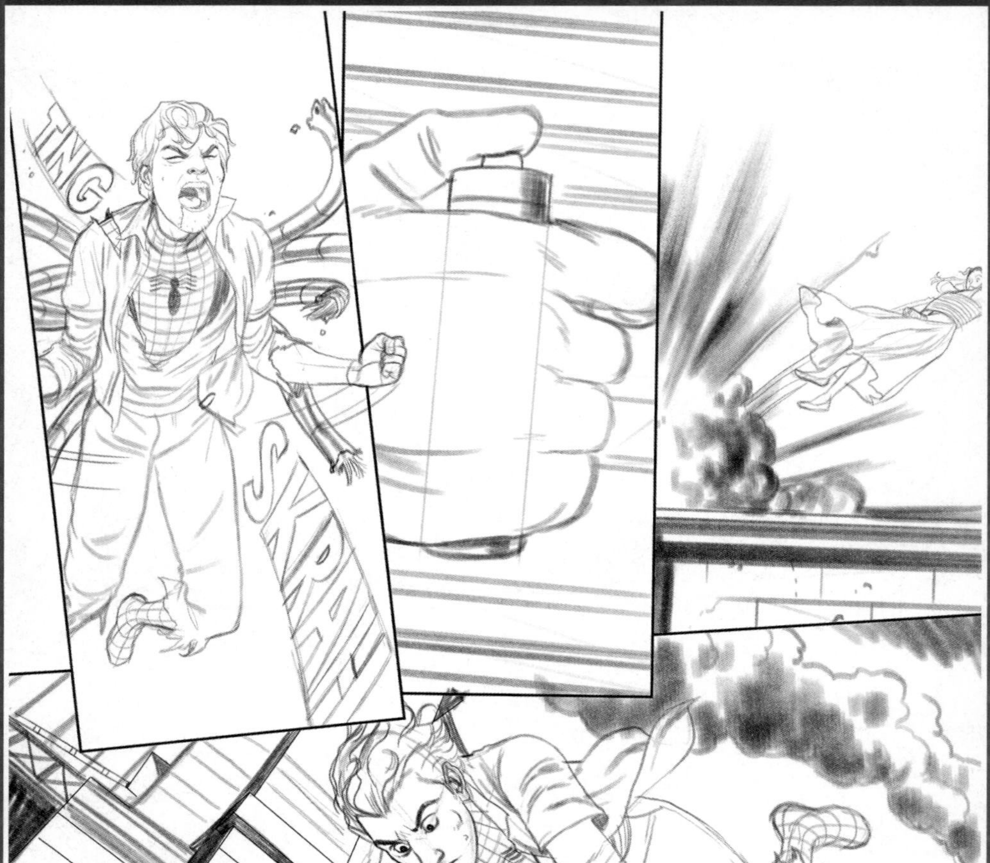
TNG
SKRAH

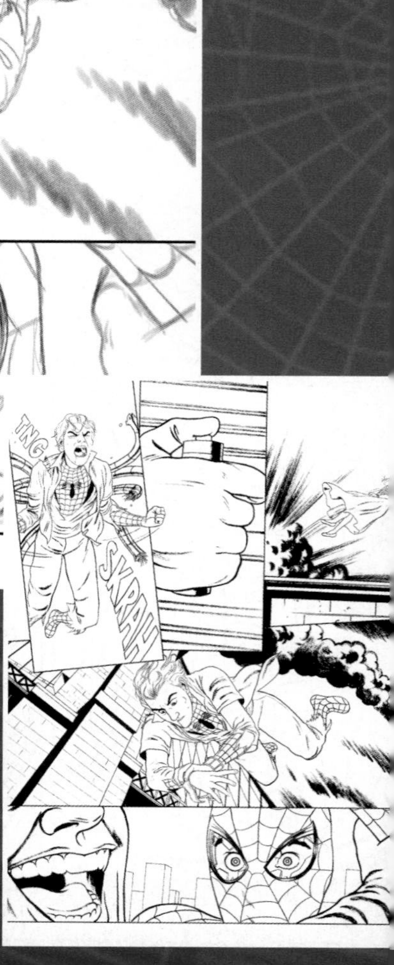
TNG
SKRAH

#303, PAGE 12 ART BY
JOE QUINONES, JOE RIVERA & PAOLO RIVERA

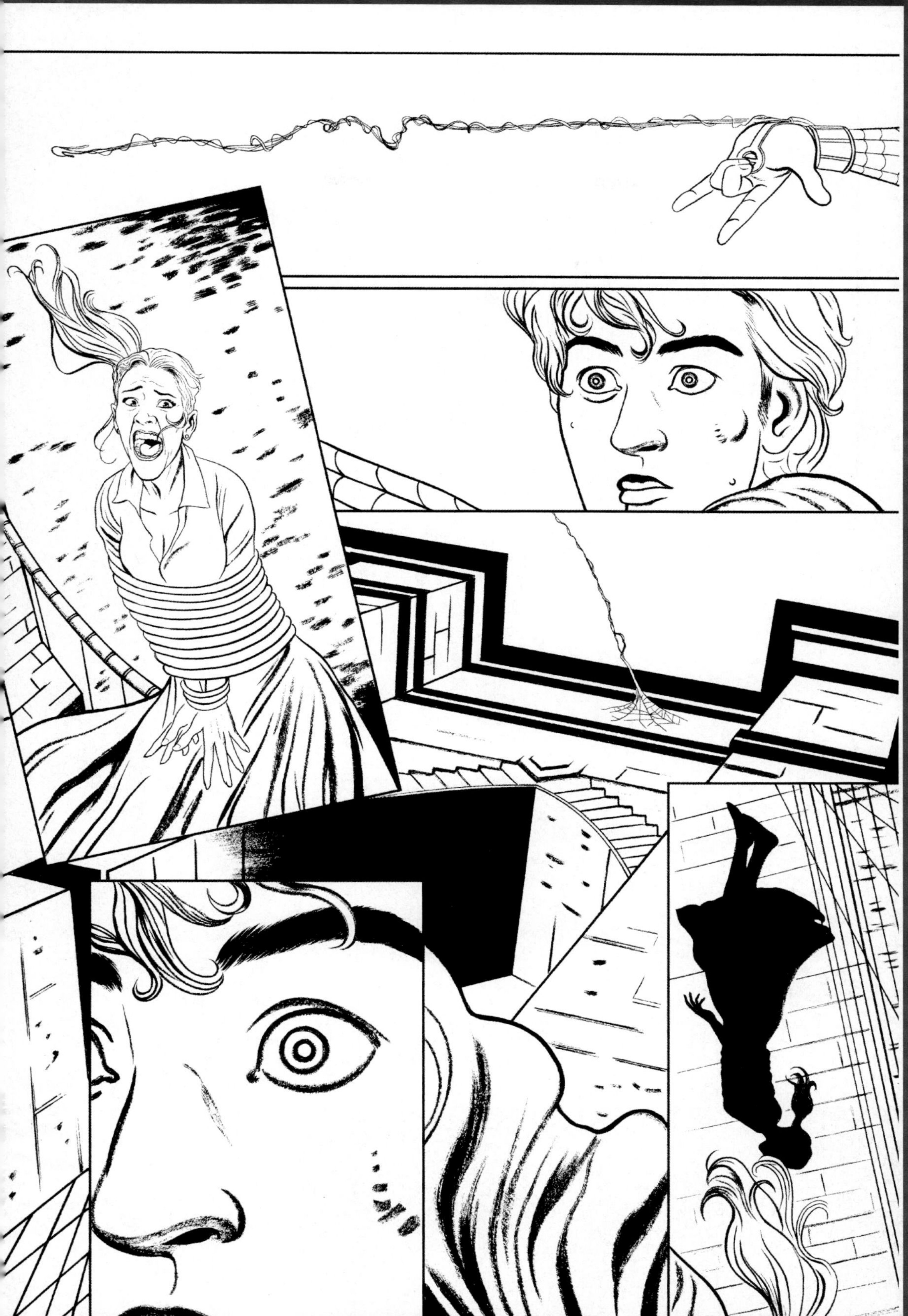

#303, PAGE 13 ART BY **JOE QUINONES, JOE RIVERA** & **PAOLO RIVERA**

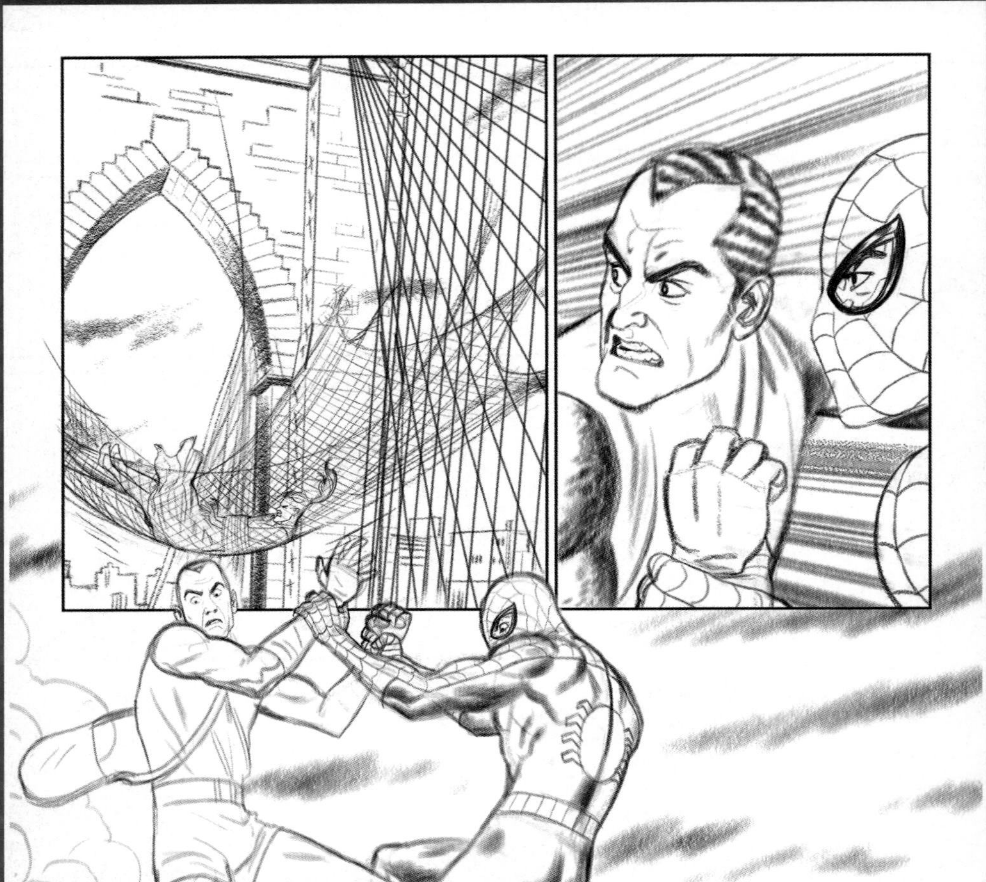
SKRAK
SKREEEEEE

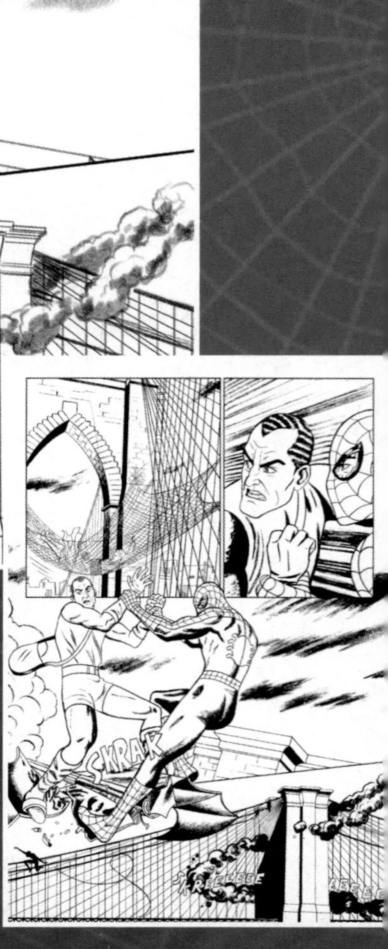
SKRAK

#303, PAGE 14 ART BY
JOE QUINONES, JOE RIVERA & **PAOLO RIVERA**